PSYCHIATRY:
A PERSONAL VIEW

Milton H. Miller, M.D.

PSYCHIATRY: A PERSONAL VIEW

CHARLES SCRIBNER'S SONS / NEW YORK

My grateful thanks to Patricia Attridge and
Laurie Schieffelin for their help and guidance
in preparing this book for publication.

To
Helen L. and William B. Miller
of Indianapolis, Indiana
THE INDELIBLE LINES
and
Harriet Sanders Miller
THE WONDROUS FREE SPACE

Contents

Preface

I'm a generalist in psychiatry. There is no part of the field that isn't fascinating for me. In particular, I've never lost the sense of excitement mixed with apprehension when I meet a new person, a new patient, and his or her family. In that first hour or hours together, you try to come so close that you sense the very breath of the people as they speak. And you stand far back to view their hopes and struggles silhouetted against the panorama of people everywhere and from all times. And you always remember what Hippocrates said: "Above all, don't hurt people."

Over the years, I've become very much a future-oriented psychiatrist, interested more in what could come next in the lives of patients (under the best of circumstances) than in detailing what was wrong before. I find that people's hopes and expectations about future possibilities determine to a considerable degree what they will recall from their past. Given good physical health, courage, and optimism about what comes next, the past looks rosier. There are times when a psychiatrist's belief in his patient's future helps restore health, clarity of purpose, and the curiosity to want to go on.

My goal in writing this book is to share with the reader my sense of awe and appreciation for the achievement of doctors, patients, families, scientific pioneers, mental health workers, and educators which in sum we call psychiatry. I want to describe as much of the field as I can because it is the breadth and interrelatedness of all the parts that make my profession unique. Psychiatry is the full panoply of human hopes, achievements, pain, and uncertainty. Psychiatry is simultaneously an explosion of scientific knowledge detailing the chemistry and physiology of mood and mentation joined with a wide variety of ageless interpersonal techniques used to alleviate anxiety and fear. In psychiatry, you confront the paradoxes in life that are as mystifying and awe inspiring today as they were for the first human beings. You celebrate the miracle and joys of what can now be done to help people; you mourn with your patients and their families life's disappointments and tragedies.

I hope this book will be helpful to readers who are concerned about themselves or members of their families, even though it is differently organized than more narrowly focused "self-help" writings. There is nothing about psychiatry that the average intelligent and interested person can't fully understand and nothing that anyone who is interested isn't entitled to know. The more the reader understands the field, the better he will truly appreciate any specific matters of personal concern. This is important because despite extraordinary progress in psychiatry, there is still a good deal of necessary trial and error in working with patients and their families. What we call "mental illness" and "emotional problems" prove often to be a very (*very*) complex mix of acute situational stress, strained interpersonal relationships, and illness in the purest medical sense of the word. I know that in my own clinical work, despite more than thirty years of experience (and a pattern of practice that makes frequent use of skilled consultants), the right answer, that which finally made the patient feel better, many times required a change or changes in the original treatment plan. One of the primary purposes of the book is to describe the *kind of relationship* between doctor, patient, and family that is essential in dealing with some of the most complex and painful circumstances that human beings can encounter. It's a relationship that is, ideally, a three-way partnership governed by the Golden Rule. It is a partnership among patient, family, and clinician marked by parity of the participants, recognition of the complexity of the problems involved, and a willingness to give everybody the benefit of the doubt.

I've had wonderful teachers; many of them were my patients and their families. This book details some of what I shared in the form of case histories, clinical vignettes, and some personal reflections. Sometimes I've been able to play a role in the emergence of understanding and reconciliation won by my patients; no less, the kindness of my patients and their families and their gifts of tolerance, trust, and forgiveness are among my most treasured experiences. I choose to make some of those personal experiences a part of this book both because they have influenced major characteristics of my practice of psychiatry and because I believe that the person of the doctor is a significant factor in the outcome of the therapy.

The first part of this book considers the manner in which it happens that people come to feel good or bad about themselves and other people. I think it is clear that a person's basic sense of himself is created and maintained by a dynamic and changing mix of biological predisposition, early life experiences, relationships with intimates, placement in society's roster of winners and losers, and intangible but crucial variables called human spirit and human intention. I believe that the pace of changing social values and in particular the current uncertainties as to what the generations in families "owe" each other have imposed stresses in North American society that threaten the most fundamental elements of personal security. Many people in America live almost exclusively with people of their own generation. They are thus cut adrift from the kinds of three-generational support and reinforcement that have regularly sustained societies through the centuries. Can people really live this way? And for how long?

The second part of the book is somewhat more clinically and technically oriented, but all chapters are well within the reader's capacity to agree or disagree and certainly to fully understand. As this book goes to publication, American psychiatrists are putting into practice a new and remarkable revision of psychiatric conceptualization and diagnosis. We call it DSM-III (Diagnostic and Statistical Manual) and it broadens considerably the way mental health professionals view and understand our patients.[1] Beyond simple diagnostic titles, the new nomenclature calls for assessment of basic personality characteristics, physical health, past achievements, and existing social supports and strengths. The new approach to diagnosis reflects the truly remarkable scientific discoveries of the last decade that greatly affect the choice of treatment and the outlook for improvement or cure. It points as well to the terrible problems that still remain in our field and underscores the enormous stake we have in a growing scientific basis for psychiatric practice. One result to be hoped for with a scientifically based understanding of the causes of mental illness is that there will be an end to the terrible guilt feelings imposed unfairly upon the parents, spouses, and children of many of our patients.

The final chapter, called "If the Patient Is Someone You Love"—and "If the Patient Is You"—is precisely that, a psychiatrist's conversation with people who trust that they will be told the truth about what the clinician believes they should do for and with themselves and their loved ones. I've included a special section of suggestions for those who must deal with the threat of suicide or the need to protect themselves from personal violence.

I hope that the entire book will contribute to the reader's confidence in making important personal decisions. Finally, I hope to share something of the exhilaration and joy that takes place in a psychiatrist's office when another person's struggle becomes yours . . . and you both win.

PART ONE

A PERSONAL APPROACH IN PSYCHIATRY

Introduction

Sometimes I have trouble remembering the psychiatry of thirty years ago. So much has changed. Yet it was then that I began my career as a student at the Menninger School of Psychiatry in Topeka, Kansas. In those days, most of our patients were so very sick that they lived out long periods of their lives in wards of mental hospitals. And the hospitals—like the patients they housed—were neglected, forgotten, abysmal, and without hope. They were sad places where broken lives were stored. In those early days, happy outcomes were painfully won; joyous outcomes were rare.

My teachers were visionaries. Karl Menninger talked of hope and love.[1] His brother, William Menninger, patiently worked to win over the leaders of the community: the mayor, the businessmen, the newspaper people, and the ministers.[2] He told them they were desperately needed as advocates for people who had been put aside and forgotten. My first supervisors in Topeka were John Chotlos, an existential philosopher-psychologist, and George L. Harrington, an extraordinary clinician-psychiatrist who could reach into the most hidden, remote, or violent person: "Hey, fellow, c'mon back, I gotta talk to you." Harrington and Chotlos told me to worry less about the symbolic meaning of symptoms and to worry more about all the life that wasn't happening for my patients. They helped me to understand that doctors and patients are caught up in the same tricky, uncertain, sometimes sad venture called "doing the best we can." My basic ideas about the kind of psychiatry I wanted to practice and to teach were well shaped in those first Kansas years. It was to be a personal psychiatry. No theory would ever loom larger than what was going on in my patients' lives. I was lucky. My early mentors taught me that from life you learn psychiatry—not the other way around.

I left the Menninger Clinic in 1953 and with my wife and three small children set off on a two-year tour as an Air Force psychiatrist. In 1955, we went to Madison, Wisconsin, where for seventeen years I was a Professor of Psychiatry (and for ten years Chairman) in a distinguished department of that remarkable university. I think of the University of Wisconsin in those years as a kind of psychiatric Camelot. Psychiatry was becoming a legitimate medical specialty. We were moving patients out of hospitals for the chronically ill. The new drugs interrupted illnesses of the greatest magnitude. By the mid-1950s psychiatrists were acquiring therapeutic instruments that allowed us to heal psychotic and depressive diseases from which mankind had suffered without remedy through all the millennia of recorded history. In those early postwar years there was also a beginning awareness of the interpersonal and social context in which the suffering of mental illness took place. The special suffering reserved for black people, poor people, old people, minorities in general and the stifling effects of sexual discrimination moved from occasional discussion topics to major courses in the curriculum at Wisconsin. I wish I had understood how much of what in those years I was call-ing mental illness was rooted in social injustice. I was slow to learn.

The Wisconsin faculty was extraordinarily rich with pioneers in many areas of mental health research. Harry Harlow's motherless monkeys were clinging to wire surrogates.[3] Carl Rogers and Carl Whitaker and their courageous patients were among the first to lift the shroud of secrecy about who did what in psychotherapy.[4,5] Sociologist Martin Loeb was pointing out that the patients who most often went home from the chronic hospitals were the ones who lived on the bus routes and had the fare to give the driver.[6] Psychologists Norman Greenfield and William Fey had established in the mid-50s beyond all doubt that a doctor of psychology was a doctor and that you didn't have to have an M.D. to be wonderfully useful to people. [7,8] Later, psychiatrist Seymour Halleck, our head of student health, and I were to work as emergency physicians in the student-run first aid stations during the anti–Vietnam War confrontations that rocked our city, as they rocked our whole society.[9] Our department was eclectic, collegial, and non-hierarchical. We loved and respected each other.

But even Camelot is not forever. One day, that was over for me. I'm not sure why. Freud said that the unimportant things can usually be explained in detail, the important not at all. Perhaps it had something to do with what Erich Fromm observed: "When a person's needs for shelter, safety and all the material satisfactions are met, then their real problems begin." I wanted to continue to practice psychiatry, but in a different setting. In 1972, my wife and I went to Vancouver, British Columbia, where I was Head of the Department of Psychiatry at the University of British Columbia and Director of the World Health Organization (WHO)–UBC Mental Health Training and Research Center, and where my wife taught painting and sculpture at Vancouver's Douglas College. In those years, I worked and traveled a good deal in Asia as a WHO consultant to the governments of Thailand and Bangladesh and as one of the directors of the Vancouver-based World Federation for Mental Health. Much of my international work was done in association with Dr. Tsung-yi Lin, a very distinguished cross-cultural psychiatrist and my colleague at the University of British Columbia. I had many experiences with patients and their families, with psychiatrists, and with the psychiatry of India, Bangladesh, Thailand, Malaysia, Hong Kong, the Philippines, Japan, the People's Republic of China, and, above all, Taiwan, the Republic of China, where I have taught, studied, and returned a dozen times in the last fifteen years. Along the way, beginning with an intensive course at the University of Wisconsin in the summer of 1968, I've learned to speak a fair Mandarin Chinese and I have come to treasure, in no small way, my friends and my life in Asia.

Working in my field in other parts of the world has helped to clarify many things for me. First of all, the suffering that accompanies the ancient and dread depressive and schizophrenic maladies is profound wherever it occurs, and these illnesses are found among all the people of the world. And no less, the emotions that go with jealousy, disappointment, and rejection, with concerns for reputation and for children and the pains that come with material possessions, are the subjects for psychiatric dialogue worldwide. Yet in each country the psychiatry is different. And the differences are considerable because there is no such thing as a psychiatry separate or separable from the values, goals, traditions, and economic circumstances of either therapists or patients. I was psychoanalyzed when I was thirty years old, and that experience helped me to understand that many of my adult ideas were shaped by the force of the instructions accepted in childhood. But even more revealing was what I discovered in Canada and in Asia, that is, how American I am and how much of what I take to be true is but one point of view. I treasure what I have shared and learned in other parts of the world. Those lessons help me understand what I really mean when I say "home."

In 1978 I returned "home" as Professor of Psychiatry at the University of California, Los Angeles (UCLA), and Deputy Director of the Los Angeles County Mental Health Department. In the latter capacity, I have direct responsibility for public mental health programs serving a population of 2.2 million people in a series of Los Angeles communities that include California's richest and poorest towns, Rolling Hills Estates and Hawaiian Gardens, and, most famous of all, Malibu and Beverly Hills.

In the last three decades I have spent thousands and thousands of hours with the sickest of my profession's patients in hospitals, clinics, and prisons in many parts of the world. In these remarkable years the balance shifted and the psychiatric visionaries became prophets. Hundreds of thousands of our patients left the hospitals and returned to their families. Ten times that number are now successfully treated every year in such a way that they will never know that only a few years earlier their "problems" would have interrupted and sabotaged their lives in a profound manner. Instead, they have trouble, they come for help, they work it out, and go on with the rest of their lives.

Even within the short span of the last decade, the progress in psychiatry and the other mental health professions has continued at a remarkable pace. We are beginning a scientific era that will be no less precise and comprehensive than the progress already seen in endocrinology, immunology, and other areas of medicine. Fifty years of study of the nature and function of the brain, the endocrine system, and the biochemistry of mood and behavior are beginning to make possible more accurate prediction, quantification, and very subtle quality control procedures in the everyday patient-care activities of our advanced psychiatric centers. The areas of greatest progress to date are in the biological fields, with precise answers emerging as to the causes of senility, of craving for opiates, of violent outbursts, of alcoholic dependence, and of the exacerbation of schizophrenic and depressive symptoms. Research into the effectiveness of the various treatment approaches has identified a growing number of the biological, social, interpersonal, and group characteristics that determine who gets sick, who could get well, who actually gets well. As our knowledge develops, the unity of biology and psychology unfold in the dual arenas of personal experience and objective measure.

I don't mean to say that all of the illnesses and all of the problems in living that appear in a psychiatrist's office will be amenable to solution through advanced scientific methodology. The human situation, a wavering between ambiguity and certainty, anoints mankind with restlessness. However, the rapidly developing body of knowledge in the basic sciences of psychiatry is of the greatest importance to patients, families, and doctors as well. It offers great hope.

And the patients come in a steady stream. Eight million North Americans consult psychiatrists every year. Many millions consult other health professionals. Many who might profit from similar consultation carefully keep their distance. Each of the people who come is different. And yet we are all so much the same.

In my work, as in this book, it is the "life experience" of the person called "patient" that is my starting place. What is it like to *be* that person whose way of living is called schizophrenic, or neurotic, or perverse, or normal? What happens in that life? And equally, what doesn't happen? Where are the hopes of the years that were good? Who are the people who counted? When the troubling complaint goes away, what will take its place?

Here we are, mysteriously, coexperiencers of life. We each have a measure of time and space, greater or lesser capacity to care, possibilities of turning toward or turning away. What and who we choose to care about, how we invest our time, the spaces we choose to occupy and avoid, whether we elect to consider at all or ignore (with determination) the mystery and wonder of our being here—these are the matters of overriding importance in my own approach to psychiatry.

> I am interested in how you spend your time and intrigued by the choices you have made. I am curious as to what will come next for you and moved by your uncertainty and pain. I will be your doctor.

When you accept the responsibility to be doctor to another person, it is your affirmation of him and your endorsement of his hopes for himself. Many times those hopes, at first seemingly remote because of anxiety, shame, or depression, are realized in full.

> What is called neurotic or psychotic anxiety is very often the "growing edge" of the person, that part which hungers for a deeper life and won't settle for a conventional, pretending, "me too" in the way most people live their lives. Sickness of this kind turns out to be a signal that a real person is about to spring forward.
>
> —Carl Whitaker, M.D.[10]

Some patients have a mental illness and then they get well and then they get weller! I mean they get better than they ever were. This is an extraordinary and little realized truth!

—Karl Menninger, M.D.[11]

People, with encouragement, often prove very adaptable. Their wish to get well and then "weller" is the central ingredient in every truly successful helping relationship. The "helper" works to mobilize and free a potential for improvement that is already there. In the treatment process, the patient discovers or rediscovers excitement and satisfaction in being the one-of-a-kind, unique, and special being that he or she is.

In truly successful therapy, not only do troubling symptoms recede or disappear, but a discovery of previously overlooked potentialities takes place as well. The helper assists the patient in the therapeutic task of unlocking chains, untying hands, removing blindfolds, commuting "life sentences," smashing trick mirrors, and turning off a searing blowtorch of guilt and shame that has been in hot and relentless lifelong pursuit.

Martin Luther King, Jr., spoke of "Free at last!"—the freedom to be oneself. To be witness to success in any individual's attainment of himself is an inspiring privilege. To be that person taking self-possession is the ultimate success.

1

Beginning at the Beginning: The People Who Count

Underlying much of what happens in life is the fact that people are both uniquely individual and yet powerfully affected by each other. Each of us is the one-and-only, never-before, likely-never-again variety of our special self. And more poignantly, each moment that we live is its one-and-only, never-to-recur point in time. Yet our individuality notwithstanding, we know each other and are mutually involved in the most basic sense. Life is "life with others," even when one is temporarily alone. And the most significant moments are likely to be those with, because of, en route to, or away from some significant other person. Human anguish and human exultation are largely dependent upon what some other person said, what he or she did or failed to do. Human nature is powerfully modified depending upon which other person is around. To some degree, most people could say of themselves, "What person I am depends upon which human being I am with. I can go from being the best of men to the worst simply by changing my companion."

Just how important people are to each other and the complex ways that they seek, grieve for, and turn from each other is something ever-present in a psychiatrist's office. In the pages that follow, I want to describe the extraordinary manner in which people demonstrate the importance of another person in their lives. Sometimes that is the central difficulty in a set of concerns and troubling events that is called mental illness. Often, however, it is from the circumstance of a person in grave trouble and great need that the most powerful and moving human relationships develop. I will try to describe this process in a series of case studies, each of which portrays an aspect of the significance of loving concern. At the same time, I will introduce as accurately as I am able a description of the manner in which a psychiatrist may work to help his patient receive, enjoy, and reciprocate the affection and concern of another person.

Some of the people who come for help are simply not willing or not able to accept and overlook what isn't happening in their lives. They aren't good sports about what they aren't getting. And for some, there is simply too much unfinished business for them to go on in search of the "what could be" in their future. One such person who felt she couldn't go on till she had gone back was a young nurse hopelessly divided in the here and then.

Case Study 1: *A Nurse in Search of Her True Parents*

Annette Wrigley, a thirty-one-year-old registered nurse, unmarried, working regularly and effectively as a general duty surgical nurse, agreed reluctantly to a single psychiatric interview because of the urging of a surgeon friend. She had confided to this professional friend her conviction that her mother and father were not her true biological parents and that she devoted most of her free time to seeking proof of this belief. Specifically, she felt that she was the child of an aging minister in her family's church and that her mother had most likely been a paternal aunt who had died some thirty-one years earlier. She had held fast to this conviction for more than six years despite angry and continuous denials by her parents, her parents' friends, and the minister she felt was her biological father. She not only believed her theory, she believed it with a desperate hope. She felt that she could not go on to other parts of her life until "the true facts are known." And to the search for the "true facts" she had committed a considerable part of her life.

She remembered her childhood as miserable and bereft of hope. Her parents always seemed indifferent to her but consumed with hatred for each other. They fought continuously and blamed Annette for having to sustain the marriage. That they were still together ten years after Annette left home was quite incomprehensible to her.

After a lonely and unhappy childhood, Annette graduated from high school expecting that she would go on to college. But her father said he couldn't support the schooling and so she went to work until she had earned enough to begin nurses' training. It took her four years. At twenty-three, she began a nurses' training program and finished at twenty-six.

Some two months after graduation, Annette became very depressed and for a period of almost a month was unable to work. This followed her decision not to marry a young suitor. She had felt herself to be in too much personal turmoil. Her depression was severe. She stayed in her apartment, cried a great deal, brooded about her life. She went once or twice to tell her parents how bad she felt but felt worse after each visit. She decided to talk with a minister whose church she had twice visited during the preceding year. He received her kindly, patiently, listened to her as she had never been listened to in her entire life. Through her own tears she saw tears in his eyes and she felt a union, communion, friendship, and peace almost unknown to her. A week later she returned and again was deeply touched by his concern. As she was crying, he reached and put his hand on hers and said, "Don't cry, my dear." It was the most important moment in her life.

She suddenly felt a total exhilaration and awe at the discovery that needed no other proof: "This is my father."

The weeks, months, then years that were to follow were, understandably, complex. There was pain, embarrassment, self-doubt, rejection, bitter denunciation by her mother, and Annette's sad decision that she should stop contacting the minister, who, though kind, had become uncomfortable with her. Yet through it all, extending to the moment of psychiatric consultation six years later, she never gave up the conviction that she had found her biological father, her true father. During the first of the days that followed her decision that the minister was her true father, she suddenly remembered a family story about an aunt, her "other" father's older sister, who had taken her own life after an unhappy love affair. This had taken place, she had been told, before her birth. At first, she couldn't believe what she was thinking, but the coincidence of timing and various other discoveries taken from her memory seemed to build too strong a case to deny that this aunt was her true mother, that she was born of a union of this woman with the minister, her father, and that the people who had reared her were her uncle and the uncle's wife. That would explain everything!

Of course, the most important matter that needed explanation was why Annette could not go on with her life. Many people have, at one time or another, considered the possibility that they were not the child of their supposed parents. Ordinarily it is a fleeting thought because knowledge of one's parents' identity is a basic part of personal identity. How can one go on to the future unless the basic facts of one's origins are settled? But no less, if the future seems menacing, an individual may turn morbidly to the past to discover an acceptable explanation for the fear. Fear of the future and preoccupation with the past seem often to be connected. At times, it is impossible to know which problem came first. I found it difficult to decide in this instance why Annette held so tenaciously to her false hope. Were her parents so bad that she couldn't identify with them? I met them and they seemed more baffled and hurt (and worried) than evil, or even unpleasant. I didn't feel that it was possible to explain Annette's delusion on the basis of "bad parents." It was more than that. In some manner, Annette was searching for qualities which she found in neither her parents nor herself. She felt she had found them in the minister and she wanted to make herself heir to what she needed.

She pursued her quest in many ways. She followed many clues. She read old newspapers in the libraries, sought various public and church records, would await a key moment in casual conversation and then mention the name of her dead aunt and the minister in close succession and intently watch for reactions. She made frequent visits to the town where her aunt had lived, tried to find people who had known her, then would produce a blown-up and retouched photo of the minister (made to look thirty years younger) and ask if he too was remembered. Some weren't sure, but maybe . . . .

And here she was sitting with me, talking seriously, intently, a woman who was intelligent, kind, polite, but wanting just one thing from me—encouragement to continue her lonely search. I asked her if she would tell me a dream and she said that on the night before our appointment she had this remarkable dream: "I was standing in a garden, a beautiful garden; I had never seen it before. There were yellow and red and purple flowers and rich, green grass and lovely spreading trees. But I was standing there crying, fiercely crying. At the same time, I was turning back the layers of some kind of bulb, like an onion, layer after layer, and crying and crying." It was a beautiful dream that said so much about her own life. The bulb was her life, the seed of the flower she was meant to be. But she sought that flower through the ritual of examination. She dared not entrust herself to the soil of her life.

If you are a therapist who wants to count for something in the life of Annette Wrigley, you have to like her, believe in her future, and gain her trust to the extent that she has the courage to trust anyone. You hope that she has the good luck to reach out to possibilities, opportunities that would take her to new and interesting experiences. It's not enough for her to "understand" her past. She has to go toward her future life. That you believe in her future is important because it helps her to do the same. She "borrows" hope for a time. And, she has to be lucky. By the time an individual has narrowed his world to pursuits that are dead-ended, morbid, and joyless, further defeats are debilitating indeed.

Annette extended the one-hour interview limit she had originally imposed and I've known her now for more than twenty years. I saw her weekly for two years and then irregularly through the next five years. I still hear from her by letter every Christmas or two and someday, when she's in California, we may meet for lunch and take turns telling each other how it has worked out.

For Annette, I know it's been hard. I think that our work together helped her avoid "dead-ending" her life in a deluded search for identity in the historical library. She says that. She says that often. But it's also true that through the years the moments of joy and freedom were matched by the times when she could almost feel her foot on the brake of her life. As I came to know her, I felt there were different causes for the various relapse periods when she would want to abandon work, friends, and general interests in favor of a return to full-time searching for details concerning her aunt and the minister. Trouble with work, friends, and sometimes anger with me seemed to make her want to go back into her past. Yet there were other times when, without apparent explanation, her mood would darken and she would become remote, almost dazed, and she would cry as much as talk. It was as if some internal thermostat regulating mood, optimism, and clarity of thought had gone awry. In a 1978 letter to me she said she felt that her problems stem from three sources. One is her stubborn and determined nature combined with a depressive disposition. Second, she felt that she was unable, unwilling— she's not quite sure—to really give up looking for a happier childhood until too late in her chronological adult life to make an adult career for herself of which she would feel proud.

Finally, her fear of producing a child—a daughter—lest it suffer the pain she had experienced, kept her from allowing any man to enter her life in a serious way till having children was no longer a likely possibility. She married when she was close to forty and has sustained that relationship to the present. Her husband—I've never met him—is a plumber, married once before, and with children from a first marriage. Annette took anti-depressive and anti-psychotic medication on prescription at intervals but often managed her anxiety by restricting her involvements for various periods. She said she still thinks there is a possibility that she was the minister's child after all, but tries not to worry about that. She hasn't taken any definitive steps toward pursuing that question for more than a decade. She discussed it with her husband prior to their marriage. He thought she might be right. But he couldn't be sure.

THE NATURE OF HEALING

As a therapist, there are really only a few things you do when meeting a new person:

First, from the very beginning, from the very first minute, you try to create an interpersonal climate that makes it possible to talk, really talk, understanding that "real talk" takes place only between people who feel equal to each other (or nearly so). The conventional understanding, which is really a profound misunderstanding, claims that many persons are patients because they can't feel equal to the demands for that kind of "real talk"; that is, they don't feel the equal of the therapist or anybody else. But I don't find it that way. I find it the rare person indeed—diagnosis unrelated—who won't match the therapist's willingness to be more than a role called "doctor" with his own willingness to be more than a role called "patient." Perhaps the therapist is the more important in giving the initial signal as to what the measure of parity, and thus the level of the discourse, is to be. After all, it's the therapist's office. But once this decision has been made, and it happens quickly, a kind of contract has been agreed to which will be hard for either the therapist or the patient to change. This is a very important matter, one that goes beyond the details of technique. It reflects the way the two people look at each other and the way they look at life.

The second therapeutic task is to listen in that unique therapist's way, sometimes with such intimacy and psychological closeness that you are almost breathing in unison with your patient, sometimes from such a distance that you think about this person in the long panorama of people with similar hopes and fears throughout the ages. Moving back and forth is important. If you're always breathing in unison, you have the limits of a close relative, lover, or athletic partner. If you are regularly removed, objective, dispassionate, and reasonable, you become as useless as all such people are. A good psychiatrist knows, almost intuitively, when to be close, when to stay back.

You listen for many things. What hasn't happened may be as important as that which is described in great detail. There are technical questions that point to further examinations that need to be performed. There are questions about past events or future hopes that may be relevant. Sometimes people have experienced mood alterations or periods when there was interference with the clarity of their thinking. Some individuals have had many other therapeutic contacts with doctors, trials of medicines, periods of hospitalization and, of course, you need to know the details of those experiences. Interruption of work or schooling and interference with the ability to live and work effectively with people are serious symptoms that require careful exploration. So is the history of suicide or its contemplation. Suicide in the family or the history of mental illness in siblings, children, parents, aunts, uncles, and in the grandparental generation is also important at times. You may even gain a head start in selecting a specific medicine if the individual has had a near relative who was treated successfully for a similar illness. Personal health history and family health history are essential. When did the patient have his or her last physical examination? What were the results? Is the patient taking any medication? Last but far from least is the present financial situation of the patient. It is sometimes the most important fact of all. Debt is a great and painful burden in the lives of many people.

You learn a great deal about people when they tell about what is usually a very small number of relationships, that is, those with mother-father, spouse, siblings, children, love(s), and boss. Much of the drama of life is lived out with that small cast of characters, and, as often as not, in the end the outcome of the therapy is determined by what happens in those key areas. That's one of the reasons that my own work with patients has become increasingly couple-, family-, and friend-oriented, with the therapy sessions including the presence of the "significant others" as often as possible.

At some summary point in the initial meeting or meetings, the therapist searches his or her own total personal experiences as husband or wife, parent, family member, and experiences gained through professional training and contacts with other patients and colleagues. You call upon what you know of families, friends, love, education, poor people–rich people, winners-losers, work experiences, illnesses, medicines, everything. And you ask yourself, "From the totality of me, from all my experiences, and after having listened as carefully as I am able, have I suggestions that might be of use to this other person?"

Finally, the therapist, or would-be therapist, makes a proposal to that other person as to how he might proceed, for how long, and to what end. I like time-limited proposals that can be extended. I like proposals that call for participation of key others. I like proposals that leave open the possibility that we're "on the wrong track" and may have to decide together to go in a different direction.

LOVING RELATIONSHIPS

If one is to talk of what is important to people, it is well to begin with love. In loving relationships, people intuit, discover, or build their meanings. The philosopher Martin Buber summed it up in these words: "Feelings one has; love occurs. Feelings dwell in man, but man dwells in his love."[1]

Without meaning to disparage any of the helping professionals, we all know (and often forget) that the most important and helpful relationships are not ordinarily offered by a doctor, nurse, social worker, psychologist, rehabilitation worker, or religious counselor. The best helper in most situations is someone who admires, approves of, understands, and loves the person, even if that person is also someone else's patient. There are many moments in life when the thing that keeps you going is the fact that someone loves you no matter what you do. Long after other kinds of therapists have come and gone, the loving relationship is likely to persist in serving, enriching, and restoring the former patient. Over a period of time, a highly troubled, disorganized, or depressed individual whose circle of relationships includes people genuinely and lovingly committed to him will fare better than a seemingly less troubled person who is without close friends or mate. This is not to deny that there are times when loving relationships are confusing, overconfining, or contaminated with unloving emotions. Neither is it to suggest that a person who is loved won't get sick or that, once sick, love alone is always sufficient to effect the cure. Nevertheless, loving relationships are an important deterrent to the development of the pain called mental illness, a restorative during the period of healing, and an antidote to this illness's long-term consequences. Few will fail to understand why loss of or serious threat to such relationships is quite often the chief cause of the anxiety, withdrawal, or distortion of life that underlies much that is called mental illness. Suicide, in young adults and older individuals as well, is frequently related to dissolution of a love relationship. Fifty

percent of the people seeking psychotherapy cite marital difficulties as their primary problem. Many others include stress
in a love relationship as among their important concerns. Trite
though it may seem, the question "Whom do you love?" is
often the inquiry that goes most regularly to the source of the
patient's greatest anxiety. Nor can a clinician overlook "acute
love" in mature and older people. Many career and major life
changes that people initiate without apparent reason prove, in
time, to have been the result of experiencing (again) "being in
love." Certainly, many of the most dramatic therapeutic
"cures" as contrasted with "improvements" center around the
discovery or the rekindling of an intense, alive, here-and-now
loving relationship. Some therapists assume an active role in
trying to increase their patient's opportunities and determination to seek love. If there are problems within a family, they
work on those. If there is no family, they work on that.

> DR. RICHARD STUART, behavior therapist: "Well, you're
> a pretty alive person, Mrs. D. How about another
> man in your life!"
>
> MRS. D., four years a widow, fifty-three, a fine musician,
> drinking too much, depressed, "alone" despite a
> circle of social friends: "Well, not just anyone, you
> know."
>
> DR. STUART: "I'm already married."
>
> MRS. D.: "I didn't mean that. I meant I couldn't love
> just anybody. If I ever get involved again, it couldn't
> be, well, how do you say, just a 'roll in the hay.' "
>
> DR. STUART: "People I know are happiest if there's
> somebody they love in their lives."
>
> MRS. D.: "Well, sure, I would be too. But there aren't
> all that many like that. I mean, I'm fifty-three and
> you don't meet too many people you could respect
> and who would respect you. And, well, it's just not
> easy at my age."
>
> DR. STUART: "So, you've been trying hard and have
> discovered it's not easy? And anyway, you could
> start with one and maybe you wouldn't need all that
> many."

MRS. D.: "Well, no, I haven't tried that hard. And I'd settle for one good one."

DR. STUART: "So, good, we're agreed. It's important to you and you should try harder. What have you considered doing to expand your circle of active, and I mean active, friends?"

Mrs. D. was my patient, and we seemed to be on a kind of therapeutic plateau after three months. I invited Dr. Stuart to join us as a consultant. Mrs. D. took that consultation seriously, appreciated Stuart's candor, didn't get mad at him (or me), and took his advice fairly literally. She made her plans, established a kind of contract with herself, and followed it. It helped her a good deal, seemed to strengthen her determination to stand up for herself, and helped her to say yes when she meant yes and no when she meant no instead of maybe when she meant either no or yes. Also, the challenge to declare openly to herself what she wanted and what she would change in order to achieve it gave her the courage to risk the most feared of all human situations; that is, appearing foolish. The Stuart exercise made her more direct with me, with others, and finally with herself.[2]

Stuart's experience in working with couples and families, and my own as well, is that if you ask a husband to make an honest list of three things he would really like his wife to do for him, and if she does even one of those three, he is likely to be a very grateful man. And the same is true the other way around. If you can have the wife state explicitly three things that she would appreciate, definite actions such as kissing her first before turning on the television, saying I love you when they make love, saying something nice about her in the presence of her family, even picking up his clothes, and so forth, and if he does one of the three, she is likely to be moved (and surprised). Small things really matter because they have to do with personal regard. This kind of therapeutic work, though hardly spectacular, can result in a significant change in the way two people relate to each other, and it can take place rapidly. You may discover that you don't have to provide a new childhood for one or both of the spouses. They may discover they don't need a new mate to be moved and excited. The therapeutic emphasis is on "how good it could be" with the two of them.

Another very remarkable therapist who is not at all vague about love and loved ones is Dr. Carl Whitaker, a psychiatrist who teaches and practices family therapy at the University of Wisconsin. Whitaker talks a good deal about the "temperature" in a marriage, and he insists that both members of a marriage have their hands on the "thermostat" and that it takes an explicit agreement between the two to raise the temperature. This would explain the paradox of a marriage that is too cold to keep tropical fish even though both partners can cite many examples of their individual efforts to warm things up. Whitaker says they have a secret deal with each other to take turns turning the heat up, then down. That way, both can make some effort but not really do all the work required to keep a marriage (and life) alive.[3]

Another Whitaker idea is that "an affair" is usually a secret agreement between a couple to "bring in an amateur psycho- therapist to warm things up for the two of you." Then, he usually adds, "You'd be better off to stick with a professional. It's usually cheaper in the long run." He thinks that every couple should have a chance to turn their exclusive and un- hurried attention to their relationship at least once every year or so.

> No, not sick couples, just couples. I'm proposing a center for couples, normal, everyday crazy couples like us and our spouses. A place to put it on the line again, to get reacquainted, to practice listening again, to exchange complaints and brag about what's good with other married people, to remember again where it is we want to be going . . . pardon me, to remember why you chose each other in the first place. I think most people choose with a wisdom that's smarter than they are.
>
> No, not sick couples, all couples, every year. Put it back up front where it belongs.

In earlier years, many therapists tended to overlook the importance of contemporary family relationships and chose instead to focus their attention upon the intrapsychic problems of the individual designated as the "patient." But that approach has many problems. Many times, the individual who was presented as the "patient" was the spokesman who said "ouch" for a whole group of people who were doing badly. And, all too often, ignoring family members during a prolonged individual therapy program was very threatening to those others, to the very persons closest and most important to the patient. In my own work, therapy almost always includes working with loved ones and a continuing exploration of the way members of the family can and do work on problem areas together.

In this respect I've changed. Early in my career I preferred to work almost exclusively as therapist to a single person. And that system has considerable merit. It's quite a wonderful thing when therapist and patient admire and respect each other and work well together. But it's much better when a therapist can help people who are already deeply involved with each other to learn how to help each other and to make their lives more openly, unashamedly, reciprocally loving. Once established, or reestablished, the process can continue and extend without outside help. The four case studies that follow explore the nature and power of loving relationships. Each describes individuals in a period of great difficulty who were sustained and protected by someone who cared for them. The responsibility of a therapist to recognize and protect the integrity and importance of loving relationships in times of great stress will be evident in Case Study 2. The reasons that a therapist should always be respectful and supportive of the love and concern that people have for each other are evident in all the examples that follow in this chapter and in many other parts of the book.

Case Study 2: *Anxious Love*

Raul and Dora were an odd couple, he thirty-seven, obese and short, and she forty-eight, fragile in appearance and tall. They had both been married several times before and had children from those prior marriages. The two of them had been together for three years, and in many respects the union was a good one. They were both wounded when they met and they had helped each other. Also, they had a degree of financial security, having pooled their money and purchased a California house with an extra lot at just the right time. Their union provided a kind of home base for several of the migrating children from their earlier marriages, and, happily, they had collected a small circle of friends who liked them both.

In their insecurity they were very much alike. Dora was a superserious woman who couldn't get over wondering about the failures in her life. She had grown up moderately well-to-do, had had a college education and then a white-dress first marriage to a young professional man. The marriage was joyless, with Dora on the defensive with her husband and his parents for sixteen years. In the end, that husband left her for a younger woman who was also the daughter of business partners of her uncordial father-in-law. She felt sure she had been voted out of the family. It was an extremely painful interlude in her life, and not the last. In general, she brought many insecurities to her relationship with Raul. He in turn had grown up poor and neglected, spent some time in a boy's correctional school, and finally "settled down" in the military. He drank a fair bit in his twenties and early thirties, and this contributed to the breakup of two marriages. But drinking was no longer much of a problem. He had his own small trucking business, which was doing well and which he enjoyed. Still, he was very self-conscious and worried about being looked down on. A psychiatrist once advised him that he was "paranoid."

Dora worked part-time in a small dress shop but spent a good deal of leisure in various women's groups attempting to seek an expanded sense of herself, continuing in her way the psychotherapy she had experienced through the years. One of the matters that her consciousness needed no expansion about was that Raul had some problems of his own, including one that seemed a threat to her dignity.

Raul had some problems with sex, at least in this union. It was very, very important to him. He traveled a great deal and arrived home at odd hours. When he came home, he wanted Dora there. And he wanted her then. She could be cooking, sleeping, awaiting the arrival of a guest or child, it made little difference to him. The ultimate provocation two days earlier was his unexpected arrival after a long absence as Dora was preparing to leave for a women's meeting at which she was to be discussion leader. They met instead with the neighbors and the police. For Dora it was the ultimate degradation. He had had tantrums from the beginning, but this was the first time that anyone had ever hit her.

The public versions from each of them were the same as they had told the police. But the private versions, unspoken even in my office, went something like this.

RAUL: "From the time I was a little boy, I've gone crazy if I felt insulted, put down, or rejected. Dora isn't the first man or woman I've hit. But I love her and curse what I've done. I don't think I'm a homosexual even if I've had a few experiences. I drove through the night so I could be with her all the way. If she leaves me, I'll kill myself. I almost did it ten years ago. I love her more than any woman I've ever known."

DORA: "Why, dear God, why did I tell my group that Raul is like that about sex. What an imbecile I am. How can I face them? I know I shouldn't stand for his attitude. He degrades me as a person by giving me no choice. I guess we should break up, but I'm forty-eight, and my mother will say, 'I told you not to marry him. He's not our class.' But so much about what we do is so good."

I felt that they were two people in a very tight corner and that the stakes were high. I didn't think we should begin by emphasizing their areas of personal sensitivity. I didn't think it necessary to quiz her on being forty-eight with a thirty-seven-year-old husband. Neither did I need more information about his fear of homosexuality as a possible sign of paranoia. I had enough data. Too much.

From a technical standpoint, this kind of crisis moment is also a rare opportunity for the therapist to help turn things around to something special. As the therapist relates to each of them, they come on to themselves and each other. People degraded fear more of the same—especially in a psychiatrist's office—and if it doesn't happen, they are often grateful and open to all kinds of constructive ideas. So the goal of our time together was not simply to heal over the very bad moment that had just occurred. It was to take a big jump, together, away from the wreckage and into (or toward) a more tolerant and supportive relationship. Repairing the old wouldn't be good enough because the old got them in trouble and would do so again. Particular thoughts regularly reappear in my mind in that kind of moment! "Physician, above all do no harm." "Then they get well and then they get weller." "The most important event in recent decades is the growing consciousness in women of their full personal potential." And, far from least, "You don't help people by tearing down their relatives."

They were damaged already and, for vulnerable people, trouble comes in twos, threes, and fours. Still, they did not require much therapy from me. We met only four times. In our second session (the second week) I asked them to "be each other"; that is, to speak as if they were the other spouse in the hours before, during, and after their awful event. I asked them to include the good as well as the mean in their portrayal. There were no Academy Award performances, but both laughed and cried and both were unmistakably searching for a kinder understanding of the other's behavior. There was a very, very painful part of that hour when Raul realized that Dora had told some of her women friends about their sexual life. Things got worse before they got better. But not really, since it turned out that Raul was already suspicious and resentful of her women's group and that had been one of the main reasons for his loss of control. I encouraged Dora to stick with her group anyway, and Raul agreed. He surprised Dora and me by enthusiastically agreeing that he wanted to share with her membership in a men and women's consciousness-raising group. That turned out to be, over the next six months, an experience he took very much to heart. He was at that particular point in his life more open than one could have expected both to the idea of Dora's growth *and* to his partial release from a very narrow and demanding idea of how a "man" was supposed to behave.

We also talked candidly and explicitly about the fact that sexual relations with Dora were a very important part of Raul's sense of well-being, security, and contentment. That part of their life together was important to Dora, too, but she knew that Raul was doing more than making love when he made love. Such manifestation of his insecurity got mixed up with her own self-doubt and she had to cope with two self-worth problems at the same time. Dora felt that she should be the kind of woman who would attract a man who would make non-anxious love with her.

I told them that they might choose to accept as needing no explanation the fact that sexual relations with Dora were a very important part of Raul's sense of well-being, security, and contentment. Dora could be, and was, a fine and full woman even though the man she was married to was not the former Duke of Windsor—and never would be. And she could be glad for that.

Dora and Raul are still together. It's been seven years since they came to see me. They never did join the procession of Californians on their way to divorce. Lately, the number of divorces exceed marriages in California: 150,000 divorces compared with 120,000 marriages annually. Nationally, there are 1,800,000 marriages and 1,200,000 divorces annually.

There are times when the power of the bonds between people is so awesome that there is no psychiatric vocabulary to describe what has taken place.

Case Study 3: *I Love You, Janie Riley*

After the tragic headlines are forgotten, the people involved still have their lives to carry on, and sometimes the aftermath is as moving and instructive as the original events. Jane and Billy Riley were still very much in love even though she had murdered their seven-month-old daughter. It was a story no less horrible than the Greek tragedy *Medea*. The combatants were Jane and her mother and, of course, Jane and herself. She drowned her baby in its bath a few minutes after receiving a transoceanic call from her mother, which was a continuation of their twenty-eight-year-old struggle with each other. Jane was suffering a severe mental depression at that time, the third such illness she had experienced in ten years. When I first met her, the trial was over and she had been released from charges but ordered deported to Australia, from where she and Billy had recently immigrated. She was in the hospital in a very depressed state awaiting deportation.

Billy was a seemingly uncomplicated man, thirty years old, a sheet-metal worker with an education that had ended after one year of high school. He had a generous heart that sought the best possible light in which to view all parts of the tragic events. I found myself tenderly grateful to him for his interpretation of the impact of the mother's call on the event that followed. "I understand it easily," he explained. "Janie missed her mother and felt more lonely and depressed that she couldn't see her." It was the more remarkable because his mother-in-law had looked down on him and opposed the marriage because he came from a very poor family.

Billy focused very narrowly on the words "a terrible illness and depression" as the total clarification for what had happened and he constantly repeated to Jane, "You c'not help yourself, Janie, the illness was too strong. It was just like our lawyer said." "You c'not see, Billy, you c'not know," she would ordinarily reply.

A few weeks later an amazing thing happened. Billy was a teetotaler, but he appeared in our emergency room at 2:00 A.M. one morning in a profoundly agitated state. At first, he appeared drunk. But he wasn't. He insisted that the police were going to kill him and that they had already killed Jane. He pleaded that he be put to death in a merciful way by the doctors rather than be forced to go through the cruel torture that was being planned. At one point, he broke away and put his hand through a glass pane in a hospital door, and he was placed in restraints and sedated. During the next thirty-six hours he continued to shout and scream whenever his sedation wore off. But near the end of the second day, he began to quiet down. At that point, we hospitalized him on the ward in the same room with his wife. After three or four days, he was fully restored to his previous manner and demeanor. He told Jane that he now truly understood what had happened to her. After that event, she did not contest him.

Prisons are more mediocre than they are brutal. You can restrict the brutality but the mediocrity and waste are constantly present. Tens of millions of dollars are squandered teaching people who hate and are hated to hate more. However, I worked for five years as the chief psychiatric consultant in a remarkable prison hospital, the Regional Medical Center (R.M.C.) at Abbotsford, British Columbia, Canada. Dr. Chuni Roy has been its director since it opened in 1973. A handful of psychiatrists, psychologists, and social workers are joined by forty female and male nurses and forty guards in working with 120 of Canada's most severely disturbed, maximum security criminals (rapists, bombers, murderers).

Case Study 4: *How Can One Evaluate*
One's First Friend?

Tom Morrant, thirty-four, had been in trouble all his life and in prisons or their junior equivalent since he was nine years old, unhappy, hostile, reclusive, and now a murderer. He didn't know whether his second victim had also died. That was twelve years ago. Now he was afraid to ask. He had been sent to the R.M.C. a year earlier because control in the regular prison meant continual solitary confinement. In the R.M.C. he had been almost impossible to manage despite drug therapy, fellow prisoner "buddies" assigned to help him adjust, visits and reassurance from a "friends of prisoners group" (the John Howard Society), and the assignment of nursing staff around the clock to help him settle down in the Center. I didn't know him in that earlier period but was asked to talk with him and his chief nurse therapist, Kathy Jones, around a year after his arrival. The problem was that Tom loved Kathy and resented her work with all the other patients in her charge. Also, Kathy was going to be leaving the Center when her husband finished school and Tom wanted a commitment that she would write. Kathy wanted to keep things straight and clear with Tom and so the two of them came for a consultation with me.

Tom loved Kathy, but I should have gone on to say that it was Tom's first love and it had helped to bring about a miracle in his life. Before seeing the two of them, I had violated my own rule about never reading other people's written reports before talking with a patient. From Tom's history I learned that Tom's life had been as deprived as any I had known. But that was before, and now Tom was different. In the interview, Kathy talked about being his nurse, not his girl friend, and Tom was saying that he could get a better girl friend than her anyway. I asked Tom how good a friend Kathy was and he said he couldn't say for sure. He had never had any other and had no way to compare. He said he knew his demands were hard on her, but she had asked for it when he gave his word to her that he would never hit her (a year before). I asked him when he would become eligible for probation and he said 1988. Looking at Kathy he said to me, in a most tender, sincere, and open way, "But I have hope."

The subjects of love, loving, and intimacy will be considered in a number of places in this book because they are so much a part of what is important in life. That was something I didn't completely understand when I started my practice.

Case Study 5: *Ellen Ryan*

I first met Ellen Ryan in September 1955. She was twenty-one, very sweet and conscientious, pretty, and she worked as a secretary in a large office. She also was overwhelmed by fears, very eccentric, and, above all, she had no sense of the power, integrity, and survivability of her own body. She told me in that first interview, "When I wear a white dress, I feel like a nurse; when I wear pants, I feel like a boy." Her sense of her self was that tenuous. Once, several years later, she discovered a dead fly in her room two weeks after it had been fumigated. With a wisdom that comes with madness, she told me in panic, "If DDT can kill a fly, it can kill me." For our next appointment Ellen's mother and father made the long bus ride from their home in southern Illinois to Madison to give me their view of Ellen's life, a six-hour trip that cost her father two days' work. The mother tearfully told me, in Ellen's presence, that one month after giving birth to her daughter she had developed a profound fear of germs and disease. She was afraid that she would convey disease to Ellen. With horror, she told me that she was also afraid that the baby, Ellen, would convey disease to her. At that time in her life the mother's fears were merciless and unrelenting. She was incapacitated at home for five months, unable to care for her child. That was in 1935. Ellen's mother had been free of gross mental illness in the twenty years that followed, but her house was very clean and few vegetables were undercooked.

I was a twenty-eight-year-old psychiatrist in 1955, and I viewed the mother as Ellen's—and thus my—

natural enemy. I felt that she had damaged Ellen so severely that she had produced schizophrenia in the daughter. I assumed that she was still a toxic force, a noxious agent.

In the twenty-five years that have passed, Ellen's illness has been cruel, awesome in its force, devastating to her life. It has taken in the recent decade a mixed manic-depressive as well as schizophrenic pattern, resistant in terms of full control to any of the dozens of medication shifts that her doctors have attempted.

I've not seen Ellen for fourteen years, but, with the knowledge and understanding of her present doctor, she calls me from Illinois not infrequently, once a month on the average. And I talk to her widowed mother once a year, maybe once every two years. What have I learned from them?

- I have been witness for more than twenty-five years to their tenacity, their dignity, and their commitment to do the best they can despite terrible adversity. I am more respectful of all human beings because of what I've learned from Ellen and her mother.

- I have great admiration for Ellen, who despite a mean and cruel disease, clings to her life, works at it, has hope. I'm glad she finally made love for the first time when she was forty-six years old. I hope she has other chances. I'm proud that she works at the Volunteers of America two days a week.

- I admire and have learned from Ellen's mother and I am grateful that she is such a staunch, loving, respectful ally and friend of her daughter. I cried with her a couple of years ago when she called and tearfully told me that she turned down Ellen's wish to share an apartment because she knew that Ellen's life would be better and bigger if she had her own place. She told me, "Of course, I am afraid she might hurt herself, but I have to believe in her life." She wanted my reassurance on the point. I told her, "You're a good lady, Mrs. Ryan, and I trust your heart all the way." Ellen's mother must be close to eighty by now.

Love, respect, inspiration, and awe form a continuum of usually positive attitudes that people may have about friends, teachers, religious and political leaders, individuals with great skill in areas that are valued, and so forth. On occasion, a doctor earns (or is assigned) respect or more by a patient and family. Even people we don't know personally can become very important in our lives.

CHARISMATIC RELATIONSHIPS

The charismatic person is defined in the dictionary as one who "restores emotion, awe, and magic to the conduct of affairs and would appear to himself and/or to others to be endowed with authority analogous to that of the original theological meaning of the word." Sometimes it's only in secret, but most people hunger for heroic figures and make their own lives more exciting by identifying with those who appear powerful and inspiring. Those who hunt and would strike down a leader express their awe and hunger, but in a mean, blunted, and perverse way. But for most of us, our heroes are treasured. Intimacy with the memory of a President John Kennedy sustains a symbol of the youth and vigor of our nation and ourselves. The memory of Martin Luther King, Jr., walking up an Alabama highway is an image not only of the man but of ourselves standing up for what we believe. There were the words of a Winston Churchill instructing his people to take a stand against the Nazis even when the enemy was at their doorsteps. They were our doorsteps as well. These men are not only historical figures, they are figures that the people of my generation can identify with. No less important is the opportunity for the architect to have been a student of Frank Lloyd Wright or Mies van der Rohe; for the artist to have worked with Hans Hofmann, Louise Nevelson, or Henry

Moore; for the philosopher to have shared dialogue with Alfred North Whitehead or Suzanne Langer. Such contacts both direct and vicarious have been important in the personal development of countless men and women. People vie to stand near the great and treasure for a lifetime an affirmation by an heroic figure.

"Living heroically" is a topic of consuming importance in the 1974 Pulitzer Prize–winning book *The Denial of Death*.[4] It was written by Ernest Becker, a distinguished sociologist at Simon Fraser University in Vancouver, shortly before his own early, tragic death. Becker's inquiry turns to the question of how anyone could live well, live optimistically, sustaining a sense that his is a worthwhile life, in the face of the absurd extremes of human existence. Each of us is poet and maker of dreams. Yet each is simultaneously an animal body committed to consuming as much other animal flesh as is needed. And in time we die. In his analysis, Becker emphasizes the importance of those who live life with style, with certainty, with so much seeming conviction about what they are doing that it would appear that there is no problem about the meaning of life. There is nothing to be concerned about! The answer is clear! It is (God, work, science, love, making money, sex, the welfare of the children, writing music, building a pension) whatever you declare it to be! Once declared, you stop asking if it really is the answer. He calls this "causa sui," that which is its own cause and thus needs no explanation. It is an Aristotelian concept. Average people can take courage and hope from those who live with genius and/or style. Identification with the great and the near-great men and women whose achievements seem as big as life itself offers comfort and hope to those who can't believe that life would be justified just for them.

Much in the tradition of medicine and the helping professions fits into the charismatic style. Whether symbolized by a mask and painted body of a tribal medicine man or a wailing siren accompanying a white-coated medic to an automobile accident, the message is the same: "He has come. A very powerful person is here! No need to question the meaning of life." Harvey Cushing, Charles Mayo, Karl Menninger,

Sigmund Freud, Anna Freud—every doctor has stories to tell about such men and women or their students or even their students' students. This writer firmly believes a story told about his professor of pediatrics, a man so commanding in demeanor that whenever he walked into the newborns' nursery, all of the crying infants fell silent.

When people are sick, discouraged, or endangered, heroic figures in reassuring stances are particularly welcome. Even half-heroic figures can be blown up to full size. When the crisis is medical, the clinician receives the patient in a medical office or clinic, surrounded by books, journals, and other tools of the trade. There are white coats, nurses responding to instructions, disinfectant smells, and other patients who are convinced. On the wall hang licenses that permit almost anything, since they are written in Latin. All this is not without importance. Power to those ordained! One chooses to forget how many patients and how many doctors are no longer with us.

Charisma provides a transient antidote to the anxiety inherent in the life of mortal beings. But the relief may be illusory. Most therapeutic charismatic poses fail the test of time.

The late Jean-Paul Sartre was merciless in his repudiation of any and all who claim by word or deed to know how other men should live. "The doctor" gets special attention in his writings. In *Nausea,* his classic first novel, Sartre traces the elements of a charismatic medical stance and notes the relief felt by all when the doctor comes to "set things straight."[5] But, as with all heroes in this illusionless view of life, in the end there is little to cheer about.

> M. Achille is joyful; he would like to catch the doctor's eye. But he swings his legs and shifts about on the bench in vain, he is so thin that he makes no noise.
>
> The waitress brings the calvados. With a nod of her head she points out the little man to the doctor. Doctor Roge slowly turns: he can't move his neck.
>
> "So, it's you, you old swine," he shouts, "aren't you dead yet?"

He addresses the waitress:

"You let people like that in here?"

He stares at the little man ferociously. A direct look which puts everything in place. He explains:

"He's crazy as a loon, that's that."

He doesn't even take the trouble to let on that he's joking. He knows that the loony won't be angry, that he's going to smile. And there it is: the man smiles with humility. A crazy loon: he relaxes, he feels protected against himself: nothing will happen to him today. I am reassured too. A crazy old loon: so that was it, so that was all.

The fine wrinkles; he has all of them: horizontal ones running across his forehead, crow's feet, bitter lines at each corner of the mouth, without counting the yellow cords depending from his chin. There's a lucky man: as soon as you perceive him, you can tell he must have suffered, that he is someone who has lived. He deserves his face for he has never, for one instant, lost an occasion of utilizing his past to the best of his ability: he has stuffed it full, used his experience on women and children, exploited them.

M. Achille is probably happier than he has ever been. He is agape with admiration; he drinks his Byrrh in small mouthfuls and swells his cheeks out with it. The doctor knew how to take him! The doctor wasn't the one to let himself be hypnotized by an old madman on the verge of having his fit; one good blow, a few rough, lashing words, that's what they need. The doctor has experience. He is a professional in experience: doctors, priests, magistrates and army officers know men through and through as if they had made them.

A little while ago M. Achille felt queer, he felt lonely: now he knows that there are others like him, many others: Doctor Roge has met them, he could tell M. Achille the case history of each one of them and tell him how they ended up. M. Achille is simply a case and lets himself be brought back easily to the accepted ideas.

How I would like to tell him he's being deceived, that he is the butt of the important. Experienced professionals? They have dragged out their life in stupor and semi-sleep, they have married hastily, out of impatience, they have made children at random. They have met other men in cafes, at weddings and funerals. Sometimes, caught in the tide, they have struggled against it without understanding what was happening to them. All that has happened around them has eluded them; long, obscure shapes, events from afar, brushed by them rapidly and when they turned to look all had vanished. And then, around forty, they christen their small obstinacies and a few proverbs with the name of experience, they begin to simulate slot machines: put a coin in the left hand slot and you get tales wrapped in silver paper, put a coin in the slot on the right and you get precious bits of advice that stick to your teeth like caramels.

Doctor Roge has finished his calvados. His great body relaxes and his eyelids droop heavily. For the first time I see his face without the eyes: like a cardboard mask, the kind they're selling in the shops today. His cheeks have a horrid pink color. . . . The truth stares me in the face: this man is going to die soon. He surely knows; he needs only look in the glass; each day he looks a little more like the corpse he will become. That's what their experience leads to, that's why I tell myself so often that they smell of death: it is their last defense.

SUMMARY

The experience of being genuinely in touch with, understood, and appreciated by another person is an important event. In many lives such communication rarely takes place. For some it never happens. What does it mean to have someone with whom one can speak of anything, unashamedly, honestly? What would it mean right now to be able to speak to that person? In day-by-day human encounters few meetings take place between people who are listening, who hear, and who understand. Instead, the apparent listener waits for the noise of the other to end so that he himself may speak, only to be also unheard.

> "Hello."
> "Well, hello there. How are you?"
> "Fine, how are you?"
> "Poorly. I've just come from the hospital. I have cancer."
> "What else is new?"

When someone is listening, this is no everyday event! To be listened to, to be understood, and to be acknowledged as interesting by a respected other is among the most encouraging and helpful experiences in the life of any individual. Carl Rogers feels that listening with the intention of hearing represents the most effective psychotherapeutic tool. Perhaps it is the only important one.[6] Somewhat afield, Ralph Martin, author of the book *The Woman He Loved*, speculates that the Duchess of Windsor may have been the first person who really wanted to know how Edward felt about his life.[7] If you want to be a psychotherapist or marry a king. . . .

Caring about and being interested in hearing from another person is not an attitude easily taught or effectively feigned. If a therapist is uninterested, dislikes or fears a patient, or if that patient is simply the vehicle for making money, such will soon be clear. When people neither appreciate each other nor particularly want to share in each other's lives, it becomes apparent even if the words spoken seem reassuring and affectionate. What we are speaks louder than what we say.

But the listening of a therapist to the words of the patient does not go on forever. What happens then? Assuming a relationship between a therapist and a patient or a family that is as free as possible of lying and pretending, what comes of it? Beyond less pain, what is the goal of a psychiatrist's help? How does it end? The patient's words might sound something like these.

When I came for psychotherapy, I had no hope other than you. When I found you, I felt you were the answer. Now, it is clear that you are not the answer and I must continue my search elsewhere. I came hoping to achieve an adjustment to life through you. Now I understand that life is not that way. One never adjusts. One keeps on searching. But I have hope. And I am glad for the chance to go on. I will miss you.

Any other ending of psychotherapy represents at best a grand misunderstanding on the part of the patient and at worst a *folie à deux* (a madness shared by two people) between patient and therapist. A therapist who seems to promise freedom from anxiety or that his message will be available to assuage the patient's anxiety in perpetuity misrepresents the world to the patient and to himself. He and the patient are "in the same boat." The world is and always will be filled with abundant reasons for profound anxiety. Whatever were the initial hopes for a perpetual link, the ending of therapy sees doctor and patient going separately, each living with the anxiety of being a finite being, each seeking elsewhere what could not result for either from the therapy. At the end therapy becomes or is revealed as "not it." "It" is what is sought as life continues.

2

Health and Illness:
An Existential
Point of View

A group of distinguished experts in the various social
and medical fields from all parts of North America had
assembled for a meeting concerning the problems of American
Indians. They were prepared to provide their findings concerning the extent of alcoholism, broken homes, venereal
disease, school failures and dropouts, street drugs, automobile
accidents, suicide, and violence among Indians. But before
the first presentation, one of the observers, an Indian man,
interrupted the meeting. He wouldn't let anyone speak. He
had something important to say: "I want to thank all of you
doctors and lawyers and people from the government who have
come here to help my people. That's very good and we are
grateful. And we do need help. But all these things you've
listed in the program aren't problems. No, actually, we
Indians only have two problems. First, we have to decide what
is a good life. That's easy. But then, we have to figure out
how you get a life like that if you're an Indian. And that's
impossible." Of course, he was right. No person and certainly
no group of people can trust someone's view of what's wrong
with them if that person doesn't know what's right with them.

What is a good life? Who has one? Who among us is to say? And what happens to the "science" of psychiatry when you start thinking about such matters?

I'm certain that there is no single theory or unitary system of treatment in psychiatry that is going to be appropriate for three consecutive patients who come in search of help. I've found that my patients are different and the treatment needs are different as well. The leading textbook of psychiatry is now published in three large volumes. The next revision will likely require a fourth. The field is extremely complex. My own therapeutic activities regularly include: listening and talking, inviting relatives to joint the treatment sessions, prescription of medications (a dozen different medication programs to consider), recommending hospitalization, setting up behavior-therapy (conditioning) programs, and offering advice to go to school, go to work, learn a new trade, go for an "encounter" weekend at a human potential center, and sometimes to stop seeking psychiatric help and take life "cold turkey." But it's no grab bag for me. I'm very careful and cautious and I take very seriously the fact that it is the one and only life of my patient that is being considered.

From the early days of my training in psychiatry, I have had a sustaining interest in existential philosophy and its application in my work with patients and families and in my understanding of my own reactions. That life is precious is a haunting conviction that underlies what I call an "existential" approach in psychiatry.[1] By "precious" I mean that the time and space allotted to each of us are the most valuable possessions we have. By "existential" I mean that I make a serious effort to come as close as possible to experiencing the way the world is experienced by my patient. Historically, existential philosophy has been concerned with two somewhat separate areas. The first has to do with the nature of experiencing itself.[2,3] How does an individual "see" and "avoid seeing" in his unique world? What is the nature of consciousness? What gets special attention and what is shunned? The second area of existential inquiry has to do with the problem of living bravely in the face of all the human ambiguities.[4,5] In a short and uncertain lifetime, what has an individual chosen as important? To what extent is a person intrigued by the opportunities potentially available to him? To what extent is he fearful? If he is fearful of disease or of attack by a stranger, to what extent does the specific fearful symptom prevent his considering the possibilities of his life and the necessity to choose among them? Sometimes the anxiety of choosing is more awesome than the fear that frightens.

An "existential" approach gives high place to the mystery of our being here in the first place and makes explicit the question: "Since you're here, what are you going to do?" It's an approach that assumes that the individual and the therapist have a lot to talk about since *neither of them* has life figured out. In that sense, it is somewhat egalitarian in perspective. It is an approach that admits, "It takes courage to live," and assigns considerable credit to people who keep trying in spite of it all.

Some existential thinkers are deeply committed to Judeo-Christian traditions of the meaning and quality of life. Paul Tillich, Christian existential theologian, wrote and preached of the life of Christ both as the ultimate model and the reason for each person to live his or her life kindly, openly, passionately, and hopefully.[6] Tillich believed that the important message from Christ's life was not a fixed prescription as to how life should be lived, but quite the opposite. He felt that every person's life is a necessary search for meaning and that biblical inspiration was just that—inspiration. No detailed, life-living road map had been charted. But there is reason and hope for the journey.

Similarly, in the experience of Martin Buber, life is made richer, more meaningful, more alive by the discovery of God's presence in a reverent relationship with objects and beings that he called "I and Thou."[7] Buber's religious philosophy emphasized the difference between the "I" that reverently and lovingly relates to the people and objects of life (the "I" of "I-Thou") and a more indifferent, less compassionate, taking-for-granted experiencing that he called the "I" of "I-It." The vast difference in the nature of those two kinds of experiencing seemed for Buber not only the models for better and less good styles of living; they also seemed evidence of the godly heights that exist in the human being. The meaning of life, its purpose, is

to be that ultimate that one already is in one's most compassionate and reverent and awe-inspired experiences.

Later in this chapter, a long passage from Hermann Hesse's
Siddhartha provides a moving summation of all religious
existential thinking: the search, your search, has worth and
meaning. There is something to be discovered. It is the unfold-
ing of your life and simultaneously the meaning of all life.

Other existential writers find no basis for religious hope. Yet
for them, the remarkable thing about man is that he keeps
going, keeps looking, keeps trying. He is the one-legged man
who hops. She is the blind woman who reads with her fingers
and walks with a dog. He is the husband and King of Siam
of whom the wife sings:

> This is a man who thinks with his heart.
> His heart is not always wise.
> This is a man who stumbles and falls,
> But this is a man who tries.[8]

Perhaps there is no better example of the role of courage in
looking for meaning in life than the late existential writer
Jean-Paul Sartre, who, in his last years, was becoming blind.
Still, he wrote as he had each day of his life. And he wrote that
there was no purpose. And he wrote.

Among my patients there have been some very hard-
working individuals who attained the external trappings of
success but who felt that their lives were empty and without
meaning. Several seemed to have been shot from the same
cannon in early childhood. They were pointed to a direction
called "the top" and given all the rules as to how to get there.
And the first forty or so years were spent living out the instructions and traveling a trajectory that provided little nourishment
for the soul. Once I interrupted a patient who was describing
his relentless, joyless climb to ask, "Did you ever think that
you'd like to get something for yourself?" My patient replied,
"Do you mean like another Mercedes Benz?" I said, "Not
exactly."

Case Study 1: *Birds Gulping Milk*

Sometimes in a psychiatrist's office, you get a vivid picture of the painful efforts of people to hide and cope with their areas of insecurity by engulfing themselves in their work. Sometimes their devotion to duty is in reality a crusade against what they most fear, that is, their personal hungers. Once I worked with a very troubled man who was also very, very successful in managing a major industrial corporation. The growing success of the corporation was accompanied by mounting misery in the man's family which reached a slugging match when he became outraged at the way his children were "gulping" milk, rather than sipping it as he had learned to do when he was a child. When he went to discipline the children, his wife came at him with her arms flying and, to his horror, he knocked her down and broke her wrist.

He was a difficult patient for me, a tall, handsome, aristocratic, ultra-conservative man with the most intense need to do "what is right" that I had ever encountered (or have to this day). He had been reared with unrelenting discipline and expectation. The milk episode was a direct reenactment of his childhood (minus any protest by a wife and mother). Although he was very successful in his management of a large company in the automotive industry, he had many phobias, including a fear of elevators, high buildings, and airplanes, which he disguised by his insistence that anyone who wanted to do business with him had to come to him. As far as business matters went, it wasn't a bad accommodation to his incapacities. He was blessed by a wonderful wife and very sweet children whose relationship to him and to each other was both a great satisfaction and much more love than he could handle. The family's troubles were related to his recurring and sometimes frantic need to compel his children to discipline themselves, to suffer and feel the kind of shame that seemed to be a constant companion to him.

Most striking in what he revealed to me was the here-and-now intensity of the hungers of childhood. It was no accident that he had come for help out of anxiety over his own children's joyous gulping down of milk. He felt that his own discipline had begun while he was still in utero. The suppressed child in him was still guilty, feeling that if only he had done better, done more, things would have gone more happily for him.

One of his most bitter disappointments was his failure in childhood to achieve a highest scouting award. He finished every requirement except one: construction of a birdhouse inhabited by birds. The birds never came, not in the early summer and not in the subsequent spring. And then it was too late for him. He wondered about writing to the scouting organization to see whether they would be willing to waive that requirement, since he was sure he could prove that others who had claimed success in the requirement had also failed to attract birds into their birdhouses.

Here he was, this forty-five-year-old president of a Canadian corporation with five thousand employees, talking tearfully with me about the pain of failure of his homes for birds, for his wife and children, and for himself.

I helped him. I made him do it again, this time in his own backyard. And the birds came. And they gulped milk. And he felt good about it.

AVERAGE, ORDINARY PEOPLE

One encounters from time to time those very special people, loving and capable, generous and wise, who are enthusiastic about living in general and their own lives in particular. Along with their reverence for others, they mostly do what they want to do, do it well, and have a good time at it. There is a kind of ambience in their lives. They are persons who are admired in almost all cultures. One wouldn't mind "being like" that kind of person. But instead we are ourselves

—less confident, less generous, and living a life with many "maybes."

In the average, ordinary state of affairs, the individual conforms closely to the standards of his or her peers. He believes what "they" believe. She does what "they" do. Both will look with suspicion at anyone who does otherwise. This conformity, this thinking, believing, and behaving like the others is not without some very obvious social advantage. It facilitates comfort and companionship in everyday life through allegiances and affiliations that offer satisfaction and safety. Being part of a "we" provides the structure for the perpetuation of ethical and religious principles and allows agreement as to the way the cultural and material legacy of the society is to be passed on to succeeding generations. In being surrounded by people who think alike and can be expected to behave in the same way, there is a sense of order, a feeling that "all is as it should be," and one can choose to be relaxed. Life will "take care of itself." Of course, there are dangers in all that homogeneity, all that sameness, all that trust of the others. One may almost disappear among them.

The German existential philosopher Martin Heidegger described this process of losing the self in conformity with "the they" in his exposition of the nature of life in "average everydayness," one of the major concepts in his classic work *Being and Time*.[9] Unfortunately, his complex formulation of existence as "being in the world" does not translate easily into the language of subjects (I, we, he) and objects, and the ideas in the paragraph that follows suffer some distortion. Heidegger is writing of the actual experiencing of life in the day-by-day going about of one's activities. He is here describing the norm, the average, the typical way in which the world presents itself as one goes along.

> I myself am not; my being has been taken away by the others. My everday possibilities of being are for the others to dispose of as they please. . . . I take pleasure and enjoy myself as they take pleasure; I read, see and judge literature and art as they see and judge; likewise I shrink back from the great mass as they shrink back;

I find shocking what they find shocking. . . . I flee from myself.

The typical man and woman do not look for trouble by finding contradictions between what they and the others believe. Nor do they seek out discoveries that would require change and thus dislocation from the others. The stranger, the strange situation, and the new idea are soon viewed as suspect even if there is a brief initial charade of hospitality and interest. In average, everyday living, people seek familiar, safe, neutral ground. Perhaps above all they try hard to avoid appearing foolish to their peers and thus singled out, individuated from the group. So they choose the known and they avoid uncertainty. Particularly suspect and frightening are reminders about the mysteries of life and death, about the ambiguities of our origin, about the certainty of our mortality. Mortality is the ultimate and dread individuation. Such matters are kept as far as possible from consciousness. The average reader of the Yellow Pages of the telephone book is both dismayed and surprised if he or she accidentally falls upon the listing of funeral directors. There are many more listed than one would have imagined! Why?

Even when it, the dreadful, has already happened, one can still, through ingenious maneuvers, postpone the moment of one's full awareness. The following paragraphs tell of the death of my aunt, who had been very close and very dear to me.

When I first learned that my Aunt Esther had suddenly died, I felt a falling, dazed, momentary confusion. The world spun away from me. Then, in a few moments, I collected my thoughts and alternated between memories of her and the practical business of her burial: She was as kind to me as anyone has ever been. Should the funeral be Wednesday or Thursday? From the time I was a little boy, she had loved me and respected me. We mustn't be shamed into buying an expensive casket. She was such a goofy, joyous woman, a kind of sixty-year-old pixie. We want to put it in the newspaper and we'd better tell that women's group she spent so much time with.

Two burial services: first, the religious service; and then, the Sisters of the Northern Lights service. What is it?

All through the religious service, I managed to be never quite with it. I was waiting instead for the service of the Sisters of the Northern Lights.

Now! A woman in a long red dress drops a red flower on the casket, tells us that red is passion and commitment and Esther was passionate and committed. White dress, white flower, purity and loyalty. Esther, that. Then, a woman stands, blue dress, blue flower, oceanic love of mankind. Esther was. This concludes the Sisters of the Northern Lights service.

Oh my God! My Aunt Esther is dead.

MATURITY: AN EXISTENTIAL DEFINITION

No one is perfect and everyone's life is surrounded by uncertainties. Over time, the similarities in people's lives grow as the law of averages catches up with individuals and with families. How, then, can one differentiate among people? What does constitute maturity? What is growing up fully and well? Any definition that rested solely upon a particular national or regional system of values would be incomplete, since what is held in high esteem in one culture may be viewed with disdain or indifference in another. For example, recall a 1944 high school valedictory address that closed with the following exhortative flourish.

> I do not know beneath what skies
> Or on what seas will be our fate.
> I only know it will be high.
> I only know it will be great![10]

And, for contrast, read "The Secret" as revealed two thousand years ago by Lao Tzu.

> The secret waits for the insight
> Of Eyes unclouded by longing;
> Those who are bound by desire
> See only the outward container.[11]

The hope of developing a single measure of maturity that could reconcile such diverse personal and cultural values is probably a vain one. Neither is it necessary to travel from continent to continent to find differing views as to what is of value. The coming of a new generation is sufficient these days to assure drastic reevaluation of what is desirable in life. Four generations in North America saw the glorification of: Horatio Alger, from rags to riches, fighting all the way;[12] *The Man in the Grey Flannel Suit*, a reasoned turning away from glory to settle for $25,000 and a good family life;[13] Jack Kerouac, vagabond Pied Piper for the rootless life;[14] and now Doris Lessing, in search of meaning in other worlds.[15] In their rebellious moments, children of the valedictorians who were predicting great things forty years ago express harsh criticism of such parental goals. "What you really meant," they say, "is to put down other people, climb over them, keep your wife in line, get more than your share, kiss up, kick down, be a 'big man.' "

Things have changed remarkably in the last decades. Extended families became too cumbersome. Then the nuclear family with children seemed not to work, so presently a great many children are reared in single-parent families. There are also a considerable number of young married couples who have decided not to have children. And other young people aren't sure they want to marry.

For a short paragraph, that is a great deal of change indeed. Hand in hand with all that, the remarkable change in attitudes about the status of women and the move of women into the work force are all part of a dramatic shift in values and goals of people in the United States. Add to all this the strong sense of indignation that is characteristic of many minority communities, which are "grateful for scraps no more." Perhaps in the midst of so much transition it is pointless to look for universal norms for maturity beyond personal survival and a general reverence for life. The great division is between those who already have achieved a secure place within their society and can envision perpetuation of a status quo as contrasted with those who have no choice but to strive for a rethinking of prevailing values that penalize them and their children. In hierarchical societies, those at the top regularly have a rosier view about the opportunities for those at the bottom than do the bottom-dwellers. In short, there are many problems in attempting to establish a measure for personal maturity that would have much credibility across nations and across cultures within any nation.

Yet I will propose a definition of maturity and emotional health that I hope will serve as a useful reference point in thinking about the many different patterns of behavior that are to be described in this book. It is admittedly my own definition taken from an existential frame of reference. And an existential frame of reference is one that emphasizes that all definitions of human events are pale facsimiles and remote approximations of the human experiences described. Specifically, openness to experience and a wanting to know whatever is true in life, the wish to choose and be responsible for oneself, and a respect for the opportunities of others to experience and choose for themselves (love) are suggested as characteristics of full emotional growth. This definition is obviously not free of either national or economic bias. It adheres most closely to the system of values in the West and, more particularly, among some educated individuals of middle and upper economic classes. Elsewhere, different values prevail. In some of the Asian societies in which I have lived and worked, for example, a reverence for tradition, acceptance of one's place in life, knowing the traditions of the ancestors and parents are high among the important measures of the educated (ruling) "man of quality." And, importantly, in both the East and the West, among those who are poor, less educated, less free to explore, less graced with opportunity, the ability to adjust and to survive in a very hostile environment is the only reasonable measure of personal development.

Of course, people with uncommon understanding, uncommon compassion, and a profound capacity to influence
and enrich the lives of those around them arise in every
culture, in every social group, and in every economic class.
There are highly sensitive and intuitive, kind and loving people
everywhere. There is in every man and woman—in mankind—a powerful thrust to make meaningful what he sees, to
understand what is before her, to create new meanings. And
while the force of social conformity is very powerful, there will
always be those whose intense personal experiencing and
strong commitment to whatever they undertake allow discoveries denied their contemporaries.

This is probably what Robert Pirsig is writing about in his
compelling and sad book *Zen and the Art of Motorcycle
Maintenance*.[16] The heroic figure, Phaedrus, seeks Quality,
equates it with the ultimate, and is made desperate by whatever
is shabby, haphazard, and of sloppy workmanship. Meaning
emerges in the coming together of man with the material with
which he works. If others will settle for less, so much the worse
for the world.

> Or if he takes whatever dull job he's stuck with—
> and they are all, sooner or later, dull—and, just to
> keep himself amused, starts to look for options of
> Quality, and secretly pursues these options, just for
> their own sake, thus making an art out of what he is
> doing, he's likely to discover that he becomes a much
> more interesting person and much less of an object to
> the people around him because his Quality decisions
> change him too. And not only the job and him, but
> others too because the Quality tends to fan out like
> waves. The Quality job he didn't think anyone was
> going to see is seen, and the person who sees it feels a
> little better because of it, and is likely to pass that feel-
> ing on to others, and in that way the Quality tends to
> keep on going.

And thus:

> The real cycle you're working on is a cycle called
> yourself. The machine that appears to be "out there"

and the person that appears to be "in here" are not two separate things. They grow toward Quality or fall away from Quality together.

Using the definition described above, the mature person is one who is open to and curious about the many potentialities in his or her life. He is willing to feel what he feels and wants to know what is true, not only in his own life but in the lives of others as well. He is not overwhelmed by the wish to conform, seeking instead Quality in his work, integrity in his love, and honesty and courage in his decisions. He is also aware that life does not go on forever, and he treasures the moments that are his. For this reason, he wants to choose for himself which of his potentialities will be selected and which surrendered. It is here that the matter of love comes into his life, since he covets not only for himself but for others the freedom to experience one's own life and to choose what is right for oneself. This love underlies his deepest value, a reverence for life.

There is yet another dimension of full human development, a quality most difficult to describe. It derives from the religious-existential perspective of Buber, Tillich, and Kierkegaard and from the mystical thinking of Indian and Asian philosophers. Akin to a reverence for things that are alive, it is a particular perspective about life, its order, unity, and continuity. It is the product of awe and appreciation that comes with the awareness of one's place in the process of all the life from all the millennia that were or will ever be. It is described by Hermann Hesse in these remarkable words.

> He took Siddhartha's hand, led him to the seat on the river bank, sat down beside him and smiled at the river.
>
> You have heard it laugh, he said, but you have not heard everything. Let us listen; you will hear more.
>
> They listened. The many-voiced song of the river echoed softly. Siddhartha looked into the river and saw many pictures in the flowing water. He saw his father, lonely, mourning for his son, also lonely, the boy

eagerly advancing along the burning path of life's desires, each one concentrating on his goal, each one obsessed by his goal, each one suffering. The river's voice was sorrowful. It sang with yearning and sadness, flowing towards its goal.

Do you hear? asked Vasudeva's mute glance. Siddhartha nodded.

Listen better! whispered Vasudeva.

Siddhartha tried to listen better. The picture of his father, his own picture, and the picture of his son all flowed into each other. Kamala's picture also appeared and flowed on, and the picture of Govinda and others emerged and passed on. They all became part of the river. It was the goal of all of them, yearning, desiring, suffering; and the river's voice was full of longing, full of smarting woe, full of insatiable desire. The river flowed on toward its goal. Siddhartha saw the river hasten, made up of himself and his relatives and all the people he had ever seen. All the waves and water hastened, suffering, toward goals, many goals, to the waterfall, to the sea, to the current, to the ocean and all goals were reached and each one was succeeded by another. The water changed to vapor and rose, became rain and came down again, became spring, brook and river, changed anew, flowed anew. But the yearning voice had altered. It still echoed sorrowfully, searchingly, but other voices accompanied it, voices of pleasure and sorrow, good and evil voices, laughing and lamenting voices, hundreds of voices, thousands of voices.

Siddhartha listened. He was now listening intently, completely absorbed, quite empty, taking in everything. He felt that he had now completely learned the art of listening. He had often heard all this before, all these numerous voices in the river, but today they sounded different. He could no longer distinguish the different voices—the merry voice from the weeping voice, the childish voice from the manly voice. They all belonged to each other; the lament of those who yearn, the laughter of the wise, the cry of indignation and groan of the dying. They were all interwoven and interlocked, entwined in a thousand ways. And all the voices, all the goals, all the yearnings, all the sorrows, all the pleasures, all the good and evil, all of them together was the world. All of them together was the stream of events, the music of life. When Siddhartha listened attentively to this river, to this song of a thousand voices; when he did not listen to the sorrow or laughter; when he did not bind his soul to any one particular voice and absorb it in his self, but hear them all, the whole, the unity; then the great song of a thousand voices consisted of one word: Om— perfection.[17]

THE ORIGINS OF MENTAL ILLNESS

Individuals vary greatly in their approaches to the everyday experiencing of their world. Some are very cautious people. They are wary of taking a false step. They are frightened of what lies ahead. They devote a good deal of attention to keeping control. When such a person finds himself outside the ordinary situations of his life, that is, in a new space, on new ground, in unfamiliar territory, he is likely to feel restless and uneasy. Such people's view of themselves, of others, and thus of their world is one that emphasizes their personal fragility and vulnerability.

Not surprisingly, these people have often grown up with a deep mistrust of their own bodies as well. And the mistrust is of the very deepest kind. They have learned not to "trust their guts." They feel that following their feelings will lead them astray, will direct them into trouble and discomfort. Such persons are obviously very restricted and handicapped as they live their lives. There are many places they cannot go, things they cannot hear, experiences they will never have. In the attempt to fuse with what is "normal," they suffer the great estrangement of being cut off from themselves. They are constantly turning away from their own feelings. Where do such attitudes begin?

While catastrophic events at any period can seriously modify an individual's attitudes, the early years of life are particularly important in setting the way a person feels about his world. Attitudes about self, key other people, the safety of feeling what one feels, and the general hospitality of the world in which one lives are established very early. At the same time the child is learning how to avoid anxiety, prevent shame, and minimize guilt, because these emotions are associated with uncomfortable bodily states such as restlessness, sweating, muscle tension, cramping pains, and the other somatic manifestations of anxiety. The child's personality is a summation of those attitudes, beliefs, and ways of relating that provide the most pleasure and fullest satisfaction, consistent with freedom from anxiety and bodily discomfort. This summation is continuously changing throughout life as new experiences occur. However, early life events and attitudes appear to exert a life-long influence on the relative preponderance of security-seeking versus satisfaction-seeking parts of the personality. The more pressing were the childhood needs to develop protective techniques, the more contingent, the more restricted, the more tentative is the child's and subsequently the adult's freedom to move in his life. "Safety first" seems to be a well-entrenched human principle. In the early years, one learns what is good (safe) and what is bad (to be shunned). Once learned, these lessons tend to be remembered always. As such, they shape subsequent learning.

One far-reaching implication of the simultaneous early and fairly permanent development of one's sense of "who I am" and "what my world is like" is that, to a large degree, one is one's world and one carries one's world along no matter where one is. It seems not to happen that a person is open, optimistic, friendly, confident, and fun loving while living in a nasty, unrewarding, dangerous, critical, shame-filled world. And physical migration to another spot doesn't usually help things very much. Further, insofar as sense of self and feelings about the world are in substantial part related to a variety of bodily tension states, the psychosomatic nature of experience and the consequence of experiencing on body function are inevitably linked. Body, sense of self, ideas about the world, and attitudes toward others are part of the same whole person. And they stay that way throughout a lifetime. The child with many fears is less likely to be as experimental, as curious, or as willing to take risks in exploring the surrounding world as the child who has a more secure (and thus optimistic) early start. And if the early fears are severe and pervasive enough, "keeping safe" by pushing away (and out of one's mind) any threat of change or even variation in routine may become the individual's all-consuming concern. Nor is it simply the people and objects of the "outside world" that may come to be feared and thus avoided. The very manifestations of one's humanness, that is, one's feelings of love, anger, admiration, jealousy, curiosity, one's appetite for touching, sexuality, food, security, one's own body parts, may all seem unfriendly, unattractive, and to be shunned. A man can come to despise his tender feelings as well as his anger if those tender feelings led him in the past to experience shame, repudiation, or anxiety. This is a grave problem because alienation from self is a core problem in all mental illness.

WHAT IS MENTAL ILLNESS?

Opposed to the openness, freedom, and expanding life of the healthy and mature individual are the varieties of experiencing and reacting that are described as the symptoms of mental illness. A diagnosis of mental illness suggests that for a given person at a given time there will be anxiety and/or depression, confusion, or physiological discomfort unless very careful precautionary steps are taken as that person leads his or her life. These precautionary steps are in the nature of avoidance techniques or mechanisms for controlling, denying, or substituting one's feelings. There is, as a consequence, less freedom to experience, less comfort in selecting from among one's various possibilities, and a lessened ability to savor vicariously the joys of one's family or fellows. The individual is often mistrustful of his own competence and/or doubtful of the friendliness and accepting nature of the environment. His or her world is one in which there is a constant danger of encountering severe anxiety and humiliating self-doubt. Much attention must be devoted to avoiding these dangers rather than to the hearty experiencing of life events. Indeed, such persons often come for help to a mental health professional specifically because they feel they are missing the good things life has to offer. If the sense of disappointment and fear of further anxiety reach intolerable levels, it may become necessary for the individual to turn away from the parts of life shared with others and to develop instead an increasingly narrow and self-centered focus of attention. Or, in the face of overwhelming disappointment and intolerable anxiety, he or she may even determine that life is not worth living, may attempt to commit suicide, or may develop symptoms incompatible with life.

Sexual awareness and sexual impulse are ordinarily experienced with interest, curiosity, and delight. Yet for a fearful person a sexual feeling may be akin to a dangerous enemy coming closer on a deadly mission. In this latter instance, the sexual feeling, although it arises from the person himself, may be dealt with by a kind of exteriorizing (pushing aside) process in which the person makes himself a stranger to his impulse and thus to himself. The inability to trust one's own feelings or, for that matter, even to acknowledge them as one's own results in a progressive narrowing of the world of experience. Such narrowing can reach disastrous proportions.

In the first of the two case studies that follow, a very desperate interval in the life of a young boy and his family will be described in some detail. The way he came to feel about himself and his reactions to those feelings led to a time when his death seemed a real possibility. He presented a genuine medical emergency. During the course of his hospitalization and in the period after, hundreds of physical, neurological, and laboratory examinations were conducted. For a time, his physical condition had deteriorated and the doctors who were caring for him were themselves obsessed with the fear that some serious physical abnormality had been overlooked. None was ever found. I think I understand what happened to him but I'm not positive. For while I value very highly the theoretical formulations offered earlier in this chapter and view them as extremely useful in directing my thinking about people in trouble, they go only so far. Theories are about people in general. In work with any specific individual, one must always keep clear focus upon that person and let the theories come along after. This is one of the reasons I much prefer to talk with a person before reading somebody else's reports about him. Person first. Theories second.

Case Study 2: *I I Must Must Not Not Make Make a a Mistake Mistake*

Jeremiah Rogers, thirteen years old, was admitted to the psychiatric hospital in Vancouver, British Columbia, on May 24, 1973, because of his incapacitating fear of being dirty. His difficulties had developed gradually over the preceding six months, beginning with tearfulness and anxiety when faced with any pressure at home or in school. Finally, his withdrawal became quite extreme. He refused to go to school, and at home he was exclusively preoccupied with the need to bathe and cleanse himself. Eating meals became a prolonged torture because of his extreme caution in order to prevent food from touching the outside of his mouth. He felt that any food on his lips was contaminating. His body weight dropped from one hundred to seventy pounds during the half-year before his hospital admission.

On initial examination, he was fearful and robotlike. He walked in a taut, stiff-legged fashion in order to prevent his undershorts from rubbing up against his anal area. This was one feared source of contamination. There were many others. The history and the physical examination made clear that the change in him was a profound one. Every concern in his life had been eliminated except for his overwhelming preoccupation with keeping clean and avoiding various contaminations. Nevertheless, in stark contrast to his general fearfulness and deteriorated physical condition, he answered all questions in a particularly sophisticated and adult manner. "Good afternoon, Doctor. I am delighted to meet you. I have heard a great deal about you. Where is your couch? I thought that all psychiatrists had couches."

In the hospital his condition deteriorated. He refused to eat because "food makes bowel movements." Gradually, he became mute, his weight dropped to sixty pounds, and he was near death because of his precarious state of nutritional imbalance. He was fed by the nursing staff, with several hours required for each meal. He received large dosages of tranquilizer medications in the effort to help him relax, and intravenous feedings were instituted in the face of his life-threatened, almost moribund condition. Then, he slowly began to respond. Over the next two months, his weight very gradually increased to eighty pounds and he became a little more active and cooperative. However, his preoccupation with cleanliness remained, and he required the full-time attention of a nurse for feeding and cleaning. Bathing, which the patient requested almost continuously with a pleading, barely audible "bath, bath, bath!" required two to three hours each day. Each bowel movement, accomplished with anguish, was followed by an urgent plea for an immediate bath. At one period, the patient spoke by repeating each word two or sometimes three times. He explained, "I I have have to to say say each each word word twice twice because because I I don't don't want want to to make make any any mistake mistake, Doctor Doctor. "

The family history revealed that the patient was the oldest of three children. His father, vice-president in a very large, family-managed department store chain in Washington State, was a tall, handsome, somewhat distant person, a Marine officer during the Korean War, a graduate of an Ivy League college. He was rational, authoritative, attentive to detail, and very preoccupied with the demands of his business. His composure was never shaken. He was always quite logical. He tried to remain objective and usually succeeded. He was, in short, a quite formidable man.

Jeremiah's mother was a very attractive, carefully dressed, tall (five feet, ten inches), excessively polite woman. Although she was more emotional than her husband, at no time was she ever seen with a hair out of place, with a wrinkle in her dress, or with any sign of wear and tear despite the enormous burdens of her child's illness. She herself was the second oldest of nine children born in a working-class Eastern European immigrant family. She wanted to go to college, but because of the severe limits on family finances she left after one semester and went to work in one of the department stores owned by her future husband's family. He was sixteen years older than she. His parents were staunchly opposed to their relationship, opposition that was continued openly up to the time of their marriage and subtly afterward. Following her marriage, the mother set out vigorously to establish her role in the newly won social circle. She tried very hard. She became active in a great many civic and church clubs. It was not, however, until after her first child's birth, approximately three and a half years after the marriage, that she had any sense of having any real chance to "make it" with her husband's family. Jeremiah was a model child. Indeed, in his mother's words, he was "a perfect child." He was deeply devoted to his mother, was something of a surrogate parent to the two younger children, was deeply religious, scholastically successful, and generally very adult oriented.

The onset of Jeremiah's difficulties appeared to be related both to his difficulties with the other boys in his grade school, who resented his "sissy ways," and to the beginning of puberty and sexual interests. One of the first manifestations of the difficulties that were to come was his request for help from the minister in order to rid his mind of "filthy thoughts." He was very troubled by an urge to look at pictures of partly naked women in magazines. He was approximately twelve and a half years old at that time.

It is not possible to say for certain what caused Jeremiah's retreat from his life. However, certain aspects of life within the Rogers family might have been important in what took place. There was an intense relationship between mother and child, accentuated by the mother's social insecurity and her use of her oldest child to acquire acceptance and status. Jeremiah was hers—was her—and the paternal grandparents' access to Jeremiah could only be through her. The mother's needs for Jeremiah to be a certain kind of child, to think and behave in a relatively restricted fashion, was thus very intense. As Jeremiah grew, his mother generally babied him, addressing him frequently at twelve and thirteen as "my big boy" or "my dear one" or "Jeremy darling." By contrast, there was a substantial psychological distance from the strong, silent father that mother and son alike maintained. In some ways, the mother was a kind of older child of the father and Jeremiah was a younger child. Jeremiah was clearly his mother's favorite. With the father it was hard to tell. What was, however, most clearly evident about this family was that from early days on there was considerable pressure on the child to be not himself but rather to fulfill certain requirements of the family situation. Perhaps the task of living in compliance with all of the demands placed upon him became impossible for Jeremiah when he was faced unexpectedly with emerging sexual feelings that had absolutely no place in his psychological view of himself. It then became necessary for this "model child" who moved so skillfully in an adult-centered world to cut down sharply on his openness to life experience, an openness already severely restricted by his overdeveloped sense of responsibility to behave perfectly.

He tried desperately to maintain the integrity and order of his world, and thus his self-esteem, by concentrating upon the matter of cleanliness. Maintaining absolute cleanliness and making no mistakes were his sole concerns. These commitments necessitated a life-and-death struggle and, at several points, the struggle nearly cost him his life.

He narrowed down his world of experience in a last-ditch effort to maintain his self-esteem, to be the kind of person that it was so desperately necessary for him to be. He was "doing the best he could" under the circumstances to assure his survival as a self-respecting human being.

Jeremiah was in and out of the hospital for more than one year before he was able to return to his home and resume his schooling. Therapy in the hospital was broad ranging and included, first of all, attention to life support, that is, nutrition, prevention of infection, and caution against suicide. A variety of anti-psychotic and anti-depressant drugs were tried and one medication, the monoamine oxidase inhibitor anti-depressant tranylcypromine (Parnate) was continued for more than a year and a half. The family psychotherapy that began in the hospital continued for almost two years after Jeremiah's return home.

Jeremiah is now twenty-one years old. He has not returned to the hospital and he has not seen a psychiatrist for five years. He has been off medication for a like period of time. After he finished high school he went away for one year to college. However, he now lives at home and works in the family business as a bookkeeper. He remains a somewhat thin and fragile person, serious about things, quiet and to himself much of the time. He doesn't date but does go to office social events and has several male friends from his early grade school days whom he sees on occasion. His father had a heart attack a year ago but recovered well. He, the mother, and Jeremiah have an apparently comfortable basis for living together. The parents are grateful for the level of restoration that has taken place in their son's life and they hope that he will improve further. Neither they nor Jeremiah see reason for further therapy at this time.

Mercifully, most of the problems that come to a psychiatrist's attention are less catastrophic than the ones presented by Jeremiah Rogers and his family. They are often, however, complex and challenging nonetheless. In some instances, an individual patient or a single family will present an interlacing variety of difficulties including a definitive mental illness, deteriorating interpersonal relationships, and complicated financial and social problems, as well as those hard-to-articulate matters associated with lack of meaning in life. There seem to be more such patients in recent years. This may be one of the consequences of the rapid social changes that have exsanguinated the meaning from the words "forever more" and offered in their place the more watery "for the time being."

Case Study 3: *The Couple Who Consulted a Builder and a Psychiatrist*

Martha Vincent made a suicide attempt, swallowing fourteen of her sleeping capsules all at once. She and her husband, both in their early fifties, had had another of their frequent arguments and she locked herself in the bathroom, took the pills, and thirty minutes later came out and told him what she had done. They rushed to a hospital emergency room for treatment. The next day the family doctor suggested a psychiatric consultation, and I asked that both husband and wife come one day later for an appointment. The husband thought it would be better if he didn't come, so he didn't attend. Mrs. Vincent was promptly sent home from the first consultation to get him.

When the consultation finally began, the Vincents were both very tense. But they warmed up while talking with me, someone who was, like them, middle-aged, upper-middle-class, a little overweight, and sociable enough to offer coffee to them. Mrs. Vincent was quite depressed, cried easily, expressed ideas of hopelessness, and described a many-month period of increasing sadness, difficulty in sleeping, and agitation. She also pouted and her conversation was full of digs at her husband, whom she felt was tired of her, thoughtless, and wanted a younger woman or at least a chance to run around.

Mr. Vincent, Arthur, a moderately successful auto sales company executive, was quietly supportive and dealt calmly with his wife's accusations, trying to be reassuring. But when he was asked to talk about himself, he became very serious and talked with feeling about the emptiness of his life. He was not much interested in his work anymore, not very happy about their two children. Their twenty-six-year-old son had quit college for the third time and was now searching for a legendary guru in northern Mexico. Their eighteen-year-old daughter, a dropout from the final year of high school, had just moved in with her new boy friend. He said that life was flat for him in general and he didn't know whether to expand or contract, that is, to make more money or less, to spend more time in his sports car, to buy a bigger car, or to give up the expensive hobby altogether, and so forth.

Both felt that the quality of their relationship had deteriorated in recent years and each tended to blame the other. They agreed as to the events that had provoked Mrs. Vincent's recent, severe depression. Specifically, four or five months earlier, Mrs. Vincent became angry and depressed when her husband was too solicitous and danced too many times with another woman at a country club party. As usual, everybody had had a lot to drink. Mrs. Vincent left the party on her own and when her husband arrived home a few minutes later, there was a hysterical scene with Mrs. Vincent running for the aspirin bottle and her husband forcibly restraining her. The next day, they made up and had a serious talk about their lives. They decided that they should pull back from their social commitments, spend more time together, make love more often, sell their big expensive house and build a smaller place. They had their home appraised and were told that it would bring $140,000. They bought a building lot the next day and Mrs. Vincent contacted an architect and described the needs she and her husband would have in the decades ahead. The next three months were good months for the Vincents. They had more sense of purpose than they had experienced in some years. But when the bids for their dream house came back, it became clear that their alternative to a $140,000 house was a $140,000 house. He was angry. She was depressed. Things deteriorated between them, and two nights earlier, following a party where there was a great deal of alcohol, Mrs. Vincent had attempted suicide.

There are several ways of looking at the events in the lives of this couple. One could focus on Mrs. Vincent and decide that she is the patient and that her depression is the illness that needs treatment. And, indeed, her symptoms were severe. One could not ignore her immediate need for "something." Mental depressions almost always feel worse than they might appear, and many times depressive symptoms, once begun, are extremely persistent. Often, depressive symptoms persist or worsen even if the apparent original cause of such emotions disappears or is corrected. Depressions develop a kind of life of their own. In this instance, I felt I had to treat Mrs. Vincent's depression actively. Treatment included careful assessment of the likelihood of another suicide attempt, a serious effort to let Mrs. Vincent know that I understood how very bad she felt, and institution of a specific anti-depression medication regime. I felt she was a clear suicidal risk even though her earlier efforts were abortive.

At the same time it would have been hard to overlook the complex interpersonal problems present in this family and between husband and wife. She had organized her life around him and them—and they were drifting apart and he didn't seem to care. She worked at it but didn't feel particularly pretty anymore and her husband's clearly diminished sexual interest seemed to accentuate her fears. She was also disappointed in the children both because it didn't look as if they were going to do much with their opportunities and because her husband blamed her for the way they were turning out. She blamed him too but felt very guilty. Perhaps, above all, she was haunted by the fear that he would leave her. She had never been alone and the thought overwhelmed her. So she found herself trying to read his mind. And the thoughts she read were not very reassuring.

Mr. Vincent had his problems too. He had been strictly reared, taught to work hard and to be intolerant of those who failed. And now he had a houseful of "failures," including, to a certain extent, himself. He viewed his wife's sexual approaches rather as if she were a baby kangaroo trying to jump into its mother's pouch, and the more desperate she became, the stronger that image came to his mind. His children troubled him both because they seemed well on their way to going nowhere and because he felt uncomfortable explaining what they were doing to his own still-critical parents and to the other couples in the Vincents' social group. Some of the latter appeared to have children who were very successful and Mr. Vincent felt increasingly uncomfortable with them. He also had some problems at work although he was reluctant to acknowledge in the presence of his wife that he was a poor third in a company with one hundred employees and that the number-four man was coming on strong.

One might also look at the Vincents in terms of the role designation that both had so totally taken on in their early years and wonder how it had worked out for each of them. Mrs. Vincent in particular had burned a lot of bridges behind her in accepting an identity as wife and mother in a home where father knows best. She had come from such a home and in her early years had had no encouragement to prepare for anything except caring for her future children and helping her future husband. Sometimes she read, sometimes she went to lunch with friends, summers she played golf. But those were "portal to portal" parts of her life, and her investment of self had been in husband, son, and daughter. She was fifty-one, very frightened about the matter of money, particularly when she compared the earning potential of her husband ($48,000 plus per year) and herself. She could type but not well. And more important, she didn't want to type well. She felt somewhat guilty that her daughter seemed to be heading the same way and was planning to talk with her about finishing high school and going on to college.

Mrs. Vincent "despised the kind of woman who is a women's libber" but was beginning to think they were right.

Viewed somewhat more broadly in an existential frame of reference, the Vincents, individually and as a couple, were finding it hard to believe in the older meanings in their lives and at the moment they lacked the courage, imagination, and hope to find new ones. The house incident was a good summary statement of the spot they were in. In their attempt to solve a problem they were confronted with themselves. That confrontation could in theory have been a stirring and creative opportunity. But it wasn't. They blamed each other for the lack of meaning each experienced. They were lucky that they didn't go on to build the new house. The Vincents had only the unused plans for the house and no answer. A good many other couples in the same boat have no answer plus a new and expensive house.

I saw the Vincents, always together, once a week over the first six months, then every two weeks for the rest of the year. Their daughter came in with them on five occasions and once I talked with her alone. (She feared she was pregnant.) I didn't succeed in meeting the older brother though both parents "tried" to a degree. Neither did I succeed in interesting the Vincents in inviting Arthur's seventy-five-year-old parents to a session. Martha was willing (eager!) but Arthur was worried that it would be hard on "them."

Still, our sessions were very helpful, as they almost always are in such circumstances. The Vincents did accept some of my recommendations. I insisted that she take the anti-depression medications exactly as I prescribed them. It took five weeks and a fairly high dose before they were effective. Also, I asked them not to talk about our sessions after they left my office and if possible to avoid the topics we were discussing outside our hours together. That always helps. It's never clear whether the instructions themselves are helpful or whether the establishment (through patient agreement) of the therapist as a person who "knows" the right regulations is the more important element in establishing such ground rules. Perhaps it's half and half. My own mode of working with people is to seek as much parity as possible, so with the Vincents I kept the overt rules to a list that included:

- I saw them only as a couple.
- I discouraged them from talking about therapy away from the office. For one thing, that decreases fights. Also, it makes for a vitality in the therapy hours themselves. Otherwise, you are dealing with a fight about what happened a week before instead of looking for new things to joy and battle over.
- Martha Vincent agreed that she (and her husband) would call me if something happened to indicate a need to change her medication. Otherwise the prescription stood.
- We had a ten-week contract to meet once a week, and after it was agreed to, all parties were to appear all ten times. In this instance, we renewed the contract once, then modified it (for less frequent meetings). In the course of our sessions, Martha started out as patient, but rather quickly, because we were talking so much about general things that affected them both—and me as well—Martha lost the primary patient status to become one of two people consulting a third about their fears, pains, hopes, and, in time, joys. And sometimes the three people were consulting each other.

The process was not altogether smooth, steady, and logical but the things we worked out (that were there waiting to be put into practice all the time) included:

- They agreed they really liked each other.
- They more or less agreed that their kids had

strengths and weaknesses but that neither of the parents could take full personal credit or assign total blame. They were *their* kids.
- And what do you mean "kids"? They were of age.
- Martha went to work and LOVED IT.
- Arthur was jealous about that and LOVED IT.
- They cut down substantially on their drinking.
- Arthur confessed he liked "R"-rated movies and they took in a few.

SUMMARY

Mental illness is for me mostly sadness about what isn't happening in life. It's a terribly expensive disease. The waste is like grain unharvested in the field, vaccines unused in a nation suffering an epidemic, the robbery that takes the savings of a person who has worked hard through a lifetime.

Among those who seek a psychiatrist's help there are many who suffer specific illnesses resulting from neuroendocrine disorders that affect mood, perception, and clarity of thinking. There are others with persisting self-doubt that arose early in life and became more pervasive with time. There are individuals who accept mandates in childhood that translate poorly over the years. They come to a psychiatrist seeking from a parental surrogate a commutation of their sentence. There are many others who live ungenerously, who know it and hate themselves for it. People who have been cheated by being born poor or by having only one parent or not even one parent have to live with all the possibilities lost already, and they struggle with the choices of giving it all away, settling for a reduced share, or trying to compete with those who have a big head start.

A person who is unable or unwilling to live to his potential pays a double price. There is the penalty imposed by the symptoms. There is the further cost of being disappointed in oneself. People know, at some level of consciousness, how special they are and they lament when they cannot be themselves.

PART TWO

THE THREE GENERATIONS: LOVE, RESPONSIBILITY, AND PROPERTY

The Beginning of Civilization: A Legend

Although handwriting as we know it had yet to be invented, for Ajote, who was now age thirty-eight, it was unmistakably on the wall. He slept uneasily in his cave, feeling closed in, surrounded, trapped. In the early morning hours, he often thought of the afternoon some thirteen summers before when he had stealthily slain the headman of his tribe. A discreet few weeks after the murder, he had taken the cave of the headman and with it leadership of the group. He had ruled during the succeeding thirteen years. But now, Ajote began to cough and to spit red, which was a certain beginning of a loss of strength and power. For a headman, such loss meant death. Ajote, frightened, had attempted to do a little political friend making, trying to warm up to some of the younger men by making friendly gestures on the hunts. But, as is usually the case with appeasing gestures motivated by fear, these efforts made him only more afraid.

He thought of fleeing, but where? The extent of his world was only the hunting area of the tribe—the caves in which they lived, the lake below, and some fifty square miles of forest bounded by the far hills. He was restrained from penetrating those boundaries, recalling the murderous treatment he had afforded a strange man who had fled from those far hills and come toward their lake three summers before. His apprehensiveness mounted as he recalled that the murdered stranger had been, like himself, an older man. Why had he come?

One day, while Ajote was coughing and spitting, he saw the most agile and unfriendly of the younger men watching him. He felt he had no hope and decided to flee from the group. That night, while the others slept, he left the cave, carrying food and a weapon. He reached the far hills at dawn and an hour later lay hidden one hundred yards from the central gathering place of the tribe that lived beyond the hills. Several of the young men in this group resembled the older man who had been slain. Ajote experienced great fear and decided to return to his own tribe.

However, he took four days to make that five-hour journey, and when he returned he had carefully practiced this story, which he told with great feeling to the people of his tribe: A dream had foretold imminent danger to the group. He had seen an image of many of their women and young people killed. He remembered specifically the crushed head of the strong young man who had observed him coughing. In the dream, a strange beast, half-mortal, half-animal, had led him, Ajote, to the far hills as instructed, and he discovered that the people there were making preparations for an attack as had been predicted in the dream.

The events that followed made Ajote the leader of the group as never before. He had foretold the grave danger. He had caused his tribe to send its younger men over the hills in time to head off the assault. In that war, the strong young man who had observed Ajote's coughing was, as foretold in the dream, killed. Ajote subsequently made known to all what was necessary to preserve the group against other enemies. All the young men were very respectful to Ajote. This was the beginning of civilization as we now know it.

3

Allegiance
and Continuity:
How Much
Do We Need?

To a large degree reality is whatever the people who are around at the time agree to. We think in the plural. Female identical twins in their mid-twenties, cousins of mine, were married within a short interval. When I saw one of them a few months later and asked, "How's married life?" she replied, "We like it fine!" She meant herself and her twin. It's like that for sisters, sorority sisters, and sisters-under-the-skin. And brothers as well. And sisters and brothers. We like to agree. We even like to agree that a subject is important enough to disagree over. We use each other to validate our world and then to relax. To turn one's back on someone is a more cruel rebuke than to dispute him. So, everywhere there are clubs and societies and people who are "in" and those who don't qualify. In most of those societies and clubs, the worst one inside, once in, is more intimately and tenderly held than the best one outside. With the passage of time, the insiders develop "language," history, and battle scars. And very important is the coming of children for whom "in" status is sought. The separation from those outside then becomes greater. So, there are families, coreligionists, social class allegiances, national and international bonds. While there is talk of a brotherhood of mankind, it is hard actually to grasp what that means. It is a little like thinking about one's grandchildren's grandchildren. Ordinarily, the "we" in each of our lives are a small number of people very similar to ourselves.

I spent several very interesting years talking with international students on North American and Asian college campuses in the late sixties and early seventies. Most remarkable was the almost exclusive cohesiveness of conationals when overseas. That is, most Asian graduate students while in North America stayed together with other Asian students from the home country whether their American sojourn was one year or ten. Equally, despite prior plans and expectations, most North Americans grouped closely with North Americans while in Asia. The explanations offered by each of the overseas student groups took the form of identical criticism of the host nationals, whose sincerity, depth, honesty, and motivation when they seemed hospitable was questioned. Unstated but at the heart of all Americans who were disappointed (and most were) was this: "They don't seem to recognize what a special person I am. My Phi Beta Kappa key and ready smile mean nothing to them. Don't they know about Amherst College?" And for the Asians in North America, there was the almost universal experience of being invited for Thanksgiving dinner, being offered an instant and intense cross-cultural friendship— "but they never called again." In the normal course of things, we tend to associate with individuals whose training and experience is most like our own, people able to understand and appreciate our efforts. This is not surprising. In the words of J. M. Thorburn: "All the genuine, deep delight of life is showing people the mudpies you have made; and life is at its best when we confidingly recommend our mudpies to each other's sympathetic consideration."

CONTINUITY THROUGH CULTURE

My cross-cultural studies that began at the University of Wisconsin in the mid-1960s reshaped my thinking not only about culture and values but about mental health and mental illness as well.[1,2,3] I learned a great deal from my colleagues in the research. They included Dr. Fikre Workneh of Addis Ababa, who was the first Ethiopian to study psychiatry (he had come to Wisconsin in 1964 for that purpose); Dr. Gwo-hwa Tseng from Taiwan, who was to become the first Taiwanese psychiatrist to pass the American Board of Psychiatry; Dr. Marjorie Klein, a psychologist, who had participated in a major study of Scandinavian students conducted at Harvard and who brought a rigorous methodological discipline to our studies; Dr. Eng-kung Yeh, Professor of Psychiatry at the National Taiwan University and a distinguished cross-cultural psychiatrist; and finally, Dr. Aristotle Alexander, a wonderfully sensitive clinical psychologist. We talked with hundreds of students from two dozen nations, conducted several thousand written surveys, and over the years followed the careers of a great many overseas students. We came to know each other, some of the people we were studying, and ourselves in a new and unexpected way. For, it turned out, we were not only ourselves. We were spokesmen for our families, our conationals, our beliefs about what life is about and how it should be lived. And in that kind of intimate exchange, you discover that not only do you believe what you believe, you *are* what you believe. A person not only lives out his customs and rituals, he becomes almost indistinguishable from them. While economics, persecution, racism, warfare, and destiny have moved millions and millions of people away from their original homes, almost all aliens cling tenaciously to that part of themselves embodied in custom and ritual. And in their first generation overseas, where possible, they group together in the same location in order to preserve what they need from the old to sustain themselves with comfort and pride while accommodating to the new.

My experiences in cross-cultural psychiatry have proven very helpful in my current work as a director of public mental health services for a part of Los Angeles County, the coastal region.* Among the 2.2 million people who live in the 450 square miles of the coastal region, there are many newcomers

* Dr. John Richard Elpers ably directs the Department of Mental Health for Los Angeles County. Dr. Boyd M. Krout ably assists me in my work in the coastal region.

grouped together to preserve and take nourishment from their traditions and customs. There are communities of newly arrived Chicanos, Cubans, South Americans, Samoans, Guamians, Fijians, Micronesians, Okinawans, Koreans, Japanese, Taiwanese, Chinese from the People's Republic of China, Indonesians, Iranians, Europeans, Africans, and now, by the tens of thousands, the "boat people," many of Chinese ancestry from Indochina. Like my own great-grandparents and grandparents who came to New York from middle-Europe in the 1890s, these immigrants brought treasured customs and nourishing beliefs and, in many instances, they could carry little else. These hundreds of thousands of newcomers to southern California, when combined with the other minority people of Los Angeles, are now the majority population here. Their political leaders are hopeful that coalitions will be formed among the various minority peoples in order to speed the process of ownership as well as tenancy in California. But linkages outside the primary group identity are usually slow in developing. Interest in the pragmatic advantages of outside connections for immigrants usually awaits the passage of a first generation spent recreating the transportable characteristics of the home culture.

In the case of my grandparents and many of the other 1880–1920 European immigrants to America, the establishment of successive generations—their children and grandchildren—into the emerging American culture has been rapid. Increasingly, the sons, daughters, grandchildren, great-grandchildren flourish in multi-cultural communities and our lives seem far removed from my father's first American home on East Houston Street on New York's Lower East Side. But my aunt, the only woman born into the second and third family generations, still lives in the original neighborhood. Hers is an important part of our family's history although I have only appreciated that fact in recent years.

I told a story to Isaac Bashevis Singer

The old folks, my paternal grandparents, lived on the Lower East Side of New York from the time of their arrival in America in 1890 till their death in the 1950s. As the years went by, all the sons got married and moved away, but my Aunt Manon, the only daughter, never married and instead remained with her parents, my grandparents, in the apartment on Houston Street. It was the general family understanding that the old folks wouldn't be happy in the suburbs of New York or Indianapolis but that when they were gone, Aunt Manon would join the brothers in the more affluent environments where they had moved. My grandfather went first, then a few years later, in 1959, my grandmother passed away. In accordance with a three-decade plan, Aunt Manon collected her possessions, gave up the apartment, tearfully said good-bye to her New York friends, and moved to Indianapolis. Two weeks later she was back in New York. Happily, the old apartment was still available.

The only woman born in the family chose and/or was assigned the life role to sustain New York continuity through the decades and then, when that continuity was not needed, she was expected to join in and try to catch up with the lives of people whom she had seen once or twice a year for twenty years. Meanwhile, the one and only life of Aunt Manon was taking place all the while. We had forgotten. A big part of that oversight was plain sexism, a denigration and undervaluing of my aunt's significance because she is a woman and because women's roles were sharply defined in her generation and culture. I feel badly about my lack of appreciation of her individuality through the years. I hope there have been many rewards and areas of fulfillment for her. I'm not certain.

In the mid-1960s, Isaac Bashevis Singer[4] visited Madison, Wisconsin, and I attended a small dinner party in his honor. I managed to take him to one side and obliged him to listen to the whole story. He was polite and when I finished he said, "People get used to the places where they live." I was somewhat put off by his brevity and said, "Isaac Bashevis Singer, you are the greatest storyteller of Jewish life in this century. Is that all you can say?" He walked off.

All changes cost something and the magnitude of social

change has been enormous these last decades. The costs are not yet fully counted. But for me it seems likely that the radical changes in expectation patterns between the three generations will prove to be the most important of all. They had been worked out over generations, centuries, and millennia through trial and error, or, if you will, through divine guidance. And, while science and technology have modified and improved many aspects of contemporary life, our basic problems in living with ourselves and with each other are identical to those that have faced human beings from the very beginning of civilization. Some of those problems are existential and religious in nature. What is this life about? Can I not in some way transcend my brief life? Others are very practical, here and now, and urgent. How do we get enough to eat? If you create something, how do you keep someone else from taking it away? How do you provide protection during the long period of helplessness of the human infant? In the end each culture develops both practical answers to the existential questions and existential meaning to the day-by-day challenges. Routine activities have embedded within them the most profound significance, and abstract beliefs need to translate into economically feasible and sensually satisfying activities. Therefore, societies, like all fine evolutionary products, are intricately constructed with the goal of survival assigned a highest priority. The various societal component parts interrelate and the roles people accept are mutually dependent. There is some room for adaptation but most of the components are there for a reason. Religion, values, customs, economic practices, codes of behavior, and the ground rules for conduct and expectation between the generations and between the sexes are of a piece. Change one element and all parts of the system are affected. That's why the elders everywhere are so staunch in insisting on the importance of the established ritual.

What started with cross-cultural studies with Asian students at the University of Wisconsin took me on journeys across the oceans and, no less distant, into the forest of my own complacency. Studying other people's values and cultural practices has a merit in its own right. But what is even better, it provides a distant platform from which you can look back at yourself and your home from a new perspective. As an introduction to the chapters that will follow, which focus upon problems experienced by individuals in different generations in North America, I want to write something about what I have learned with the help of my friends and colleagues in Asia and other parts of the world. I hope to illustrate that, cultural differences aside, the important problems beyond sustenance and shelter that all human beings face are the same and that the solutions developed by one group of people are understandable and familiar to all others.

I made my first visit to Asia in 1965 and then, in 1969, had the opportunity to live and work in Taiwan as a Visiting Professor at the Department of Psychiatry in the National Taiwan University Hospital. My subsequent research and various teaching assignments have allowed me to revisit Asia often, particularly Hong Kong and Taiwan, where a number of friends have permitted members of my family and me to share in their hopes, loves, celebrations, and sorrows. The history of the Chinese in Taiwan has unique characteristics, but basically, it is a part of the extraordinary Chinese story of more than four millennia of human experiences and achievement.

The chief ingredients of a traditional Chinese world view were articulated thousands of years ago, and for many, many millions of people the tenets of that ancient understanding of life still apply.[5,6] First and foremost, unity and continuity characterize Chinese ideas about the universe. Dead ancestors and unborn descendants share a destiny with the living, and the living have the responsibility both to do what is right and to correct what is wrong. From the ancient Chinese perspective, events in nature and the feelings in the hearts and minds of people are connected and sustained in a delicate balance. For things to be right for man, they must be right in the universe. So, traditional Chinese societies have developed extremely well-defined values, roles, and rules covering all aspects of life. Diet, ritual, weather, medicines, current and past relationships, family history—all need to be considered in circumstances where things are going badly. It's not only that the Chinese teach and emphasize interdependence within the family and group; if their basic ideas about life are correct, each person *is* dependent upon the others, including some still unborn. In a closed universe, you live forever with the messes you make. Worse, in a closed universe, you live with the messes your family makes, made, or will make.

Given that definition of life, the necessity for family continuity is evident and the logistical requirements for providing that continuity are extensive indeed. The well-being of the family requires that there be a generation-after-generation acceptance and successful fulfillment of family responsibilities by the family leader and by all other family members. Ordinarily, the number one son carries that leadership responsibility until his first-born son takes it from him. With the responsibility goes honor, financial control, and the intangibles that come with hereditary designation as the special one in a family. When there is no son to assume the role, a son must be found.

Case Study 1: *I Am My Uncle's "Son"*

In 1935, in Hong Kong, Ke-sying Shu was born. He was the third child in his family, the second son. The family were moderately well-to-do landowners, part of an extended family that included Ke-sying's parents, his paternal grandparents, his father's older brother and wife, who had two daughters but no son, and his father's younger brother, who was married and had three sons and two daughters. Ke-sying's older uncle was the first-born son in that generation, and when he fell gravely ill with no male heir, it was decided that Ke-sying would be adopted by the dying man as his son. Ke-sying was three years old at the time. The adoption was carried out over the most strenuous objection of the dying man's wife because the new "son" would be the full heir to his uncle's estate, and her two daughters and she herself would be the financial losers. She took legal action to interrupt the process—unheard of in Hong Kong at that time. However, the laws favored the rights of the dying uncle to have a "son" and the rights of Ke-sying's paternal grandparents to preserve control of monies and to ensure that there would be an appropriate first-born son of the first-born father to carry out the religious ceremonies and other acts needed to assure the family security in this life and beyond.

They chose well. Ke-sying grew to be a traditional and responsible "son" and "first grandson." He was also respectful toward his "mother" through the decades though she rarely spoke to him and has continued her legal efforts for forty years to have his status as her "son" revoked.

The decades passed. Her own daughters were married. Ke-sying had married and had a family of his own. But, through the years, she lived with Ke-sying and now his wife and their children as the "honored" if unloved "mother" because in the Chinese tradition, the mother who is widowed lives with her son. When last I heard, the arrangement continued. For forty-four years now, "mother" and "son" have lived together. Litigation is still under way.

The selection of Ke-sying must have been inspired because it would be hard to imagine a person more serious and committed to the maintenance of continuity, tradition, and family dignity than he. He successfully manages the several-generation family business, furniture manufacturing, and has developed an extensive export-import company as well. He has preserved continuity between the generations from his paternal grandparents to his own children, and it is likely that he will ensure that continuity through his children's children, his grandparents' great-great-grandchildren. And since I know his adult children and the sense of Chinese family responsibility they have already assumed, I would wager that the continuity sought will carry through at least one generation further, that is, to the great-great-great-grandchildren.

This is an amazing feat, really. But then, the Chinese are a remarkable people. And they are a remarkable people in part because of their extraordinarily compelling unity of world view, religion, customs, educational systems, and, importantly, the understanding between the generations as to what the requirements of each to the other will be through this life and beyond.

I need not labor the fact that it costs a great deal in terms of human commitment and the expenditure of time, effort, and income to honor the hopes of the great-great-great-grandparents. Whether that is a good way to spend human time and energy is a separate question. Also, the feasibility of sustaining extended family responsibilities in a rapidly industrializing Asia is unclear. But what is evident when one considers what hundreds of successive generations of Chinese have tried to perpetuate is the depth of the need for continuity systems.

Of course, I'm not really writing simply about Chinese life. The needs of Grandmothers and Grandfathers Jones and Smith are in many ways similar to those of Ke-sying's grandparents. It's good to be loved and valued and looked after when you are old. It's good to feel relevant at all ages. It would be nice to be remembered after you are gone and there is something rather touching about the idea of people taking time out to think of you and saying good things about you. This doesn't even mention the matter of money and possessions, and it would be good to hang on to some of those for as long as possible. It is reassuring to believe that the product of one's labor will enhance the life of children and grandchildren.

Case Study 2: *A Chinese Daughter-in-law?*

One of our sons, Jeffrey, studied medicine in Taiwan and while he was there I often found a way to visit him. He had many Chinese friends and one who was very special was Miss Tseng, a kind and happy twenty-five-year-old schoolteacher who was very fond of him. She was always very kind to me and took special effort to explain those aspects of Chinese culture and tradition that she knew would be of interest. Once when the three of us were together in a small family restaurant in Taipei, I asked her to tell me about the handsome, small, red-lacquered shrine that stood on a special table at one side of the room. Some fruit and a cup of tea had been placed in front of the shrine. She explained that most Chinese families maintained a commemorative area in a place of honor in their home in which ancestral plaques telling of the family's history were stored and toward which reverent behavior would be directed. Without being too specific about it, perhaps the spirits of the ancestors might be attracted to such a place and might take pleasure at respectful good wishes or even a cup of fresh tea being offered. She went on to say that the responsibility for such honors was usually assumed by the daughter-in-law and granddaughters for the husband's parents and grandparents. Of course, while the in-laws lived on, the daughter-in-law would bring such honor in her everyday living. I asked her whether all the girls her age, in her group, with her level of education, would really undertake such activities for very long. She replied by looking fondly at my son and, ignoring my question about other women's attitudes, she said to me, "Yes, for all of my life I would honor my husband's parents. My children and their children will do the same."

Case Study 3: *In a Million, Million Years, Much of This Will Be Forgotten*

A few years ago, we invited the new dean of the medical school and his wife for dinner. He was an Oxford (England) graduate and, in addition to being a distinguished medical educator, had written a book of poems, spoke often of Shakespeare and Chaucer, and, in general, seemed something of an English version of America's William Buckley. His wife was a physician as well and was reputed to be a gourmet cook.

We weren't casual about selection of our other guests. We chose some old friends: an English professor whose hobby was collecting medieval glass and his wife, who was a French teacher. I wasn't entirely comfortable with the prospect of the evening but I felt if I poured enough alcohol and kept busy by pretending to help serve the dinner, my level of illiteracy might not show.

I love my parents and they are remarkable. But their surprise telephone call from the airport announcing their arrival two days earlier than expected put the evening's dinner party in a new perspective for me. I decided God had developed a perverse sense of humor.

I must confess that I don't recall all the details from the event, just smatterings from here and there. I do remember my father comparing Churchill's speeches with those of Franklin Delano Roosevelt (unfavorably), and I think my mother did find my report card from the fifth grade on which the teacher had noted my leadership ability and special appointment as recess monitor. She happened, by chance, to have it in her purse.

Actually, I have a well-practiced technique that I use in such moments. I close my eyes, pinch my leg, use an old meditation formula, and repeat over and over to myself, "In a million, million years much of this will be forgotten." This particular evening ended with a grand finale when my mother grasped the dean's arm as they were leaving to ask that he take care of me.

What was surprising, but not really, was that after that evening there was that special added relationship between the dean and his wife and my wife and me that comes when you know people's people.

And when their relatives came to town, they always wanted us to come over to meet them.

I forgot to mention that our other friends, the English professor and his wife, brought a small house gift, a piece of old glassware. Somehow, it was later broken.

In its way, Rip Van Winkle is the horror story of all time. It is probably too far from what people can face to be a successful movie. *Star Wars* and *The Empire Strikes Back* are much closer to our experience. There is the need to preserve for all time and through all conceivable changes the continuity of a recognizable me, us, we, also them. The Ten Commandments are the guide not only to how to live together, but to how to live together forever. Every culture has them. Every culture is them. While there are legends about warriors who left the culture to discover the rest of the world, it was also clear that there were those who remained and sustained the familiar. They included the old people, the children, and certainly the women.

What we call mental illness is inseparable from the need and capacity for people to sustain continuity in their lives through affiliation, ritual, and multi-generational linkages. Through the centuries, the worst pattern of tragedy was often a personal failure to embed oneself and one's posterity in the process of continuity. There were the cast-off wives who could not produce the male heir, the cast-off daughters who were not that heir. There was Medea, who murdered her children in revenge. The ultimate plague imposed by the God of Moses upon the Pharaohs was the death of the first-born sons. On a lesser scale, there have been the countless dramas through the countless ages when a child, because of great strength or great weakness of character, failed to live out the expected continuity or refused to mate with the person pre-selected. Or refused to mate at all.

The next chapters consider in more detail the contemporary break in continuity and the repudiation of cultural expectations by millions and millions of people in North America, Europe, Asia, Africa—everywhere. The rapidity of social change and the relatively short space of time in which so much has taken place preclude the summary statement, "Despite what one would have expected, this is what actually happened." Instead, one can choose to look at it in either way. One can conclude that people today seem to be living on in vast numbers, surviving the putting asunder of continuity and tradition as if such matters were a trivial facade cloaking a pervasive life force that survives and does all right no matter what. Conversely, one could take note of the devastating pain and absence of confidence in so many contemporary lives and wonder whether life is bearable in this era. Or, one could take a more sociopolitical view and point out that life has always been easier for some, harder for others.

4

No More
Grandmothers,
No More Grandfathers:
Learning from Peers

When his remaining two grandparents died in close succession, twelve-year-old John Lorton told his father, "You're next, Dad, and then me. Our Grandmas were a screen that shielded us both. I'm afraid."

An ancient Chinese blessing is the wish that "the Grandfather goes first, then the father, then the son."

For generations and generations, almost every individual's sense of "who I am" has been cast within the broad frame of "Thomas, son of John and Mary, who were in turn son of Martin and Louise and daughter of Sidney and Rose."

To be born outside that frame or to be orphaned was (and is) to be at great risk, at times to the point of death. Through the centuries, the privileged child was simultaneously grandchild, nephew, niece, godson, goddaughter, first, second, third cousin, and/or betrothed to the daughter of its father's oldest friend and classmate. This order within relationships described the past and fixed the present as the route to a prearranged, understood future. The lineage of families like the lineage of kings was both legend of what had been and a promise of certainty in a world fraught with ambiguity.

In many stable, long-established societies, grandparents provided a preserving, conservative input, one emphasizing traditions and telling the history of "our" people. They both offered a reinforcement of the authority of the children's parents and attenuated the tension between parents and children through love and advice offered to each. The matter of love is still important because all too often that which makes life bearable is the fact that somebody loves you no matter what you do. You can earn respect and affection in the street gang or with one's peers, but you have to earn it every day. Unconditional love is sometimes easier for grandparents than parents because they have less complicated responsibilities and because they may see more clearly the continuity of their life in the grandchild. Further, in extended family situations, grandparents often provide more flexibility for struggle within the family (without leaving it). Children who come to feel that their job in life is to get rid of their parents can run away from home and go to grandmother's house.

Grandparents assumed responsibility for inculcating, reinforcing, and romanticizing belief systems that form the basis for the young person's lifetime understanding of:

- *This* is who I am.
- *This* is what I believe.
- *This* is why I choose to behave as I do.
- *This* is what I believe in even if my appetites, instincts, and fears would lead me elsewhere.

Perhaps more important than the teaching of specific rules for behaving was the fact that an environment was provided in which *the child learned to believe in believing, learned attitudes that might facilitate survival in the face of the most disheartening and disillusioning events.* The continuity of grandfather and grandmother through parents and through children is inherently reassuring. There is promise of more to come. Traditional systems taught not only rules. They made clear that life is continuous and that life and believing are synonymous.

We take for granted that everybody believes or could believe in something. This is not the case. The complex nature of both *belief itself* and *belief in believing* has been articulated by the distinguished American psychiatrist Jules Masserman in a remarkable 1953 paper, "Faith and Delusion in Psychotherapy."[1] He pointed out that the life of almost everyone now living and everyone who ever lived has been made more comfortable and satisfying by faith in the validity of one, two, or three deeply held beliefs. First, many hold to the existence of a transcending God or Gods, a divine spirit who offers meaning, inspiration, guidance, and hope for everlasting life. Other persons demonstrate faith in the inherent worthwhileness of the work of man, his industries, her writing, his farms, her science. They see obvious purpose in developing this planet and even in efforts to repeat the process on some other star satellite. The third major belief is in the essential truth of brotherhood, love, sexuality, loyalty, fidelity, and the communion between fellow beings.

An overwhelming majority of people in every society are deeply committed to the "reality," the "correctness," the "proven" status of one, two, or three of these ideas; that is, that God, work, and/or love are *real*. But not everybody. Many of those who are called "schizophrenic" live lives in sharp contrast to the majority of their family and neighbors in that they refuse to believe in such assumptions. They behave as if they believed, and sometimes they directly say, "No God, no work, no love. Outright lies! Or at best, trivial." Such individuals are very threatening to others. For verification of the power of such a threat, the reader might ask, "How would I feel, personally, about someone living in my midst who believed neither in a meaning to life nor in the value of any person's work, or who could never appreciate and demonstrate how good it is to be together?"

Masserman pointed out that all three of these fundamental beliefs may actually be "delusions," the vain hopes that enable the "normal" men, women, and children to lead anxiety-free lives in villages and megalopoli around the world. When an individual has repudiated or abandoned the beliefs and the style of life that others lead, the possibilities of living together are diminished. No less, the possibility of living with oneself and life itself may be equally threatened. What would transpire in a world of societies where the individuals either believed in very little and/or where there was little similarity in what they did believe?

Inevitably, life is not easy. There are moments in every person's history when the very best one can do is to hang on to hope, to await another day, to be optimistic or stoic or inwardly turned or to seek to hold another's hand. Even the most successful person will face despair if he encounters all of his personal critics on the same day. Most who are in jails, many who drift into the skid row areas in contemporary cities, most who contemplate taking their own lives, many who become sick with the symptoms that are called mental illness are individuals who lack either the talent, the experience, the instruction, the internal resources, and/or the faith (belief) to:

- Keep trying.
- Hang on.
- Await another day.
- Be optimistic.
- Be stoic.
- Be speculative.
- Turn one's thoughts inward.
- Seek release from anxiety through
  a clasping of fingers with another person.

In the moments when the best one can do is not to give up and/or not to make things worse, memories of what grandparents had to say and demonstrate can become very important: "We made it through bad times by sticking together, by believing in ourselves, by helping each other, by showing love, by working incredibly hard, and by living the life that we believe in." The finest technology in the world diminishes not one whit the importance of a personal value system that guides the individual, group, and society through moments when the exigencies of life strip away all that is casually worn. In every life such moments come. That suicide is now a growing choice of many young people in many Western societies is an ominous sign. It may reveal that freedom from the burden of the aged with their nostalgic messages may be more than the young can endure. Many have spoken of effects upon grandmothers and grandfathers of being separated from the succeeding generations. There is now growing evidence that such separation may be equally destructive to the young. The grandparental role in society has been an imprinting that taught the young person that living is living out beliefs. For many, that input has been largely interrupted. The family, which formerly included grandparents, aunts, uncles, great-aunts, great-uncles, and godparents, has now become the two-generation (nuclear) family plus "friends." The "we" of young people is much more likely to be a reference to their own generation rather than to a family system of self, parents, and parents' parents. Since many parents are busy and tired, divorcing in record numbers, and not too certain anyway about what is of value, it is now the boasting of peers and the safe-adventure ditties on television that have largely replaced the stories grandparents had to tell. Those stories were force-fully and repeatedly told from the child's earliest days. They were reinforced by believing peers, amplified by ritual, choice food, song and dance, and ultimately personally consecrated in some initiation rite.

CHILDREN ON THEIR OWN

No summary statement can begin to encompass all that has happened to the 225 million people living in North America in the last twenty years. Almost all of us have lived through and been changed by the extraordinary events of the times. Even those who attempted to barricade themselves and their families from surrounding events found no way to stem the tide of change. Our curiosity as a species is too great. Someone is always turning on the television and then you're in the middle of it. Television makes it difficult to live quietly alongside the carnival while the rest of the world rides the roller coaster. There are some families who, to an extent, have sustained their traditional way of life without much concession to all that was going on around them. The family stayed cohesive. The mother stayed home. Religion remained important. Everybody had his job to do. The hierarchies stood. The parents carefully monitored the children's associates. But there aren't very many families without defections. There are the children who left to find a better job and those who left because they didn't fit. Both are away.

Young people growing up in the sixties and seventies differed in important respects from their predecessors of earlier generations. To begin with, there are a great many of them. Half the people who ever lived live today, and half of these are twenty or younger. The children who grew up in North American are among *the first in the history of the world* to be educated by people neither approved of nor supervised by the local people—parents, teachers, religious leaders, school board, tribal or city council. These children learned to trust what they saw on television because of the dependability, tenderness, and honesty of Captain Kangaroo and Mr. Green Jeans, story ladies, and *Sesame Street*. Then they were watching Walter Cronkite and the TV specials on the shootings at Kent State, the funerals of Martin Luther King, Jr., Jack and Bobby Kennedy, the ugly stories from Vietnam, Watergate, Three Mile Island, and Iran. Not only were they greatly influenced by what they saw, but the mode of presentation made the on-the-spot history lessons different from the ones their parents had received three decades before. Television says, "Here are the facts we have and here are the pictures. Some things aren't certain. These you will have to decide for yourself." The "extended family members" introduced by television dramas also served to demonstrate to young people how they have a "right" to be treated in the home and at school. No injustice to a child is left uncorrected beyond the second commercial.

Since the late 1950s children have been much more on their own. Affluence, moves to the suburbs, working mothers, and the fact that there was less need for the labor of children left many free to travel, play, or whatever. There weren't many things they *had* to do. Their parents were busy. Teachers were no longer particularly feared. Sundays were given over to watching football games. There was, in most families, a lessening of executive functions of the older people. Even in families where father continued to "know best," the children were reared with classmates and friends who raised questions and offered attractive alternatives. Of course, the 1 million children whose parents obtained divorces each year were often first among the group thrown on their own.

The "cult of the wonderful adolescent" reached a lofty high in the late 1960s, then retreated abruptly in the 1970s. It was an intoxicating era in which the music of the Beatles, Bob Dylan, and Janis Joplin, the two generations of writers after J. D. Salinger's *Catcher in the Rye*,[2] and the young filmmakers following in the tradition of Bergman, Fellini, Antonioni, and Warhol all starred the young hero. The "progressive educators" who carried the message of John Dewey, Columbia University Teachers College, and the givers of advice who came after the durable Dr. Ben Spock all kept a spotlight on the young.[3,4] They were contributors to young people's discovering "I'm very important." For many of the young people of the sixties and early seventies, the intoxication, group intimacy, and heady blend of drugs and lots of leisure supported the illusion "I'm creative as well." It was an era when many traditions were abandoned.

Of course, not all traditions deserve faithful compliance. For example, the decades after World War II saw a considerable reduction in the level of shame and guilt about sex. This is quite an important matter. Guilt over sex and shame about one's body have been traditional among educated people for a long time. There has been so much modification of the attitudes of secrecy, shame, and punishment associated with sexuality in such a very short period of time in North America that what follows will seem bizarre to the young reader, half-forgotten by their parents. But all of that wasn't long ago.

As a case in point, if a bit stylized, consider the following paragraphs taken from a mischievous book called *Plain Facts for Old and Young*. It was written by a doctor in 1891.[5] Thousands and thousands of copies were sold. It was passed from generation to generation. It added to the level of misery and unhappiness of most who read it. My grandmother gave it to me at the time I married. I was glad not to have had it earlier.

Cure of the Habit

The preliminary step in treatment is always to cure the vice itself if it still exists. The methods adopted for this purpose must differ according to the age of the individual patient.

In children, especially those who have recently acquired the habit, it can be broken up by admonishing them of its sinfulness, and portraying in vivid colours its terrible results, if the child is old enough to comprehend such admonitions. In addition to faithful warnings, the attention of the child should be fully occupied by work, study, or pleasant recreation. He should not be left alone at any time lest he yield to temptation. Work is an excellent remedy; work that will really make him very tired, so that when he goes to bed he will have no disposition to defile himself. It is best to place such a child under the care of a faithful person of older years, whose special duty shall be to watch him night and day until the habit is thoroughly overcome.

In younger children, with whom moral considerations will have no particular weight, other devices may be used. Bandaging the parts has been practiced with success. Tying the hands is also successful in some cases; but this will not always succeed, for they will often contrive to continue the habit in other ways, as by working the limbs, or lying upon the abdomen. Covering the organs with a cage has been practiced with entire success. A remedy which is almost always successful in small boys is circumcision, especially when there is any degree of phimosis.* The operation

* A condition in which the foreskin of the penis is tight and cannot be drawn back.

should be performed by a surgeon without administering an anaesthetic, as the brief pain attending the operation will have a salutary effect upon the mind, especially if it be connected with the idea of punishment, as it may well be in some cases. The soreness which continues for several weeks interrupts the practice, and if it had not previously become too firmly fixed, it may be forgotten and not resumed. If any attempt is made to watch the child, he should be so carefully surrounded by vigilance that he cannot possibly transgress without detection. If he is only partially watched, he soon learns to elude observation, and thus the effect is only to make him cunning in his vice.

In adults or youth a different plan must be pursued. In these cases moral considerations, and the inevitable consequences to health of body and mind, are the chief influences by which a reform is to be effected, if at all. These considerations may be urged with all possible eloquence and earnestness, but should not be exaggerated. The truth is terrible enough.

Good riddance. Who needs that heritage? However, how goes the emancipation? What happens when children are out from under the relentless imprinting of values that grandparents, uncles, aunts, ministers, and parents formerly provided? What happens when the shame, guilt, and fear associated with sexuality is largely lifted? What happens when the principal teachers of young people are young people? What happens when young people decide to decide for themselves?

In many families, the effects of all these events have been devastating. I think that as a group, the North American children of the sixties and seventies were the hardest to raise of any in this (or any) century. The general disappearance of grandparents as ultimate authorities, the pace of life and variety of activities of contemporary parents, the Pied Piper effects of identification with youth culture, and the catastrophe of drug abuse have exacted a considerable toll on the young and those who cared for them.

Many, many of the middle-aged individuals who came to my office to talk over their divorce plans or their sense of purposelessness were people who had lived through dreadful experiences with their children. Drugs, sex, police, violence, wandering off, quitting school, and lack of respect on the part of young people have led to the dissolution of many contemporary families. Disappointment about what happened to their children caused many parents to blame each other. People like to stay with and return to people with whom they have shared victories and celebrations. Ex-partners in bankrupt businesses avoid lunching together.

Of course, one of the big businesses of families is their children and the manner in which they grow to adulthood. There is something between parents and children that is before and beyond words, a "given" of existence, a fact that is already there when it all starts. It may be true that many young marrieds in America today are saying that they don't want to have children of their own, and they mean it. But, even if they don't, somebody else will—to the joy and affirmation of different sets of grandparents.

What made the raising of children very hard for parents in the years that followed World War II and the reason that so many feel that they have failed miserably in their parental role was that their assignment was almost impossible. Two parents alone, however dedicated, just cannot have the same power and pervasive impact that the army of adults who were part of the extended families of earlier generations could muster. Most in the parental generation in the fifties and sixties had been reared, taught, and disciplined by the armies of agreeing adults who have always reared children. The parents of the fifties and sixties believed that it could be done in the nuclear family (with both parents busy). It can't be done. Of course, there are a hundred other reasons why many contemporary parents exert less influence and power over children. But the net result is a widespread sense of parental failure that reached its peak in the early seventies and moderated a bit since as more and more parents have discovered that they have lots of company. It's really been very sad. People of great sincerity, competence, and achievement in other parts of their lives found themselves set up to be parental failures in stark contrast to their other successes. Of course, a good many of the young people who "failed" their parents were and are great successes by other standards, some by any standard except the narrow one defined by inflexible parental demand.

But by any measure, reasonable or otherwise, many times it has been very, very difficult.

ARE THESE OUR CHILDREN?!

Not so long ago, I was asked to served as a consultant to a family psychotherapy program that wasn't working out very well. The young therapist had started with one of the teenagers, then expanded the program to include the parents and older sister, and, at my suggestion, had asked the grandparents to participate as well. They were strangers to me but I recognized them by name as members of a prominent local Jewish family. I walked into the room where they were all sitting and realized that someone was smoking marijuana. It was the daughter, about eighteen. The younger boy, seventeen, wore a large crucifix. The grandparents were worried. The mother was nervously smiling. The father was slumped in his chair. I looked around and started to laugh. The mother said, "I feel exactly the same way. I'd be laughing myself if I wasn't so busy crying."

Other times, there was no possible way to laugh. Many youngsters who left home because there was no meaning there fared much worse in a world of strangers. For some of them, the confrontation with what was missing in themselves awaited completion of a migration across the continent to the West Coast. Then there was no place to go. The suicide note on the next page was left by a twenty-four-year-old woman far from home. It was addressed to her boy friend. One of how many thousands of final messages that came back to heartbroken families, to be read and reread, it said everything and nothing.

> Dear Tom,
> You must forgive me and carry on. You have so much strength in you and I would hate to see your ability go to waste. And never, but NEVER blame yourself for what has happened. My lows are so outrageous that I can't see living with them for the rest of my life. There would never be peace of mind for me. This was my own decision. I know I promised I never would but my soul never ceases to ache except when I am stoned or drunk. Please don't shed any tears for me. I know you will but please don't worry for long, because I won't be suffering. It is the best thing, believe me. Love you.
>
> Love,
Jane
>
> P.S. There's probably more I could have said, but I can't think of anything. Except forgive my selfishness and may God forgive me. Say good-bye to everyone for me.

Many of the millions of young people on the move, toward Vancouver, to California, to Kabul, to caves and communes in Greece, or to unreceptive hosts along the Ganges River in India, found themselves in water over their heads. Some discovered unknown strengths and learned to swim. Others couldn't. There have been many, many of those others.

A Sudden Silence at Mrs. Van Warren's Country Club Lunch

At seventy-four, Mrs. Van Warren is the last of the way it was, and an invitation to one of her famous luncheons is always a mixed blessing. One's social status is affirmed during a boring, tasteless, ceremonial, and overlong meal. Rich from birth, from marriage, from remarriage, Essie Van Warren has no way of discovering that she is not an expert on all subjects. So, she speaks only "ex cathedra."

The lunch, Sunday, after church, was to have been for eleven, but the Reverend Baxter's wife didn't come. She had to skip church to have an excuse, but that was small enough. She'd been to lunch before. Mrs. Van Warren, who didn't like the clergyman's wife anyway, was glad. Seating eleven people means you can't have alternate seating for man, woman. With ten, it's possible.

The guests included the Nolands, he the executive vice-president of the town's major banking firm and she formerly a Duncan, a very good family. The Nolands, in their early fifties, had three young adult children, two of whom they would not speak of at Mrs. Van Warren's luncheon. The Wentworths, oil and real estate, were also there, hoping that questions about their only daughter would stay superficial and that the subjects of abortion, trial marriage, marijuana, and something called "coke" wouldn't come up. The Richards, owners of the biggest department store, in their mid-forties, wanted not to come. But they came because his dad told them to. That was something Mrs. Richards was going to bring up with the marriage counselor on Tuesday. The fourth couple was new, the Sloans, he a writer and the token outsider. But not really. Sloan's wife had formerly been married to a cousin of Mrs. Wentworth's. Very wealthy people.

Grace first. Then a frantic but hopeless dive into a second mild aperitif. A crabmeat cocktail. Then a jellied consommé with a garnish of sour cream and caviar. Then, the second sermon of the day as Mrs. Van Warren began to talk about the young people, their lack of morals, their poor dress, the weakness of parents of that kind of degenerate youth. Mrs. Noland spoke up about the way caviar improves consommé, and Mrs. Sloan was eager to agree. (What's she hiding?) Mr. Richards guessed the crab came from

Mexico, but Mr. Wentworth thought California. Mrs. Van Warren continued to say that simple things, clean tastes are disappearing and that the leaders of the church should consider who should receive communion. A baked herbed chicken arrives. And then, like a bomb, she asks, "How are all your children doing?"

There is a sudden silence at Mrs. Van Warren's country club lunch.

Just about the time when I have convinced myself that really nothing major has changed and that the pendulum will swing back and some of the older traditions will again prevail, I come across an article in the newspaper like the following.

Cambridge, Mass. (UPI) The traditional family is quickly being replaced by singles, and by 1990, mom, pop and the kids will be in the minority, a new study concludes. . . . "The traditional family as we have known it will become a minority," said George Masnick, coauthor of the three year study entitled "The Nation's Families: 1960–1990." Masnick, a population expert at Harvard University, said in 1960, 75 percent of all American families were "traditional, nuclear types." He predicted by 1990 about 50 percent of all U.S. households will be "husband-wife" types, with about half of those choosing to have children; the remaining 50 percent of households will consist of individuals living alone. Of twenty million new households expected by the end of this decade, more than 16.5 million will be unattached individuals, said Mary Jo Bane, Associate Director of the Joint Center for Urban Studies.[6]

And it is certainly true that the way many younger people are envisioning their lives and carrying out those visions is far different from what their parents had planned.

The Expert Comes Home

The rapid pace of social change is making it hard for a person like myself to do very well on the radio and television talk shows. I had a grim experience not long ago when I went back to my hometown, Indianapolis, Indiana, to give a talk and was invited to make an appearance on a widely viewed supper-hour TV news program. My parents, long-time Indianapolis residents, were quite high about my planned appearance and I overheard my mother making telephone calls to a long list of friends and relatives.

The moment came and it turned out that they had allotted five minutes for my interview minus time for a commercial in the middle. I thought that was all right. However, after a brief introduction the youthful appearing, very confident TV commentator had a complex question for me. It went something like this:

"Well, Doctor, I know our viewers will be very interested in your reply to this controversial situation. It came up earlier today on one of the call-in shows and I very much want to know what you think. I assume, Doctor, that you accept marriages between same sex people if they are consenting and of age and what I want to ask you concerns children in such unions. Now I'll be right back with that question after this word from our sponsor."

"Now, Doctor, this is a lesbian couple who have a stable and satisfying relationship that has continued for more than two years. They are talking about having a baby and one of the women's brothers has agreed to provide sperm donation for artificial insemination for his sister's mate. Do you think that's a good idea?"

I replied that I didn't have the slightest idea. He thanked me and said it was good to talk with me. I drove back to my folks' house. Everyone was very quiet. They had started dinner without me. No one looked up. The TV was off.

The sixties and seventies saw a trade-off of independence, equality, candor, and mobility at the expense of a sense of continuity, tranquillity, order, and ritual. There have been many casualties. Has it been worth it? Certainly the young people, as they finally grow up, develop qualities that should contribute to a good life for themselves, their children, and their neighbors. In particular, their allegiance to and affection for each other is impressive. They don't seem to experience the kind of rivalry with (against) each other that marked earlier generations. In my own growing up, so much loyalty was committed to parents and other adults that there wasn't much left over for peers. I owed it to my parents to succeed, to study, to work harder than my contemporaries, and to surpass them. By contrast, fewer of today's young people are reassured when their peers do badly or fail. And it is with their peers, here and around the world, that they will need to live and work and share. I'm also a new convert to the active participation of young fathers in all aspects of child rearing, including preparation for and presence during the actual delivery, sharing in the earliest days of care, and in all the days following in the lives of the children. That is an attitude I've learned from young people, including my children. I think it will make for considerably healthier families.

5

Living as an
Older Person

For someone reared in a society that respects, elevates, and honors older people, the aloneness, relative poverty, and sense of irrelevance of so many aging North Americans seem unthinkable. A young Korean physician who was about to return home came to talk with me about his feelings concerning the separation of the generations. He had lived for three years in the United States.

What is hardest to understand is how your country-men treat old people. I think it is very cruel. We are a poor country but no one would put his mother or father in a different home to live out their old age. It is our responsibility to take care of our parents. Didn't they take care of us when we were young? Think how they must feel living away from their children and grand-children. My mother lives with us and even during the war [the Korean War] when we had little to eat, we were glad to have her. My father died in the war. Every morning I go before his picture and pay my respects to his memory. I don't think I would like to be an older person here. Many other ages would be fine, but not old age.

Actually, he had underestimated the complexity of our generational problems because each of the three generations is incomplete without the other two. Young children and adolescents lose if there are no grandparents around to serve as culture bearers and unambivalent love figures. No less, the current generations of parents without grandparents have had serious trouble raising their own children and, as well, trouble staying married to each other. And, without doubt, separation of the generations has been very hard on the older people.[1,2] So much that has happened has gone against them. They have suffered from the generational divisions and from the speed of technological change which made their skills obsolete and left them nothing to teach the young at work. A terrible inflation has dissolved their savings and in many instances made insignificant their already paltry pensions. They suffer from skyrocketing costs for medicine, housing, transportation, and from several decades in which old people themselves believed that the television and radio concentration on the young reflected their own lack of worth.

But there is another important truth about seniors in America. The American milieu with its blend of ingenuity, independence, willingness to participate, and basic openness to life has produced a special kind of person. Millions of Americans sustain into their senior years a vigor, sensitivity, and integrity that makes them our most unique national product.

Case Study 1: *The Media Watcher from Long Beach, California*

The city of Long Beach is one of the twenty-eight cities of the coastal region of Los Angeles County (there are, altogether, eighty-six cities that make up Los Angeles) and I've come to know a good deal about it. It's a fine and proud city with a beautiful harbor in which the famed ocean liner *The Queen Mary* has come to stay. Long Beach, California, vies with St. Augustine, Florida, for the distinction of being home for the largest percentage of citizens more than sixty years of age, approximately 22 percent compared to an 11 percent national average. In addition to my appreciation of some very extraordinary citizens who live there, I admire the city itself. Situated on the sea with a unique "southern exposure," Long Beach claims the best weather in America; that is, just right in the summer and even better in the winter. Its major urban renewal program is creating a higher quality of housing and a greatly enriched artistic and cultural milieu. Not only have many older people created imaginative and satisfying lives here, but waves of immigrants from Europe, Mexico, Samoa, Fiji, South Asia, and now the boat people from Indochina have come to Long Beach and added to its rich multi-cultural tradition.

Still, it is one's experience with special individuals that provides the deepest impressions of a place, and Long Beach is no exception to that rule. I'd known Cora Cocks for several years without quite realizing what a celebrity she was. A little woman, shy of five feet tall, she had introduced herself to me at a citizen's mental health advocacy meeting as "a great-grand-mother and a Gray Panther." The Gray Panthers are a nationally organized group of senior citizens and young people actively working for a better deal for old and young. They work with the same passion and determination as panthers of another color. Somewhere during our first meeting, Cora told me she was seventy-seven. I have seen her many times in the last two years. Sometimes she is a negotiator or lobbyist for mental health funds for seniors. Sometimes we were together because she is a member of my own citizen's advisory council overseeing programs and priorities in mental health for people of all ages. She is a gentle person, warm, thoughtful, and dignified. She has been a widow since 1975.

Cora grew up poor. Her mother died of tuberculosis when she was four months old and her stepmother died when she was four years old. Cora had an older sister, one year her senior, with whom she grew up. Her father was a coal miner who wanted to take care of his two daughters, but most of her childhood was spent in foster homes or orphanages. Usually her sister was with her. Cora is a happy person, but her memories of childhood are predominately unhappy ones. She is very much involved with these memories, which she contrasts with her experiences in adult life and old age. She feels it is a wonderful miracle that her life worked out so well. Even the opportunity to experience old age seems a bonus since, to her knowledge, no member of her family, including both sets of grandparents, her father, sister, and two mothers, lived beyond a fiftieth birthday. Her own marriage of fifty-one years was a very happy one, though the early years of the marriage spanned the Great Depression and had been difficult financially. She worked as a teacher till her children came and at intervals during the Depression when her husband was out of work. But in the middle and later years of the marriage, her husband had a good job, and the family always had enough for basic needs, including the education of the children. Cora had cared for him at home during his final illness. That was his wish and hers. "I was always proud of him and he was always proud of me. He would be proud still."

Cora would be inclined to find a different word, but she is a humanist and no age group escapes her interest and concern. Her commitment to the well-being of fellow seniors is sincere and compelling. She has close friends who are one hundred years old. No less, she has been an active leader for many years in efforts to end child abuse. Some of the pioneering work in the field was carried out in Long Beach and Cora was a leader from the beginning. Beyond the children and the seniors, Cora has had an active involvement in the establishment of a Long Beach Shelter Home for

Women, a haven for those beaten by husbands and boy friends. This is another program important to people in Long Beach. Cora has been part of many advocacy activities for seniors in Long Beach, in California, and throughout the nation for more than thirty years.

One of her major activities at the moment is media watching. She is very concerned about the image of older people that television portrays. She is personally offended by a famous comedienne's depiction of a toothless and senile senior in a rocking chair trying to remember what the pleasures were—while people laugh nervously. She is offended as well that older people are so often portrayed on television only as the afflicted in denture, hemorrhoid, constipation, and sleeping potion advertisements. She feels such depictions essentially villify seniors. She tries to interest the banks, buses, department stores, restaurants, and service organizations of Long Beach in the special needs of senior citizens. She is currently taking the lead in trying to encourage the doctors and hospitals of the city to accept the usual 80 percent payment of medical bills usually allocated by insurance carriers as payment in full if the patient is a poorly fixed senior. She is frequently asked to talk to groups of retired people, college and high school students, and service organizations on the topics of death, money, indifferent children, problems in finding a caring doctor, and, always, sex. On the latter topic, she achieved some notoriety, about which she is a bit uncertain.

She was being interviewed on a network talk show (prime time) early this year by a psychiatrist* who asked her if she had started to date since the death of her husband. She said yes and when he asked her whether she was making love again she said she was. He went on to ask whether, at her age, she could still have an orgasm and she not only said yes but repeated

* Dr. William Rader, Los Angeles TV station KABC.

the word. She told me that her adult grandchildren were unambivalently proud of her interview on the television. Her children? Well. . . .

Cora plans to do what she can to battle against ageism because "It's just so unfair." She feels good about her present life and she feels clearly that, for her, the later years are far better than the years of childhood. She appreciates her freedom to be herself and to need to make no apology to anyone. She says she's no typical old person, only because there is no such thing as a typical old person. "We're all," she insists, "as different as snowflakes."

Among the quarter of a billion people on the North American continent there are many different kinds of "older individuals." No single description is sufficient. For some few, like Cora Cocks, old age is one of the finest periods of life. It is a time for enjoying life, a time of mattering, a benevolent period of living fully to the very end. For such persons, old age brings its own rewarding variety of joys, deeper understanding, and interpersonal fulfillment. But this does not happen automatically. Older people, like everybody, need others who care about and admire them. How a person feels about himself is also not easily separated from such matters as income beyond Social Security payments, the quality and location of housing, and the ability to climb stairs, chew food, and move without fear of falling. Above all, their sense of well-being may depend on whether the mate is living (or whether they have a new love).

WHEN OLD AGE GOES WELL

There are special satisfactions that may come in later years, particularly if both members of a couple are living and in reasonable health. Not many achieve all that they had hoped for in their youth. Few who aspire to such positions rise to the very top. But the discovery that life offers satisfactions and joys even when one's goals are "scaled down" can be very reassuring. Older people usually come to understand the absurdity of the person who methodically and painstakingly plans all things. They learn about a tombstone in a Miami cemetery that lists 1925 and 1969 as the dates of birth and death and bears this inscription: "Man plans and God laughs." They have learned that "this too shall pass" and serenity may come in their lives. If they are among the lucky parents whose children stayed married, there is the reassurance that "he has a wife and she has a husband to look after them now." It's as though school let out and vacation has started.

Among the joys of the older years may be the rediscovery of one's mate. Couples who have lived with the pressures that accompany rearing children, including PTA, bad grades, other children's angry parents, accidents with the family car, "What is she doing out past 2 A.M. with *that* boy?" "You're quitting college?" "You lost your job and your wife is pregnant!" and so forth, often have fallen out of touch with each other. Their reacquaintance may be very meaningful to both. And a long-kept secret about older people is that their life together often includes a part that is sexual! Children have traditionally had a great deal of trouble accepting their parents' sexuality. This is true whether the child is fourteen and the parents thirty-eight, the child is twenty-four and the parents forty-eight, the child thirty-four and the parents fifty-eight, the child forty-four and the parents sixty-eight, and, yes, there are sometimes parents in their late seventies whose relationship includes active sexuality to the discomfort of their fifty-four-year-old children (whose sexuality in turn is denied by their thirty-year-old children). When both mates are alive and when the physical and financial realities are not overwhelmingly nega-tive, then older people can say, "All of life is worthwhile, but I cherish in a special way these last years since the kids are raised and we are back together and we get along so well." Obviously, the loss of such a relationship through death of a mate is a particularly cruel experience, one likely to place enormous stress on the survivor. The loss of a mate is the ultimate test of a person's wish to go on living. The frequency with which the deaths of long-married individuals occur in rapid succession attests to the fragility of life without another.

Many times, however, even the loss of a mate does not rob an older individual of his or her sense of relevance and meaning. Some very fortunate families enjoy relationships that span three of four generations, enriching the lives of young and old alike.

My family was graced by the presence of grandparents and great-grandparents. We celebrated three golden weddings. These people were very important in my life and in the lives of my children. I came to know a good deal about "geriatric medicine" from my family experience. When I was a second-year medical student (with a new blood pressure cuff and stethoscope), I was consulted by several members of the family who were worried about Grandma Molly, aged sixty-eight. Grandma had been somewhat apprehensive about the presence of unfamiliar workmen in the house and had hidden her money in a purse, which she put into the oven. At supper time, some unexpected smells were produced. "Medical" assistance was sought.

I gave Grandma a thorough examination, noted her high blood pressure, and paid particular attention to her problems in solving certain mental tests that I gave her. For example, she did poorly with the task of remembering numbers. I would call out a series of five or six numbers and ask her to repeat them. She often forgot one or mixed up the sequence. A bad sign! On another task designed to reveal waning mental prowess she did equally poorly. This test consisted of the simultaneous recitation of the alphabet and numbers (A1, B2, C3, D4, and so forth). Grandma's mind seemed to want to go in one direction or the other and the task of switching back and forth from letters to numbers was difficult for her. Grandma acknowledged the memory trouble that I was discovering and then, as was often the case with her, she began to tell me in great detail about some events in her early childhood.

One of Grandma's favorite tales, told over and over during the last two decades of her life, was an "audience participation" story concerning an event that happened when she was eight years old and a second grader. The teacher asked a question that Grandma alone in her class was able to answer. The question was this: Which word should be emphasized in the following sentence: "Is God upon the ocean as well as on the land?" Each of those queried by Grandma over a thirty-year period, her daughters, sons-in-law, doctors, lawyers, businessmen, family friends, and others, always guessed wrong! Perhaps forty times during her last twenty years, Grandma challenged me to solve that problem. I would guess *is, upon, ocean, land* and then go into the small articles and prepositions until finally Grandma, with glee, would declare, "No! The word to emphasize is *God!* You see, you aren't so smart."

My medical report to the family was rather dire. The future was clear and all too ominous. Grandma gave many indications of organic brain damage. The problems of senility and deterioration were imminent. We were all sad.

Twenty years later, in her eighty-eighth year, Grandma Molly, alert, imaginative, and great fun almost to the end, passed away. At family parties during those years, Grandma was always in evidence. Two or three times each year, she could be counted upon, rather shyly at first, like a young teenager, to step into the middle of the living room to sing and dance "After the Ball Is Over" with my father, with me, or with our friend Harry Myers. And each time, on the second or third chorus, we would all join in: Grandma, Grandma's children, her children's children, and her children's children's children. We knew we were sharing something very special.

We took very good care of Grandma. She was "under doctor's care" over the years and things never got out of control. She was on blood pressure medicine steadily for twenty years. Once, she became very depressed as a side reaction to one of the blood pressure medicines and she was promptly switched to another. She was always busy and she lived in her own home. She had help with cleaning but she herself was the one who was responsible. She cooked most meals for herself and sometimes for the whole family. She had many stories to tell and she instilled a sense of the history and folklore of our family in her descendants.

In my grandmother's life, continuity was of the greatest importance. She derived her sense of dignity not only from her own actions but the actions of her family. She was proud that she was a daughter in the Klein family, known for generations for their honesty in business, a reputation she felt still survived in "the books" of all who had dealt with her father and great-grandfather. One's standing in the community was of the greatest importance to her. She felt that her children's children's children would benefit from the good life of her mother and father and their parents before. She was a very good woman. She was a good neighbor.

BITTER OLDER YEARS

Most grandparents and their families aren't as lucky. Rather than emphasizing what is right with them, many live with a sense of self that emphasizes their losses, their loneliness, and their growing incapacity. For them, old age is the time when things go wrong. Above all, in an increasingly urbanized, progress-oriented, and affluent society, one of the things that went wrong is that they are *poor*. One-third of the nation's older people live "below the poverty line"—they are poverty stricken! Older people also are poor in terms of prestige, influence, and power in an affluence- and youth-oriented society. They lack voice. Sit-ins, protest marches, strikes, and voter registration campaigns are not the concerns of older people, even if they are the concerns of the times. Living separately from younger people, away from "where the action is," they lack information that would make the contemporary society of interest to them. This separation from the growing part of society is costly. The contemporary historian and balladeer Bob Dylan reminds us, "The times, they are a-changing." And he adds, "Them's not busy living, them's busy dying."[3]

Overshadowing all losses are those that make for loneliness. The world fills up with strangers. The death of old friends and the migration of others leave giant gaps in place of people who admired, reaffirmed, and understood. Whether one is seven or seventy, having someone your own age to talk to and play with determines the quality of life. Friends listen to us, nod their heads, laugh at our stories, and affirm our judgments. That affirmation is essential for survival.[4,5]

In all probability, the most impressive lesson of the twentieth century relates to the discovery of large, unnoticed, undervalued, and deprived social and racial groups in our midst. In each instance, better food, better clothing, better opportunity, and greater acceptance made it come to pass that those others were more like us than we had realized. There were the mentally ill, the mentally retarded, the poor people, the black people. Now we are discovering the Indian people and the old people. Next, perhaps, the people in jails will begin to look more familiar. In every instance, the human and social needs of each person and group were just about what common sense would have suggested.

In most large cities, there are various social programs for older individuals sponsored by the city, state, province, or church organizations. We prefer to believe that these programs are useful in meeting the needs of older people. However, a dissenting view follows. It was voiced by a social worker, a therapist employed in a "golden-age center" in New York City. Her name is Shirley Silbert.

I wish I had never gotten into this work. It terrifies me. This is the seventh year that I have been a recreational therapist here and I can tell you that there is nothing golden about growing old. It's not very pleasant. Oh, among the thousand or more people who we're involved with each year, there are twenty or thirty who are like the ones you see on television, lively, happy, with something to give, and able to laugh. But believe me, they're really the exception! When you talk about old people, forget the word *happy.* The lucky ones are those who are able to manage and who are content, I mean resigned.

Old age is mostly a time of fear. There is fear of dying, of being alone, of being sick, of having no friends, of not having any money. And loneliness is the most terrible part of old age. Little by little, they lose their friends. People move away. People die. Even the neighborhood changes. The little shops are torn down and up go high-rises. There is nothing familiar left. Another problem is the muggings and the holdups. Most of the older people I know are poor and they have to live in a tough part of town. Then, because they're not able to fight back, they are a good target for the kind of thug who would kill anyone for $1.35. All of them are afraid to go out at night. They are prisoners after dark.

Our center provides almost every service you could think of. The most popular is a doctor who comes in to take people's blood pressure. And there's a newspaper that's published, the *Golden Years.* We have a lot of dances, birthday parties, discussion groups, workshops in art, needlepoint, singing, card playing, bus trips, guest speakers, a small library, a financial counselor, and just about everything. And there are ministers from every denomination who work with the social workers. But, like I said, there are only very few old people who seem to have a good time at the center. Most of them don't. They come hoping for the greatest thing in the world to happen to them. What is that? It's for someone to listen while they talk about their ailments, tell how lonesome they are, and maybe brag about the children they never hear from.

I'm fifty-eight and obsessed with the notion that one day I'm going to be like them. I don't think I'd like to live like that. But as bad as it is, even though their lives don't seem to have much meaning, very few of them want to die. I guess I'll feel the same way. So will you. Just to be on the safe side, take care of your teeth.

HEALTH PROBLEMS OF AGING INDIVIDUALS

As life proceeds, transient and minor bodily difficulties usually progress to a point where they are persisting health problems. The body is rediscovered, but this time in a nostalgic way. The value of teeth, of freely movable arms and legs, of unclouded vision, precise hearing, easy digestion, and plenty of energy is best appreciated by those who are older. Older people's bruises heal slowly and recovery from a fractured bone takes an eternity. Accordingly, they have an understandable protectiveness about their bodies. As one great-grandfather said, "When I'm asked to do something, I not only have to decide whether I want to do it, but also whether my body wants to. Sometimes, we disagree." An older person has to take into consideration matters that would never occur to a young person. "Can I digest that? Will I be able to see that fine print? Can I hear the actors' voices from the balcony? Can I, and should I, walk those steps? Is the journey worth the tiredness I will feel when I come home?"

Certain kinds of physical illnesses are particularly devastating. Conditions that long immobilize and require placement in an unfamiliar institution are very difficult. Consider, for example, the consequences of a fractured hip. There is the injury itself, followed by transportation to the hospital, a series of X rays, and ultimately the bad news that hospitalization of weeks or months is necessary. Further, the individual may learn that at least two operations will have to be performed. Even worse, the outcome is uncertain. Life inside a hospital means enforced dependency, separation from loved ones, sharing living space and the most private matters with strangers, and an unfamiliar and often uninteresting diet. Pain often grows worse at night and disrupts sleep. There are also the inevitable personal slights that are experienced by those who must be cared for by three shifts of nursing and medical personnel. The very indignity of being a man or woman deprived of erect locomotion is in itself a considerable affront.

Individuals who are immobilized, whether by fracture, stroke, or heart attack, are particularly susceptible to the mounting level of anxiety, narrowing of personal interests, and loss of hope that accompany mental depression. Depression superimposed upon a preexisting physical illness is extremely demoralizing and its development makes the diagnosis and management of it doubly difficult. Depression also impedes recovery from physical illness by taking away appetite and decreasing cooperation. Perhaps more important, those healing forces subsumed under the heading "the will to live" are destroyed if depression is not treated. Vascular disease is another serious threat to older people, and since blood vessels are a vital part of every organ, it is an enemy that may strike anywhere. The disease is particularly devastating when the heart, brain, and kidney are affected. Kidney disease is associated with elevated blood pressure, which in turn makes damage to the heart and brain more likely. Damage to brain tissue produces unpredictable consequences, depending upon the place and extent of injury and the preexisting personality of the individual involved. The process may be acute or quite subtle. If the changes are gradual, the individual can, to a certain degree, compensate for and mask (for a time) the humiliating and confidence-destroying symptoms of memory loss, confusion, disorientation, and mental depression.

Case Study 2: *A Man Who Held Power to the End*

Mr. Reginald Vance, Sr., was seen by a psychiatrist under rather extraordinary circumstances. He was seventy years old and chairman of the board of a large industrial corporation. He had decided to change his last will and testament in order to eliminate both of his sons, whom he felt had turned against him. His attorney was uncertain as to how clearly his client was thinking and decided to ask for a psychiatric report at that time. Mr. Vance was not enthusiastic about subjecting himself to such examination but did so at the firm insistence of his attorney.

Reginald Vance was a very distinguished and impressive man. He spoke with assurance, looked directly at the psychiatrist, and started out in the psychiatric examination as if he were calling to order a meeting with the junior staff members in his office. This impressive start notwithstanding, he was actually quite confused, disorganized, and deluded. Beneath a rather haughty and disdainful facade, he was a man who was uncertain as to the date, the city in which the psychiatric examination was being held, and the reason for the examination. He attempted to cover his first several mistakes by angrily accusing the doctor of trying to confuse him and he stood up to leave. He was persuaded with great difficulty to remain, and then only after the doctor agreed to call in Mr. Vance's wife, who had been waiting in the outer room.

In general, Mr. Vance presented many of the classic signs of chronic and severe brain damage. These signs included a decreased ability to understand, to remember, to calculate, to judge, and to learn. For example, when asked to perform simple mathematical problems he proved to be quite impaired. He demanded a paper and pencil before answering the question of how much change a buyer could expect if he gave the clerk a $5 bill and made purchases in the amount of $1.75. His final answer, $3.75, was incorrect. He was also unable to perform tests such as subtraction of serial 7s from 100 (93, 86, 79, 72, and so on). He did not understand the task for a time, then finally replied, "Of course, 100 minus 7 is 93. And 93 minus 7 is 84, and 84 minus 7 is 67. And 60 minus 7 is 53, and 53 minus 7 is 56." During the examination, Mr. Vance became angry several times, and at one point, after failing to answer a question, he began to cry.

Mr. Vance was struggling desperately to maintain an outward appearance that masked his sense of impending disaster. He was a proud man attempting against odds to maintain his dignity.

The suspicions Mr. Vance had developed about his sons were "delusions"—fixed, false ideas that were not open to change. Specifically, he felt his sons were trying to poison him with gas released in buildings in which he walked. He stated that their purpose was to wrest control of the family business in order to assist communism. As he spoke, his wife, aged sixty-eight, sitting slightly to the side, shook her head negatively, indicating her disagreement with the husband. She was, however, reluctant to disagree with him publicly.

His delusion about his two sons was not entirely without basis. They were both in his business and were soon to follow their father in leadership. But in the meantime, they were in the position of protecting their father while simultaneously reassuring exasperated employees who faced the confused, angry, and accusatory old man. This dual role made it difficult for them to "talk straight" with the father. He sensed their "deviousness" and felt that it hid malevolent intentions. The delusion provided a kind of face-saving solution. He could maintain that the changes he was experiencing in himself were not the result of his advanced age and waning powers. Instead, they were the consequence of an evil plot, one developed by his own sons. He projected all responsibility outside himself. Otherwise, he would have been required to face his own fragility, loss of powers, and impending death. This was not possible for him.

The problem of differentiating between mental depression and other problems of old age is a very difficult one and will be considered in the chapter on depression. But there were many instances in my own practice when an older individual was thought to be hopelessly senile when instead he was primarily depressed and the depression accentuated all other problems. In these many instances, effective treatment of mental depression, usually with medications, relieved not only the various physical and mental symptoms of the older person but eased considerably the problems between the generations which were thought to be unreconcilable. This fact, the prevalence of a treatable mental depression that compounds the problems of older persons and the people who love and care for them, needs much wider recognition.

SERIOUS ILLNESS AND THE DENIAL OF DEATH

When death impends, there are often powerful forces at work that conspire to rob the dying patient and the family and friends of what might be extraordinarily meaningful, life-enhancing experiences. The central fact is that in urbanized North America there remain many cultural taboos against any sign of recognition that a threat to life is signaled. The rules of good sportsmanship about death impose a tragic charade on many who are seriously ill and upon their relatives. Each pretends not to know what is happening even though each knows full well. One need not go far afield for evidence of the powerful restrictions imposed on the dying and those who attend them. The dehumanization of the dying patient in the name of sparing feelings is still very common in almost every hospital! Everyone knows that the patient faces a life-threatening situation, yet no one speaks of it—not friends, not family, not doctor or nurses, and, ordinarily, not the patient either. Suspecting that he is critically ill and may be dying, the patient either does not try or is unable to get anyone to acknowledge this fact. Grotesquely, all the signs may be present that others await his death: diet restrictions are abandoned, the room is changed from ward to private, blood pressure is taken more frequently, visitors with swollen eyes are allowed beyond the ordinary hours. Yet nothing is said.

In effect, all concerned conspire to deny the reality of what is inescapable and pervasive. The effect of stripping the approach of death of its meaning, of pretending that such a palpable risk doesn't exist, is to treat the patient as if he did not exist—as if he were already a non-person. His encounters are deprived of all human warmth and candor and the time that remains in his life is thereby rendered inauthentic and meaningless. Sometimes, however, it works out differently, as is revealed in this story told to me by Dr. Carl Whitaker.

> I went to see Jake about a week after the operation. They had all told me not to tell him what he had, but I walked through the door and began to bawl like a baby. Jake looked up and said, "It's okay, Carl, I know." I walked over and took his hand and said, "You bastard, I'm really going to miss you. You're one of the few people I've ever been able to talk to. A big part of me goes with you." Jake sat up in his bed, smiled, and told me, "It's good to have somebody to

talk to. The rest of them buried me about two weeks ago. I don't have courage enough to tell them I'm still here for a few days." We talked for an hour, one of the best hours we ever had together. We cried a little and he laughed when I told him I was going to name a goldfish after him. He was dead a week later. His wife wrote me that he had talked a great deal about our being together and she wanted to thank me.

In a similar way, the next of kin are often ignored in hospitals until it's time to request an autopsy. All studies show, however, that they are a very high-risk group, prone to a host of diseases, to severe depression, to suicide, and to life-shatteringly poor decision making during the mourning period. The interval of the serious illness, the terminal illness, the time of death, and the period of bereavement are parts of an inseparable whole. Honesty and candor in the relationship between doctor and patient, between patient and mate, and between patient, family, and doctor during the earlier periods in the patient's illness will have real significance during the later (mourning) period. However, when the patient, the family, and the doctor are successful in their denial of what is imminent and inevitable, the effect can be disastrous.

Case Study 3: *He Didn't Say, So She Didn't Ask*

Mrs. Florence Teague, aged sixty-three, was admitted to the psychiatric unit of the University Hospital seven months after the death of her husband. She was depressed and expressed a sense of never having found herself after her husband's death. The husband's illness had begun five years earlier when he was discovered to have a prostatic cancer. Over the succeeding years, there were three major surgical procedures. Extensive radiation and chemotherapy treatments were given at several intervals, and there was a two-month period of hospitalization immediately before death.

Mrs. Teague had a very dependent relationship with her husband which continued with little overt change during the illness and up to the very day of his death. *At no time did she or her husband discuss the seriousness of his illness, her fears about the prospect of life without him, or even practical issues with regard to the payment of bills resulting from his hospitalization.* Nor was the doctor (or group of doctors!) useful in helping the patient and his wife prepare together for the consequence of his illness. Everyone kept his thoughts to himself. The wife who wanted (and simultaneously didn't want) to ask her husband many things, to tell him many things, remained silent. On the day before his death, from his hospital bed, the husband filled out the checks for the monthly bills. This had been his custom throughout their marital relationship. He died without ever advising his wife on any matters, without acknowledging to her that he was dying. He had mentioned that his will was in his lawyer's office. That was all!

A BRIEF REFLECTION ON THE FUTURE OF AGING

There was something unnatural and sick about the middle years of the twentieth century in America. Many older people fared badly. It was a time when their special needs, hopes, and contributions to the society were low priority matters in many homes and in the national consciousness. Cartoonist Paul Conrad of the *Los Angeles Times* summed it up in a sketch called "Speaking of American Cults" which was a pyramid of "I," "ME," "MINE," "MYSELF."[6] Things are out of balance when there are no older people in the picture. As we worry about the ecological balance in nature, there is reason to worry about the ecology of the contemporary life-style with its generational cleavages that make children strangers to their grandparents.

Where all this will lead is uncertain. There is no going back to the three- and four-generational family farm. At the same time, it seems unlikely that grandparents and grandchildren are destined to remain strangers through very many generations. It costs everybody too much.

We are in the midst of such rapid social change that it isn't clear what the short-term and long-term impact of the divided generations will be. I have a distinct impression that another ten years will produce the data necessary to prove that three generations is much better than two and that one generation can't make it. I think we have that information already in the mounting number of suicides of the young.[7]

Common sense should make clear that to devote the first half of one's life to rearing, nurturing, and investing one's passion and compassion in the young and the last half of one's life alone and lonely is not an ideal social arrangement. In the preceding chapter I noted that one of the lessons of television was that young people discovered early how they were "entitled" to be treated. I suspect that as they approach the halfway point, they'll think of something.

PART THREE

PEOPLE WHO FAIL, TROUBLE, AND DISAPPOINT

6

Violence and Weakness, Rebellion and Surrender

On our balcony off the dining room, six feet from my usual chair, in a pot with a cactus blooming, and before my very eyes, two pigeons chose to set up housekeeping, ignoring my repeated but weak gestures of "Shoo, shoo, go away pigeons." Three weeks later they deposited two eggs and right now they are providing a demonstration of parenting that makes me cheer for them. I am proud for them. I wish them all well. And I am in awe at the beauty and urgency of the process. The relentless determination that it be just right, absolutely right, so that those two baby birds have a chance, surpasses any power of logic. The nesting, shielding, regurgitative feeding, guarding, teaching, and the partnership of female and male carry through an incredible master design.

By contrast, what a rotten start so many human babies have. The fetus may be pounded from the outside, gorged with nicotine, alcohol, Valium, or heroin. The mother is sometimes obtunded by ambivalence or worse. The father is many times unseen.

Anyone who is witness to the process as it was intended will sorrow for those who have a *lesser beginning*. Have they *any* chance at all?

Many of the people who come or are sent to a psychiatrist's office believe they have failed, have troubled and disappointed themselves and others as well. They tell of events that span the full range of human possibilities. I remember the boy who became psychotic when he couldn't get into Harvard, only MIT. He felt his life was over. And I think of the girl whose frantic parents opposed and stopped her marriage to "a nobody" artist who went on to become rich and famous. There were how many boys who didn't want to go into their father's profession and how many girls who did. I think of the many brave young women in the fifties and sixties who disappointed their families by acquiring a college education instead of a husband. There was also the long line of people who fell in love with people who were the wrong religion, the wrong color, and now the wrong sex. There was one couple who were married twenty-two years but didn't know how to make love with each other. After they found out how, they divorced. There was the remarkable man with severe cerebral palsy who became mentally depressed because he was progressing too slowly toward his doctorate. And I remember with sadness the young doctor who destroyed his career with drugs because he felt doubt about his ability. How many hundreds, by now thousands, have I seen in clinics, alcohol and drug centers, jails and prisons who had against them the three strikes of poverty, broken home, and minority status at birth. But it's not just the poor who are at high risk. I often recall that remarkable woman, kind and funny, who at thirty-five learned there was a fifty-fifty chance she would develop Huntington's Chorea. She was pregnant at the time and she wanted that child. She won! The dread disease skipped her (and thus her son). I remember the rich girl whose maternal grandmother hated the son-in-law and left her entire estate to her three-year-old granddaughter. But the curse intended only for the father (and mother) took the life of the girl. She was a heroin addict at fourteen, dead at twenty-one.

The causes of "failure" in our society are too many and too complex for easy analysis and summary statement. But it is a terrible shame that millions in our midst feel defeated, despondent, and hopeless about themselves. Many of those people are set up to lose by poverty, social deprivations, economic exploitation, or by the greed and competition that dominates some families. Some who feel defeated torture only themselves. Many strike back at family or at passersby. Either way, it costs a great deal when people feel unappreciated and abnormal in their world. Ernest Becker wrote, "Of all the wicked acts that are performed, none are more hurtful than those carried out by people who are trying to appear normal."

Case Study 1: *The Mother of a Normal Child*

In Los Angeles, there is an annual special art fair for handicapped children and thousands attend. It is a profoundly inspiring yet still a sad event. What was most touching for me was the absence of any reason to differentiate degrees of handicap on a hierarchical scale. Those deaf, crippled, slow learners, thalidomide victims with missing fingers and arms, children with cerebral palsy, and a cretinous child were all there together without apology. None was made uneasy by his association with the others. Almost none.

My artist wife was doing a workshop at the fair. She had stones and sticks and small strips of plaster gauze which were converted by the children into small puppets that were then painted and carried off. Eight or ten children would be working at any given time, and there was that extraordinary mixture of élan and seriousness that is characteristic of the meeting of a child who wants to succeed and a teacher who is certain of the child's success. Then, a strange thing happened. I saw a woman walk over to whisper something to my wife. She pointed to one of the children working at the puppet-making project. My wife said something back and the woman abruptly left, pulling the protesting child after her. Later I found out that the woman had come to say that her child was normal and my ordinarily supergentle wife told her, "Your child is beautiful but its mother's head is all fucked up."

There are many individuals whose lives seem overwhelmingly, almost unbelievably filled with bad luck, trouble, and failure. Some emerge from the straight, detourless route of poverty, broken home, foster home, girls' or boys' correctional school, jail and prison. Over the years, they build or accrue nothing and instead involve themselves with drugs, alcohol, violence, and unpaid debts. They offer little help, joy, or encouragement to any other and in the process of making the same mistakes over and over, they are resigned to and accept failure.

There are millions of such persons in North America. They are largely anonymous strangers. The people who know about them are police, social welfare workers, bill collectors, hospital emergency room personnel, tavern owners, Alcoholics Anonymous workers, parole officers, and such family as still keep in touch. They are people who fail, trouble, and disappoint, all the way. One can rationalize about them but almost nobody would want to live the life they lead.

Many social institutions have been created to care for or deal with such individuals, the overwhelming majority of whom have emerged from less privileged backgrounds. Whether one studies infants born with birth injury, badly burned children, battered children, the mildly retarded, school dropouts, inmates in juvenile detention, broken and disorganized families, inhabitants of the alcoholic skid row, individuals prematurely old, or convicts awaiting execution on death row, those from poor and deprived backgrounds are inordinately represented.[1,2,3,4] It would be an oversimplification to equate financial stability with mental health. However, it becomes clearer all the time that to be deprived of a full share of society's opportunities is destructive to personality and spirit. Of course, this is a matter that everyone clearly understands—but in just such a way as to forget. Most psychiatric textbooks skim or skip the subject. It is boorish to speak of it in most social circles. Selective inattention to the plight of life that is not "me and mine" is part of the madness of being sane.

The view from a psychiatrist's chair is a necessarily restricted one. But the psychiatrist who pretends that the social and economic realities that make so very many people miserable are not his concern is, in my opinion, not a psychiatrist. Fifty years ago, Bertolt Brecht wrote:

> *For even saintly folks can act like sinners*
> *Unless they've had their customary dinners.*[5]

WHO NEEDS WHAT KIND OF HELP?

R. D. Laing is a Scottish existential psychiatrist, writer, and poet of great skill.[6] He has allegiance to those on the "outside" and, in a way, he is their spokesman. He makes a virtue of nonconformity by pointing out the terrible things that some people come together to do to other people.

He does not think there is anything the matter with him because
One of the things that is
the matter with him
is that he does not think that there is anything
the matter with him
therefore
we have to help him realize that,
the fact that he does not think there is anything
the matter with him
is one of the things that is
the matter with him.

Throughout the centuries there have been those individuals whose styles of living confused, confounded, worried, and infuriated their contemporaries. Sometimes they are called immature or antisocial, sometimes lazy or evil. Their selfish attitudes, unwillingness or inability to exercise control, unwillingness to work, unusual sexual interests, or inordinate use of intoxicants place them apart from their peers. In other instances, they are simply one of a whole group of poorly regarded people who fare poorly in the society in which they are minority members. Still others are the black sheep who know what the white sheep expect of them but don't come across.

An individual so designated is usually understood as someone with whom something is wrong. Depending upon the favored theory as to what causes evil, deviance, or inadequacy in the particular era, the explanation chosen will vary. During the Middle Ages in many parts of Europe there were men, women, and children who were thought to be suffering from bedevilment in the concrete sense of the word. The task of "redemption," that is, their forced conformity, fell to spiritual leaders who began by trying to drive out and, if necessary, burn out the devil. Different eras have different devils who, nevertheless, work, as devils do, to produce behavior and beliefs unacceptable to the majority. In the contemporary period, many causes of deviance have been detailed. There are proposed genetic abnormalities, complex sociocultural factors, interfamily and interpersonal struggles offered as explanation of the behavior of those who don't fulfill family and societal hopes.

Psychiatric diagnosticians have attempted to sort out what it means to fail, trouble, and disappoint. In the process, they have had to wonder what it means to succeed, please, and come across with what others demand. As a case in point, consider the young man described below who grew up to become a psychiatrist. He does not fail, trouble, or disappoint. He "treats" some of those who do. But . . .

Case Study 2: *From Little Boy to Psychiatrist in a Straight Line*

He is a boy of ten and his potential is boundless. His parents are educated, have money, love each other, and love him. There are so many things he can do and be and feel. As to career, his future seems without limit. He can be a doctor, a lawyer, an athlete, an engineer, a minister, and, indeed, at various times in his thoughts, he is all of these. Without knowing why, he knows he must be "a useful and successful person."

His personal wishes at age ten are likely to conform closely to the ideas of those who are most influential in his life, that is, his parents, his minister, and his teachers. He meets people and they say to him, "How old are you?" and "What are you going to be when you get older?" They seem to care about his answer and about him. To which college should he go? He begins to ask the question while still in grade school. Perhaps his college will be Harvard or UCLA, Indiana or Stanford, McGill or MIT, Wisconsin or Chicago. And later he chooses. And in doing so he makes a certain surrender. He moves further in a life plan, the outline of which was sketched by the people he loved when he was a child.

The broad, general educational possibilities at the university allow him to sustain into his second semester the potential for all the careers. But then there comes another point, a moment in which he must choose again. He chooses medicine. In this choice there is much surrendering and he does not make the choice easily. Perhaps he slightly hedges the commitment, planning to combine law and medicine in forensic medicine by subsequently adding the law degree; or he resolves his conflict between the ministry and medicine by deciding to study medicine to become a medical missionary. But still, he chooses. And, in doing so, he moves within a life plan conceived with family and friends.

About this time, another matter captures his attention. His determination to stay a bachelor, play the field, and marry at a mature thirty-five, is tested in his twentieth year by a young woman, also a student in the college, perhaps in music or the arts. She is sweet and soft, not unlike his mother. He discovers she is fun to split a steak-for-two with. Soon he feels she is getting too serious, repeatedly warns her against this. Six dates a week are too many. They each should see other people. He urges maturity, good judgment, even offers to help her find other dates. Instead, she arranges her own. And then, in a long, solitary, soul-searching day of considering bachelorhood to thirty-five, playing the field, and being practical, he chooses her. He hedges the surrendering slightly. Perhaps their engagement will be a long one. Perhaps she will work over the years and the baby or babies will be delayed until after he is able to complete his medical training, his internship in Hawaii, his training in obstetrics at Johns Hopkins or, better, in psychiatry at the Sorbonne.

The first baby, his exhilarated parents' first grand-child and his proud grandmother's first great-grand-child, came at the end of the first year of medical school and the second during the early months of his internship. His surrender of the possibility of studying obstetrics at Johns Hopkins or psychiatry at the Sorbonne followed an interview with an insurance man, the one who sells "insure now and pay later" policies to protect "that lovely wife and those two swell babies of yours."

Some things were not surrendered but were traded. The year of internship in Hawaii was traded for the second child, Annie; the year at the Sorbonne was replaced by the coming of the third child, Susie. And the notion of yet another year of psychoanalysis for himself, this time with a woman analyst, was abandoned in favor of a house and an acre in the suburbs.

At age thirty-two, his training over, he is a physician and a psychiatrist. He pays the insurance man for the years of coverage. There are many things that he is not. He is not an alumnus of Harvard, UCLA, or MIT. He is not a lawyer, engineer, minister, sociologist, professional musician, physicist, anthropologist, or base-ball player. Despite many things surrendered and many potentialities lost, there are also many positives in his world. He is recognizably the grown-up boy who once wondered, "What will I be?" He is proud of who he is, where he has been, and he is confident about where he is going. He enjoys his work and is conscientious about doing it well. He is encircled by family and lifelong personal friends and feels a closeness on many sides. In surrendering, in choosing and in caring, in following through, in staying with the plan, in fulfilling a number of commitments to loved and admired others, his life sustains its meaning for him. There is seeming continuity to it. There is a unity of past, present, and future. For him, life makes sense. One does what one should. One works. One cares for the family. Perhaps his children will be doctors too. He wouldn't have it another way.

But is his a good life? Is this the way everyone should hope to live? Won't this rather conforming man look back and wonder why he was so obedient, so nonexperimental, and so responsible? Won't he ever want to raise a little hell? Should he have accepted so totally the values he was taught? And how good a psychiatrist can he really be with his straight and serious approach to everything? He plays in a game where he wins all the time. Could he ever truly understand people who fail, trouble, and disappoint? Could he—who plans his life in intervals of years—possibly understand a person who lives from moment to moment?

Even more to the point is the question of whether anyone who lives in a world of plans that work out and promises that are kept can understand the world of those who know only NOW. They really are two different worlds. The clock of the person who has nothing to wait for reads both NOW, NOW, NOW and NEVER, NEVER, NEVER. Sometimes, on fast glance, it advises NOW or NEVER. When the doctor meets the person who has learned that plans don't work and begins to set up some plans, this time his plans don't work either. The same occurs with prospective employers, really with everyone. And it goes no better when two people locked into a NOW life meet and need something from each other. To begin with, there is no sense of kindredness between them. They may be the two most oppressed people in town, but rather than being drawn together, each is likely to see the other as a threat.

One learns in earliest years to walk, talk, read, and write. In the same years, one is learning that promises are kept and that plans work out. When that does not take place in the life of a child, it often follows that he or she becomes the adolescent and adult who lives impulsively and violently.

LIVING IMPULSIVELY, LIVING VIOLENTLY

Some people handle tension poorly. An uncomfortable moment seems an eternity. Unable to wait, to hold back, to control instincts, they act impulsively to relieve the tension. In the history of many such individuals, there may be a long series of comparable moments, that is, moments when they were overwhelmed with the need to fight or to flee! In a life that is interrupted repeatedly, one never fully develops a sense of continuity of personal history. The urgency of the demands of the moment is so powerful that it is impossible to feel a sustaining sense of responsibility to others or to prior goals. Instead, life is characterized by its discontinuity. This kind of moment-by-moment existence is particularly characteristic of individuals who grow up in disconnected, deprived, broken, or stormy families. In the following case histories, consider the lifetime absence of "input" suggesting a purpose of life, a sense of continuity, and the feeling that "I am among friends." The first is that of a young ghetto dweller who was interviewed while in jail awaiting sentence after his conviction for the fatal stabbing of a policeman. Contrast his life with the life of the young doctor just described (or with your own). What follows may seem like an extreme example of deprivation and its consequences; however, it is only extreme. It is not unusual, it is not unusual at all. There are many, many thousands of such individuals.

Case Study 3: *A Young Man Who Always
Landed the First Blow*

John Washington, aged eighteen, jailed, was awaiting sentencing after conviction for stabbing a police-

man to death. He was probably on drugs at the time of the assault. According to testimony in the court, a policeman walked toward a group of young people standing on a street corner at 11 P.M. and asked, "What are you boys doing out so late?" Whereupon John pulled a knife from inside his shirt, ran toward the policeman, and stabbed him six times. When others in the group, his friends, pulled John off the policeman, he tried to stab one of them. John was jailed and convicted of murder.

He was of uncertain parentage, raised by various aunts and grandmothers, and from the very beginning there was no home that he felt was his home, no room that was exclusively or dependably his own. There were many males in and out of the various homes where he stayed, but he had a sustaining tie to none of them. He was on the street a great deal, a street filled with aggressive, unhappy, and neglected young people, and with rats as well. At times in his life there was not enough food. When hungry, he seemed especially liable to misadventure. When he was eight years old, he was injured on the street, struck by a car, and was unconscious for three days. In school he did very poorly and was behind two grades by the time he was eleven. When he was twelve he was arrested and placed in a correctional school for truancy and theft. No teacher ever liked him and no adults except his grandmother and one aunt ever talked at length to him about anything except what he had done wrong or what he was forbidden to do. He had been stabbed twice and beaten up many times in fights with other men, arrested a half-dozen times by policemen (white and black), had seen one friend killed and many taken off to prison. He viewed the entire white community with suspicion, fear, and hostility. Girls he also viewed with hostility and suspicion because they frequently laughed at him.

Life for John Washington was very much a here-now sequence of confrontations, a series of *High Noon* showdowns. The future was the next challenge to fight.

His past was a collection of humiliating memories. He knew for certain only that the winner of the fight was the one who landed the first blow.

Another person whose life seemed to center around the prospects for violence and avoiding humiliation was John O'Connell, a twenty-eight-year-old divorced and unemployed laborer. I first saw him when he was admitted for the third time to the psychiatric unit of Vancouver General Hospital.

Case Study 4: *A Brawler Who Sought Approval from All*

He was a sturdily built, five-foot-ten-inch Caucasian man who weighted 225 pounds. He swaggered as he walked, scowled menacingly when encountering strangers; when relaxed and among friends, he talked incessantly of how many people he had sent to the hospital after they had picked a fight with him. He presented himself in the emergency room at 2 A.M. in an intoxicated state and expressed the fear that he would kill himself or someone else. He was depressed because his girl friend had called the police when he attempted to "talk to her." He was out on bail at the time after having scuffled with police. Two earlier hospitalizations had occurred under similar circumstances, times when he was having disputes with his former wife. There were two children from that marriage, but John had lost touch with them and did not contribute to their support.

He had grown up in a stormy, deprived family. His father was an alcoholic who died after a tavern fight. John was eight years old at that time. His mother remarried and divorced twice, then lived for a time in a common-law marriage that had been ended a few years earlier. She also drank heavily. Her mother, John's grandmother, lived in the same community and at intervals over the years took over responsibility for John and his three older siblings, all girls.

From earliest years John was preoccupied with his sense of discomfort, embarrassment, and fear of being singled out for humiliation. He endured the excruciating role of "the dumbest kid in class" and quit school when he was fifteen. There was only one thing he could do well during those years and this was his ritual of recess fights. He was physically large for his age and after he had fallen behind in school, he was bigger than all his classmates. He loved to brawl. And in adult life the one thing he could do well was to bully and brawl. He had been out of school since the age of fifteen but had never held a job longer than four months. He had numerous arrests for being drunk and disorderly and had spent six months in the county jail for nonsupport of his children.

John was not a very versatile person. He was a repetitious and boring patient who seemed only to know how to pout, to storm around, and to threaten. At the same time, his need for approval was very great. He wanted women to admire him and after being rebuffed in his seductive approaches to the nurses, he centered his efforts on gaining the attention of the female patients on the ward. He challenged one male patient to fight after a group therapy meeting in which a female patient had expressed her admiration for the qualities of the other man. His occasional helpful activities on the ward were aimed at evoking admiration and praise. His motto seemed to be "Admire me and make me feel good—or fear me." At times, when confronted with having misbehaved, he could acknowledge his mistake but could not see how he could have behaved differently.

John Washington and John O'Connell are two of a large number of individuals with a low tolerance for frustration, lack of versatility, resentment of authority, and a willingness to launch physical assault when angry. Over the years, such persons have been called "psychopaths," "antisocial" or "asocial" personalities, "passive-aggressive" personalities, or, less dispassionately, "bad apples." They often cause a good deal of trouble both to themselves and to the people and institutions in their environment. They are so obnoxious and disappointing to others that one usually overlooks the fact that theirs is not a very good life to live. There is pain, shame, injury, and jealousy. Usually, there is poverty as well. They develop a poor record in school, with police, with employers, and also in their close interpersonal relationships. Nor are they easily influenced to change their style of living by any of the "reforming" or "healing" agencies of society. In the year that followed John O'Connell's psychiatric hospitalization, he worked irregularly, drank continuously, tried several more times to make up with his ex–girl friend, and landed in jail each time. He had been offered outpatient appointments with a psychiatrist but he appeared only once, and then only to escape prosecution when arrested again for bothering his former girl friend.

During the period of hospitalization, John was interviewed once in the company of his mother, who commented, "John and I are a lot alike. I had a lot of trouble growing up till I was forty or so. I think in a few years John won't drink so much and will settle down." This is not an infrequent pattern. Indeed, if still alive and not a severe and chronic alcoholic ten years later, the "antisocial character" may well have become a rather conventional and usually law-abiding citizen. It is unusual, however, for such individuals to acquire much depth or breadth of personality. Maturity in a significant sense never happens. Instead, "settling down" follows the scattering or disappearance of the old gang, the extension and worsening of the hangover periods, and, if the individual is very fortunate, a rediscovery of the woman or man who is still waiting at home.

We know enough to predict that our society could produce far fewer individuals who end up thinking, believing, and behaving like John Washington and John O'Connell. This would require specific attention to maternal prenatal care, avoidance of premature birth and birth injuries, and the provision of adequate physical and psychological care for the infant and family. As the child grows, intellectual stimulation, loving (nonviolent) and stable maternal and paternal role models, and youthful playmates would be needed. The school system that received the child would attend to the special needs of each child and to the general needs of the group. Intellectual and emotional growth would be carefully observed without making the child feel like a failure. The child would receive careful yet tender indoctrination in terms of "what we believe." The violence of television would be drastically reduced. Racism would end.

Children who are going to have serious social and educational problems usually announce themselves no later than the early grades and then progress along a course of mounting difficulties.[7] There has been a major shift in the last ten years in thinking about children in the United States. For a long time, property rights were thought to apply to children and "society's rights" to intervene were seriously contested. Brutalization and neglect of children in the parental home was "overlooked" by teachers, pediatricians, and neighbors because the idea that children are only "on precious loan" to the family was not backed up by legal statute or sufficient public consciousness. Those who tried to "intervene" were often discouraged by the legal and therapeutic outcomes. The interventions were usually overturned in the courts and the therapies were ineffective.

The therapy that regularly failed for multi-problem children doing poorly at school was too narrow in its concept. The child was sent to a therapist and nothing much came of it. In contrast, there are therapeutic programs developing today in many school systems which are much more broadly conceived. Some of them are impressively successful. The child in trouble in school may be hyperactive, may suffer a specific and correctable learning disability. He or she may have suffered minor brain injury at birth that makes for trouble in patterning time, that is, in anticipating and putting events into sequence. The child may be anxious, hungry, partially deaf, overwhelmed by fear and unhappiness about what is going on at home. He may feel ashamed of his clothes. Then there are the matters of the teachers, their workload, their attitude and understanding of the child who is making known its vulnerability. And the parents.

If there is to be successful intervention in behalf of a disruptive, troubled child in school, the program needs to be a wide and wise approach to the system in which the child lives, studies, and plays. It needs to be an intervention that correctly diagnoses what is wrong with the child and then specifically treats any physical deficiencies and in other matters assists the child, its teachers, and the parents. It needs to be a system intervention that has the endorsement of the top leaders of the school system (principals, school board, commissioner), and there must be continuity in relationship over a period of years between the mental health workers and the school system.

When those conditions are met, some very remarkable results are achieved. Twice the number of well-treated vulnerable children succeed in continuing their education through high school graduation when compared with untreated classmates. Only one-third the number of expulsions for disruptive and violent behavior occur among the treated group. There are now many reports of successful interruption of school failure—and all that goes with it—IF the therapeutic approach can be wide enough in scope.[8,9]

What is the treatment? Heaton, Safer, and their colleagues, reporting a seven-year study in a Baltimore County (Md.) school system where they worked with seriously disruptive students, describe a broad approach that included: major subjects taught in morning periods by regular teachers and some individualized instruction; special, individualized reward for compliance programs (behavioral therapy approaches) including the opportunity for early release from school and extra play time (during school hours) and similar programs of conditional rewards worked out with parents at home; a clear and precise school discipline program ranging from warnings to brief exclusion from the rewards program; counseling, discussion, personal support, and the added extra of genuine availability of mental health staff to teachers, parents, and children in moments of crisis so that one problem did not escalate into an avalanche.

In brief, in Baltimore County and wherever you can achieve a sufficient competence and cooperation and continuity, it is possible to head off in the schools some of the lifelong failures in the making. Important? There is nothing more important.

There is newly enacted federal legislation that is defining such assistance to schoolchildren as a "right," with such provision a "responsibility" of the school authorities. There are obvious problems, including the enormous costs that can be easily built up in evaluation and hospitalization of a child. But in time, ground rules will be worked out which will provide a maximum return for the invested dollar.

LIVING PASSIVELY

The person who attempts to live his or her life compliantly and with someone else in charge rarely achieves much personal maturity. There are many such persons. They have been variously labeled as "passive and dependent character disorders," "inadequate personalities," "constitutional inferiors," or, if particularly reclusive or eccentric, "schizoid personalities." They are often products of a disturbed, unhappy, or broken family and it is there that narrow and nonassertive approaches to life are learned. Early life experiences teach the child what sort of person he is and what sort of people he or she can expect to encounter throughout life. One's essential trust in self and in others takes form very early, beginning with the discovery that mother and the important people who come later can be trusted to return. There is a basis for security in important relationships. There is no more significant lesson for the child. That kind of optimism about others is best learned in earliest childhood, reinforced when the mother goes away to the hospital and returns with a sibling, relearned with teachers and friends, firmly experienced in one's life with a mate, and then reexperienced in a different light when one is oneself "the trusted other who returns" to one's own children. There appear to be critical cutoff periods beyond which the richness, meaning, and generalizability of "the trustworthiness of the other" becomes sharply curtailed. The ability to trust another person, achieved in childhood, is the foundation for a lifetime of interpersonal relationships.

Similarly, it is with and from the mother, the father, and young peers that the child learns the joy of making discoveries. He learns to "trust his guts" because she, the mother, and he, the father, trust him and are pleased by the discoveries made and reported. The child learns and discovers good things about himself. He or she is a person more likely to go right than wrong. The child fortunate enough to come from this kind of background carries a fundamentally optimistic outlook about his undertakings and, as a consequence, feels freer to explore life's possibilties.

Of course, "stop," "don't," and "awful" are parts of the necessary learning of any child. Laing calls such learning a confrontation between "twentieth century mother and stone age baby." And from childhood on there is the hard lesson that everybody doesn't love you like mom and dad do. For the lucky child, the earliest blows are cushioned in the familiarity and security of family, and later in the circle of peers. Many children do not come from this kind of cushioned beginning. They are the poor and relatively uneducated children of poor and uneducated parents. Or, they are the children of no parents at all.

However, it is not exclusively through deprivations associated with poverty or "second-class citizenship" that the development of personality may be hampered. Just as there is a very high incidence of inadequate, asocial, or antisocial behavior patterns associated with the lower socioeconomic groups, there is also a contrasting form of passive, ever-expecting, never-really-trying kind of attitude among children in certain upper-class families. Of such persons Hannah Arendt wrote:

> Necessity and life are so intimately related and connected that life itself is threatened where necessity is altogether eliminated. Necessity serves to prevent the apathy and disappearance of initiative which so obviously threatens all overly wealthy communities. Through the success and material provision supplied by the all-successful parent the struggles of life are diminished during childhood. The elimination of necessity, far from resulting automatically in the establishment of freedom only blurs the distinguishing line between freedom and necessity.[10]

Case Study 5: *A Man, Thirty-eight, and His Mother, Seventy-three*

Gerald Cotton, aged thirty-eight, presented himself for "advice and counseling" at the university psychology clinic. He was enrolled as a graduate student in engineering but after one semester was thinking of quitting. Before leaving school, however, he sought an interview because "it seems like everything I start, I quit." A brief review of his job history and of his interpersonal relationships supported this description. He had graduated from college at the age of twenty-two, sixteen years earlier. During the intervening years he once returned to school for one and a half semesters and he had held nine or ten other positions. He had worked variously as a teacher, counselor in a boys' school, overseas administrative officer, personnel officer for a manufacturing company, assistant credit manager of a department store, and in other jobs. He was never fired but always grew tired of the work and moved on.

He was a nice person, soft, gentle, and very courteous. He had traveled widely, met many people, had many superficial friends but few intimates. He had contemplated marriage three or four times during his life but somehow or other "it never quite happened." He had experienced several heterosexual relationships, but none during the preceding year. He denied homosexual experiences.

There was only one significant human being in the life of thirty-eight-year-old Gerald Cotton and that was his seventy-three-year-old mother. She had been widowed for thirty-six years and had never remarried. Gerald was her only child. His complaints about her meddling were intense in contrast to his bland manner with all other topics.

At the request of the counselor, Mrs. Cotton willingly traveled across the country for a series of joint therapy interviews. She was a woman from another era, something of the "grand lady." She was the volunteer curator of a historical museum in the town in which she lived. She was also a connoisseur and advocate of the arts, gracious dining, and all the other features of "living as one should." Her interest in her son was enormous and there were few details of his life about which she did not have an opinion. In fact, she had intervened on several occasions to help arrange new jobs for him when he became dissatisfied with the work he was doing.

Dialogue between the two was unusually spirited. It went something like this: "Gerald dear, if you had stayed with the job in the private school as I advised you at the time, I am sure that when the headmaster resigned only one year later you would have been considered." To which her son, with great anger, replied, "The headmaster did not retire one year later. He died of a heart attack three years later. And the man who was chosen as the new headmaster was his assistant, who had been with him for twelve years. I never would have been considered!" There was the quality of old married people about the two of them. Despite the frequent disagreements and arguments, they seemed very much to enjoy talking with each other.

I saw Gerald Cotton on five occasions before his mother's visit and seven times after her departure. At no time during interviews when the mother wasn't present did he evidence any amount of vitality, enthusiasm, or commitment. He was involved, really involved, only when she was present! His approach to his life was one of limited commitments, waning interest, and partial involvement. The one exception was his relationship with his mother. With her, he lived out a complicated ritual of inviting her into his life and resenting her intrusion.

The magnitude of Gerald Cotton's investment in his mother made it difficult to accept fully a second woman in the world. This is a form of Oedipal complex. As originally introduced by Freud and narrowly interpreted in this case, the Oedipal complex implies that this man's involvement with his mother included fantasized sexual (genital) contact, as a consequence of which he lived with great guilt and fear. Viewed more broadly, however, one might say instead that his relationship with his mother contained both loving and angry feelings and that the intensity and strength of those feelings (plus and minus) were nowhere duplicated in his life. She was his main source of joy and anguish. It was hard for him to go on to other situations with much enthusiasm. His great moments were with or against, because of or in spite of her.

One could, of course, view Gerald Cotton's background as one in which, beyond the indulgence of his mother, there were also significant deficits. He lacked a father. Also, the over-solicitousness of his mother robbed him of the opportunity to be alone in his own life. She was always there or waiting to come in. He was always seven, six, five, four, three, two, or one day(s) away from the time he would (or would not) make his weekly call to her. His many failures—his inability to prosper in a job, to marry, to complete school, and so on—he accepted as a matter of course. They were a series of victories through defeat. But at least the defeats were his own. Any significant victories in life would undoubtedly have been "owned," that is, taken over, by his mother.

Viewed from a different perspective, passivity and passive resistance allow the individual to answer any questions about the meaning of life by focusing on a specific person or group. No need to worry further. No need to think deeply. It's him! It's them! At times this form of relating in the world becomes rather complex and involves a large group of actors who are actually thinly disguised substitutes for mothers, fathers, or an early love that went badly. The "problem" becomes the whole life.

Case Study 6: *A Man Who Suddenly Wound His Wristwatch*

Thomas Ryan was twenty-six. He was a very eccentric person. He was thin, small, often smiling through tightly clenched teeth. He did no work, though for years he seemed about to get a job, or at least this is what he reported by long-distance telephone to his mother during each weekly call. At the end of the calls, lasting fifteen to thirty minutes, he would signal the operator while the mother was still on the line and they would ask the telephone charges. Then she would send that amount through the mail. In that way her husband, Thomas Ryan's stepfather, wouldn't find out about the calls.

This young man lived the life of a hermit, but a hermit who wore a seersucker suit and carried a cane. He had no friend except his mother. He loathed his robust, outgoing stepfather and resented the athletic prowess of his half-brother and half-sister. His step-father's mother—he called her "the witch"—he hated most of all. He visited her often in her nursing home and rubbed her hands because he knew how she would have hated it, and perhaps still did through a senile fog. He was a source of unending pain to his step-father, who was a minister in a large and affluent church in Washington State.

He, Thomas Ryan, was a master at making people with power or authority trip themselves up. He had developed the art of standing near a bus stop alone. Then, as the bus approached, he would move forward in such a way as to make the bus come to a stop. Suddenly, he would look up as if surprised and walk on. One driver, twice burned, jumped from the bus and chased him down the street.

Mostly he did nothing in particular. His mother sent him $300 monthly, possibly an inheritance from his father, possibly a bribe from the stepfather for living in Canada away from the family. The stepfather viewed him as "the worst boy who ever lived."

As a patient, Thomas Ryan sometimes kept his appointments and sometimes didn't. He liked me, more or less, and liked having someone to talk to. Also, the fact that the therapy was paid for by his mother pleased him even though he knew there was money for only one appointment per week for one year of treatment.

And that, essentially, was his life: Sleep late, get up about noon, dress in a seersucker suit (he owned two), and go for a walk. In restaurants, he would play small games with himself predicting whether the waitress would select an "establishment face and physique" or take customers as they arrived. He attempted to persuade himself that successful-looking people (like his stepfather and mother) were more likely to receive better service and thus "the world opens up for them." So he was exquisitely attuned to whether the waitress filled his water glass, coffee cup, and so forth. If he saw any suggestion of favoritism, he left no tip. Eating out was a tense experience.

Once in a long while he would get up early enough to go to church on Sunday. Then he would join the line of people bidding the minister a good day, and when it was his turn, he would chatter on for a bit and then finish with some deflating sentence designed to make the minister feel bad or disappointed. He might say, "We couldn't hear the sermon in the back rows" or "I think you repeated yourself a little today" or "I think the drop in attendance is due to the weather."

Thomas Ryan made no apology for his life. He felt he had been treated brutally as a child, felt his mother should never have remarried, felt that he lacked the physical qualities of successful men, and saw no reason why he should battle against destiny. He saw his therapy as a reasonable attempt on his part to clarify certain questions that would otherwise have been answered in normal family relationships and felt he owed no one thanks for putting up the money for the treatment. Finally (after six months, one-half the time originally planned) the treatment ended when I insisted that the patient had to take one step (any step) in the direction of broadening his life. He could choose to find a job, return to school, make a friend, perform a voluntary service role, anything. Anything. He refused and the therapy ended.

Two months earlier, however, we shared what was for me one of the most remarkable therapeutic encounters I have ever witnessed. At my insistence, his family came for one joint session. We had spoken on the phone but I had not met them before. They were as described. The mother was beautiful at fifty, appeasing, hopeful. The stepfather was tall, handsome, strong willed, contemptuous of his stepson, and long ago had given up hope that anything that included Thomas Ryan would be other than painful. The half-brother had refused to come for the meeting and Thomas's half-sister, newly a mother, brought her three-month-old baby along and managed to be busy if any questions were directed her way.

But Thomas Ryan was a different man during that hour. He looked harassed, his face was flushed, he sat restlessly on the edge of his chair. His attention turned rapidly from mother to stepfather and he countered any statement of either parent with an accusation. But he was clearly frightened and frantically trying not to be cornered. I had never quite appreciated the desperate other side of his life.

He always wore a wristwatch. It had never been wound or set before. But on that day, to my astonishment, his watch was set to the right time and he limited the length of this particular encounter. He furtively glanced at the watch many times during those ninety minutes. The rest of his life was timeless. It didn't count.

Life became serious only when the real contenders were on the scene.

There is something else that I should say about Thomas Ryan and that's his "diagnosis." I felt he suffered a paranoid schizophrenic illness and so did the psychologist I asked to see Thomas during the initial evaluations. That's a serious diagnosis reflecting the seriousness with which I viewed every aspect of his life. First of all, he had interrupted the gainful part of all activities (no work, no love, no real goals), and that is very, very ominous for any person. Second, he had narrowed his interests and actions to a narrow and morbid range. He was attending to a smaller and smaller set of experiences and since they were basically mean and ugly events, not much good could come out of his findings. Mostly his discoveries were distortions. For example, he was attempting to depreciate people who lived "ordinary lives" by describing them as sheep who were led (by evil people like his stepfather). He cited as an example an experiment of his own in which, while waiting with a group of others at a stoplight, he suddenly walked against the light and noted that three others followed his lead, for a few steps at least. He asked what I thought about that and I told him I'd hate to be his partner in a tall-building window-washing business. He said, "Is that all you have to say about that?" and I told him, "That's all it's worth. It's for the potty." He said, "You're mad at me!" I told him, "Damn right!"

The other part of the paranoid schizophrenic diagnosis relates to Thomas Ryan's agitated and desperate condition in the family interview. He had no margin. If he were backed one step off the road he habitually walked, he felt in grave danger. And his anxiety was profound. That was what his psychological tests seemed to show. When he looked at the Rorschach cards (inkblots) he began with a small joke and then saw only eyes looking out at him, indications of evil, human parts (but no humans); on the cards with color, there was blood and worse. At times during the examination, he would concoct a kind of general story to explain his morbid replies, but each of those stories was farfetched, ugly, and basically the same. The "things" that Thomas Ryan "saw" in the world of inkblots were what he saw in his daily life. So he narrowed his world down to manageable size and tenaciously held that ground. It would have been possible to seriously underestimate the magnitude of the illness and the desperate kind of person with whom you could be dealing if the pressures on Thomas became too great.

Most of the people who fail, trouble, and disappoint aren't as precariously balanced as Thomas Ryan, and there is more reason for hope that their efforts in psychotherapy, rehabilitation, and job training will have a better outcome. Thomas Ryan was very sick and it is unlikely that any society would have been sufficiently healing, supportive, or understanding to prevent the onset of his illness or to restore him to full function. It is likely that he suffered some kind of genetic predisposition to schizophrenic distortions. Similarly, there are a good many people among the long-term unemployed, long-term psychologically disabled, long-term prisoners, and chronic alcoholics and drug abusers whose problems are not simply social, economic, and educational deficiencies. Problems of mood, difficulties in the clarity of thinking, and poor impulse control can be the major causes of a particular individual's poor life adjustment. Usually, it's not either/or. Those with significant emotional deficits have a vulnerability to social maladaption just as those with serious social and economic deficiencies have more than their share of psychological stress and symptomatology. Every nation in the world has a significant share of mentally ill citizens. We have much to accomplish in our society, but even extensive social change will not completely eradicate mental illness.

7

Making the World Come Alive: Making the World Disappear

We are beginners at a dart game when it comes to understanding or doing very much about alcohol and drug abuse, food excesses, and smoking. Yet they are major killers, stalking the contemporary life-style just as epidemic diseases struck down the generations before. Our hungers are lethal. Our resistance is low. Patients, doctors, and other helpers fail more often than they succeed when trying to modify excesses of drinking, drug-taking, eating, and smoking even though extensive research efforts and elaborate therapeutic programs have been developed in each area. The bottom line is that we are extremely reluctant to give up our habits, and more often than not we don't.

For a long time, the people who were expected to stop pleasure-linked behaviors but didn't or couldn't were alcoholics and drug addicts. Their failure to stop their costly habits was taken as a measure of their moral weakness. Now the revelation that smoking and overweight are very severe health hazards has confronted tens of millions of Americans with the challenge to stop their (our) pleasure-linked behavior.

For the great majority, it has been difficult, very difficult. "Life-styles," "values," patterns of intimacy, and a stubborn determination that "this is the way I want to live" are basically systems that have been developed to protect the ability to "turn on" or "turn off" in the ways that are most satisfying. How a person "feels" is the overriding reality in life. Like trump cards in gambling casinos, "feeling good *now*" beats the risk of "feeling bad later" in that big game of chance called "life."

In the last decade, the body chemistry, particularly the chemistry of the brain that coincides with "feeling good" and "feeling bad," has been studied by scientists in laboratories all over the world. Nobel Prize laureates work in this field. It has become the most exciting and promising area in biological research. Studies of the transmission of impulse in the brain, the action of important brain transmitter substances called catecholamines, and the interaction between the brain and the endocrine system through the pituitary-hypothalamic-gonadal axis have greatly altered our understanding of the major mental illnesses. This type of basic brain research has been combined with genetic studies of multi-generational family histories and sophisticated follow-up studies of children adopted out of and into families with psychopathology. The evidence now strongly suggests that there are significant "linkages" between the major mood disorders of mania and depression and abuse of alcohol, heroin addiction, various patterns of violence, and certain eating disorders. In another development, the recent discovery of naturally occurring morphine-like substances in the body (called endorphins and enkephalins) has spurred research into the manner in which the brain signals pain and pleasure and causes the individual to experience contentment or anxiety. There are specific receptor sites in the brain that have now been pinpointed where both endorphins and externally provided opiates (morphine, heroin) have high affinity. And now, substances have been developed which block opiate activity by occupying those sites within the brain that provide the "high." Incredible![1,2]

One result of this work is that any heroin addict who chooses to withdraw from the drug can now do so without suffering the intense withdrawal symptoms that formerly always occurred. Presently, most such addicts don't choose that option. They crave the heroin experience in their life. Still, the new success in controlling anxiety during heroin withdrawal may become a model for the control of other kinds of anxiety and panic states. These remarkable developments not only give hope of improving the currently poor prospects of the heroin addict, but also give impetus to the development of further techniques that may quell the pathological hungerings, mood fluctuations, and extremes of anger and anxiety that are a part of other addictions and pathological life-styles.

This area of research also helps to explain the biological bases of passion, exhilaration, and joy. Studies of mood, heroin craving, and heroin blocking agents suggest similarities between satiation with heroin and the processes of sexual consumation. Brain research scientists Mirin, Meyer, Mendelson, and Ellingboe hypothesize:

> The dramatic effect produced by an injection of heroin have been well described by both clinicians and users. A brief but very intense euphoria, followed by tension relief, seems to be the common denominator in the heroin experience. Chessick called this sequence of events the "pharmacogenic orgasm" and addicts themselves often describe it in sexual terms. In the case of intravenous heroin, the immediate postinjection "rush" is frequently equated to sexual orgasm and subsequent feelings of tension, relief and relaxation have been likened to "being wrapped in warm cotton," "returning to the womb" or similar allusions to warmth, security and being cared for . . . [they are] important factors in the decision to initiate and maintain drug use. . . . At the present time there are sufficient data to explain the brief (30-60 second) but intensely pleasurable rush the immediately follows intravenous heroin administration. The mechanism most likely involves massive release of catecholamines at both central (brain) and peripheral sites. The rush is followed by a less intense but more sustained period of relaxation and tension relief lasting 2-4 hours.[3]

Of course, craving and yearning are not simply neuro-chemical events. They are very complex sociocultural, inter-personal, as well as biological matters. Still, the ongoing research into the linkages between the neurochemistry of pleasure-pain, the craving for drugs and food, and the mode of action of medications that prevent the experience of anxiety is a matter of great importance.

Alcohol, heroin addiction, Valium abuse, cigarette smoking, obesity, and pathological dieting: do they belong together in the same chapter? "Does my being 20 percent overweight just like one-quarter of all Americans over thirty years of age mean that I'm 'weak' like a drug addict?"

In two important respects, all the hunger, craving, and excess consumption conditions are more alike than different: First, the results of therapy in all areas achieve only very limited success. Second, conditioning techniques (behavior therapy) are popular at the present time in treating almost all these problems.[4,5]

ALCOHOL

One of my very close friends is an alcoholic man. He's forty-five years old, a gentle gentleman, married to a fine woman, and they have three children. The history of alcohol abuse goes back at least three generations in his family. His father and one brother both died in separate alcohol-related accidents. He carried his personal battle with alcohol very nearly to the end. On two occasions, his drinking exacerbated a severe pancreatitis and both times he was critically ill. That second episode wasn't long ago and now he doesn't drink at all. We're together fairly often in social settings where almost everybody else can and does drink, and in those moments I feel a sadness for my friend because taking a drink is a bonus in life no longer available to him. He feels that loss. He'd like to take two drinks and quit but he is sure now that he can't. I'm sure as well. If I didn't like and admire him very much, I'd probably have little sympathy for his needing to deny himself this seemingly small thing. But he is my friend and I've been forced to think about the fact that alcohol is *quite a bonus* in millions of American homes and tens of millions of homes worldwide. Moreover, fermented beverages and other intoxicants have been a valued part of individual and communal life through the ages and in many parts of the world.

I tell this small and obvious story because—I must confess —it wasn't obvious to me for many years that to want to take a drink but to have it forbidden is not a trivial deprivation. Neither is it obvious to many working in the health professions because they regularly come toward alcoholic patients in a critical, condescending, and/or exhortative manner. *Very few* doctors, nurses, and other health workers can avoid moral indignation as one part of their response to their alcoholic patients. In return, *very few* humans will tolerate a doctor or nurse who is ambivalent about them. That's probably one reason that fewer than 10 percent of the nearly 10 million Americans who suffer from alcoholism or alcohol-related disorders are receiving therapy for their alcohol problem. Still, it's not easy to love an alcohol abuser unless you loved him a great deal before the drinking started.

The prejudice against drinkers combined with the individual's own sense of shame keep most alcohol problems hidden for long years. By the time an alcoholic's problems do surface, they are usually deeply set and very complex. The family members who could intervene to insist that they do have a stake in controlling a spouse or other relative's drinking too often keep a conspiracy of silence to "protect" their family member from embarrassment within the family. Others subscribe to the sick contemporary value system that says we are not responsible for each other and that everybody has the right to drink, drug, eat, or smoke himself to oblivion.

Alcohol and other intoxicating drugs are used because they temporarily change the way people feel. Any individual can "make the old world disappear" and in its place make new and often friendlier feelings about the self and others or about one's past, present, and future appear. Although wide variations occur at times in the same person, intoxication often is accompanied by heightened self-confidence, increasing conviviality, and a kind of euphoria. Ordinary social restraints seem less binding and, instead, the events of the moment acquire preeminence. Alcohol is actually a central nervous system depressant, but its ingestion frequently produces a kind of high. Alcohol provides a way of temporarily getting "out from under" worries, tension, and anxiety.

Currently, 75 percent of adult American males and 60 percent of females drink. An estimated 3 to 5 percent of the men and 1 to 2 percent of women in the United States are said to be alcoholics. But what is alcoholism?

The most authoritative definitions aren't really very informative. The American Medical Association states that "a complicated interplay of physiological, psychological and sociological factors . . . leads to the origin and development of alcoholism." From 1952–1972, the World Health Organization definition of alcoholism was as follows: "Alcoholics are those excessive drinkers whose dependence upon alcohol has attained such a degree that they show noticeable mental disturbance or an interference with their bodily and mental health, their interpersonal relations and their smooth social and economic functioning or who show premonitory (early) signs of such developments. They therefore require treatment."[6] The new WHO definition attempts to draw a distinction between alcohol dependent conditions manifested by habituation and withdrawal symptoms and a second category of alcohol-related disability, which could include impulsive or episodic drinking associated with destructive behavior but with no habituation or craving between episodes. There is, obviously, a great deal of imprecision in our understanding of many aspects of alcoholism including its cause(s), the nature of its progression, and the effects of various treatments. But on the matter of the penalty that people (and society) pay for alcohol abuse, the facts are all too clear. The price is enormous.

An estimated 200,000 Americans die annually because of alcohol and alcohol-related violence. Among them are the victims of homicide, suicide, and accidents, the latter being the number-one cause of death before age forty. Alcohol is the frequent accompaniment of many or most of those individual tragedies. Auto accidents, drownings, burn deaths, and serious falls are often alcohol related or alcohol caused. An estimated

20 to 25 percent of all hospital admissions are thought to be alcohol related. If one adds the cost of property damaged, law enforcement and probation, insurance expenses, and so on, societal expenditures for the alcoholic man or woman may well approach $10,000 per year. This would not include the loss in productivity and would not begin to compensate for the damage to the spirit, emotional stability, and educational development of the millions of children who grow up in environments negatively influenced by alcoholism. The costs of child abuse, child neglect, and child abandonment are paid in the generation(s) that follow. Perhaps the most cruel of all the data about the damaging effects of alcohol are the now conclusive studies of babies born damaged because their mothers drank heavily during pregnancy. A fetal alcohol syndrome with a variety of birth defects and the possibility of delayed motor and mental impairment and/or future alcoholism is well established. There is similar evidence of damage to the babies of mothers who smoked heavily during pregnancy.[7]

Recent research has also revealed persisting deficits in brain function in alcoholics who are in their mid-thirties. Clinically, it is easy to overlook deficits in sober alcoholics. But subtle signs of brain damage may signal a "preclinical phase" of mental deterioration.[8] Of course, it has been long known that damage to the heart, gastrointestinal tract, cirrhosis and cancer of the liver, pancreatitis, accidents with head injury, and a hundred other physical consequences accompany alcohol abuse. And since alcohol abuse is now frequently combined with other forms of drug abuse, there are associated risks of hepatitis, seizures, suffocation, and more! Much more!

Case Study 1: *An Alcoholic Man, Forty-six, Who Smoked Marijuana Every Morning*

"Well, Doctor, you ask me why I always smoke a little [marijuana] when I first wake up. It's a kind of habit, you might say. My wife is constantly on me. She has such a lousy attitude. She doesn't understand anything. That's exactly what they told her at AA, but it didn't do her any good. You should see her, Doctor, and try to talk a little sense into her.

"You want to know why I always light up a joint first thing in the morning. She doesn't sleep with me anymore, so I'm there on the back porch by myself, and since I'm not working much because of the economy, I may sleep a little later. Everybody is gone when I wake up about 10 or 11 (A.M.). The last thing I do every night is lay out a joint on the stand next to the couch. And my lighter. When you first wake up, there will be a few moments when you are surprised it's morning, and you aren't just sure where you're at. Sometimes, you don't feel too good. Maybe your head hurts or you remember all the crap that went on the night before with her. Well, that's a good moment to light up and smoke. Just lay there and smoke. Then, in a few minutes—it's faster than a belt of whisky—I get up and use the john, brush my teeth, and shave. Then I fix myself coffee. On the weekend, she's there and all the crap starts. You should talk to her, Doctor. Talk a little sense into her."

This man, like many severe alcoholics and chronic drug abusers, mixed his intoxicants. After twenty-five years of hard drinking, he had reached a point where he couldn't work. He was picking up momentum on the downhill ski slope. The life of every member of his family was made dreadful by his drinking. Neither I, nor the family, the police, the judge, the jails, the "dry-out" centers, the mental hospital—nothing—interrupted this man's plunge. Mercifully, only a relatively small percentage of those who abuse alcohol reach that level of impairment.

Case Study 2: *Valium, Martinis, Despair, Valium, and Success*

Hy Ross was forty-seven years old and a very successful businessman. I saw him first while he was in a hospital following an alcohol-related seizure. He was being evaluated to make sure he had no brain tumor. There was none. He was one of the founders of a small "door to door" life insurance company. But after a few years the company wasn't small anymore. He managed several mergers with other companies and now they were large enough to be listed on a stock exchange. Mr. Ross had acquired a house along the sea, another house in Mexico, and a furnished condo. He and his girl friend fought regularly about the condo. She lived with him in the sea house now, but earlier in their relationship she had lived in the condo. She didn't know why he still needed that place. He winked as he explained it was an "investment." He had been married and divorced and he told me he paid over $3,500 monthly alimony. He had one child, a daughter thirteen years old who sustained a birth injury and suffered severe cerebral palsy. She walked with a staggering gait and her speech was hard to understand. But her intellect was unimpaired. He cried as he spoke proudly of her achievements and of her open affection for him. She was the one person in the world he fully loved. He had had a bitter divorce after a bitter marriage. In the end, he hired a detective to prove his wife was unfaithful. She hired accountants to prove he was hiding his wealth in order to cheat her. He fought for custody of their daughter, claiming his wife was unfit and immoral. Then he offered her a quarter of a million extra dollars for custody. His wife hated him more for that. The divorce had taken place ten years earlier but Mr. Ross was still outraged, feeling he had been robbed of his daughter. However, he saw her every second weekend and she lived with him for one month in the summer. He was very concerned about that situation. His wife was considering returning to court to change the arrangement because of his drinking. He claimed he still hated his former wife, but noted that his girl friend was very jealous of her because of the many mean, hour-long telephone discussions the two conducted over their daughter. They argued about her doctors—she had two sets—adjustment of leg braces, choice of school, speech instruction, and the bad influence on the daughter of each parent's new relationships.

Mr. Ross had been an only child. His father, also a very successful businessman, had died of a heart attack at forty-eight. Four years earlier, his mother had died at sixty-four of a malignancy. They had had a poor relationship. Prior to the development of the malignancy, he hadn't seen her for two years. He resented bitterly her lack of interest in her only granddaughter and said he came drunk to her funeral for revenge. Also, he acknowledged coming drunk to many events. His father's family were described as gifted, erratic, high-strung; two of his father's three brothers had been heavy drinkers. One had died in the fifties of a probable heart attack and the other died in an automobile accident that took place after he had been drinking. There was no history of drinking or mental illness in his mother's family.

His daughter's name was Erin and he wanted to talk with me about the wisdom of finding a psychotherapist for the daughter to help her with the problems he anticipated she would face in later adolescent years. He wanted her to have a mature professional friend. He was certain that he would die soon and, in his sober and intoxicated moments alike, the thought of his daughter at the mercy of the world was more than he could bear. He had in mind that I might start to see Erin on the days she visited him, that is, every other Saturday. I asked him, "Why don't you speak for yourself, John Alden?" He replied, "I'm a dead duck. My heart is going to go. It's her that can be saved. Don't worry about me. I've got a lot of money."

He repeated what his internist had told me. He mixed Valium, alcohol, business, and more alcohol in what appeared to be a nonstop race to his death. He had an additional girl friend who came regularly to see him in the condo, but he said that relationship wasn't serious. He was mildly diabetic as his father had been before him. He was forty pounds overweight. His blood pressure fluctuated but was often quite high. He smoked a pack of cigarettes and took between twenty and fifty milligrams of Valium daily, a fair bit. He told me that he drank throughout the day, every day. He had two martinis or more at lunch, a drink or two after work. He took a nap before dinner, then drinks and a bottle of wine with the evening meal. If he didn't fall asleep first, sometimes he took a nightcap. He said he'd been drinking heavily for fifteen years. He wanted to cut down but not stop because his business and family problems were great and he enjoyed alcohol. He had taken "treatments" several times in a famous sanitarium, but the last time they discharged him for getting drunk while there.

Mr. Ross was still moderately active at work, though he had been advised to retire by his partners. He enjoyed supervising his company's salespeople and there was always someone to fire, suspicions of premium theft, constant efforts to avoid loss of "lists" of potential customers to other insurance firms, and so forth. He had an income of $10,000 per month. In addition, he had "stock options" that he was converting into a trust for Erin. He was so drunk the second morning I came to see him in the hospital, we didn't try to talk. He walked out of the hospital without permission later that afternoon.

The patient's internist was also his old friend and, though it had been complicated, he was as well the personal physician for the patient's former wife, Erin's mother. He was also in contact with the present girl friend, Ross's fiancée (the woman living with him in the sea house), who, he said, had been part of Mr. Ross's life for seven years. She was desperate about his drinking, which she felt was totally out of control. The doctor was very concerned about his patient-friends and when I suggested a six-way meeting (doctor, Erin,

Erin's mother, Mr. Ross, the fiancée, and me) he said he wouldn't miss it for anything. I told him to stand firm on the importance of all the participants coming. A day later he called to say that everything was set and that the surprising thing was that the three adults were eager for the meeting. Erin's mother promised to bring her along. Mr. Ross was firmly instructed that he was to stay off Valium and alcohol for twelve hours and he agreed.

I should say something about the inclusion of Mr. Ross's girl friend in the session. Her presence was originally opposed by Erin's mother, who didn't want to extend any unnecessary dignity to "that woman." But at her doctor's request, she finally agreed. I have discovered, painfully, that excluding an individual from discussions that might significantly concern his or her life is a grievous act. You are never forgiven, and, more to the point, that person has no choice but to take revenge by defeating any program that is agreed to in his absence. Also, in this instance, Mr. Ross's fiancée had been a person in Erin's life for almost seven years. I discovered at our meeting that she was a very remarkable woman in her own right and that her concern for Erin and Erin's father was best described as that of a second mother and loyal wife. That was the reality of it, though it was unconsummated legally.

Erin was worth every penny of the quarter of a million dollars offered ten years earlier. With inflation, the price on that day would have been no less than a million. To everyone's surprise, Mr. Ross had observed one week off both Valium and alcohol and he seemed to be a different kind of person. In the hospital, he had flaunted a coarse bravado. He was colorful as usual, but much more reserved, honest, and open. I began the meeting by asking what each participant hoped would come from the day, that is, the very best that could happen. I started with Mr. Ross's fiancée. She seemed very uncomfortable. But she said in a strong and decisive way, "I want Hy to stop drinking today. I want Hy to marry me next week. And I want to have a delayed honeymoon in Spain next summer with Erin coming along." Hy Ross squandered his wishes. His former wife retaliated with two rather petty observations, then surprised everybody by saying, "Most of all, I hope you can stop drinking, Hy." The internist wanted Hy to go back on antabuse to help control his drinking. Erin, who was a very loving child, a young woman really, spoke in a labored way to say she worried that her Daddy had been in a hospital. Also, she wanted to go to Spain.

I saved my wish till the end of that session and then asked for five more meetings with all participants present. All agreed.

At the next meeting, I knew we were into something big when Hy's fiancée, Barbara, announced that Hy had put the condo up for sale.

When the therapy of an alcoholic man or woman is successful, it is almost always because one or more of the following has happened: The patient sinks to but recoils from a kind of rock-bottom situation, a now-or-never moment of experiencing starkly and undeniably the expense of drinking; a serious physical illness develops and it is clear that drinking will soon mean death; there is a conversion to religion and/or to Alcoholics Anonymous, usually with the dedicated help of an AA group and/or a particularly persistent minister or doctor; the spouse or a close friend locks the outside door, throws away the key, and makes it stick that "we stay here till you stop drinking or I die trying." However, even when all these circumstances take place simultaneously, the result is very often disappointing. It isn't easy. Working with an alcoholic man or woman and his or her family requires enormous determination, an ability to live through periods of disappointment, and the availability of support systems to sustain jobs, hope, and family relationships. Alcoholics are people who live out the rule that "trouble comes in twos, threes, fours, and fives."

Since the 1960s, the American Medical Association and the American Psychiatric Association have designated chronic alcoholism a disease, and there is now a good deal of evidence that supports that concept in the instance of at least some alcoholics. Evidence of a genetic predisposition to alcoholism has come from studies of the high incidence of alcoholic relatives of individuals with severe mood disturbances, that is, depression and mania. This is particularly the case in mania. Further genetic evidence of a hereditary tendency for alcoholism has come from a number of studies of the families of alcoholics including studies of adoptees from alcoholic families who left their biological parents early in their lives but developed alcoholism nonetheless. One of the most interesting reports in recent years was that of Wolin and associates, who compared the effects of alcoholism in the parental generation on the children as they grew up. They demonstrated that there were fewer children who became alcoholics in families that, despite alcoholism, sustained traditional and ritual practices.[9]

There are many other areas of continuing alcohol research including efforts to find "biological markers" in blood or urine, measurable physiological characteristics (blushing, sweating, and so on), allergies, food idiosyncracies, and so forth, which would give further evidence of the causes of alcoholism, hope of new techniques for early diagnosis of vulnerability, and better modes of treatment.

Although there have been reports over the years suggesting that "some" severe alcoholics could become social drinkers, the prevailing opinion has been that few individuals successfully achieve that status. This is a major tenet of Alcoholics Anonymous. "You are only one drink away from being a drunk again" is repeated millions of times each year by deadly serious AA members to themselves, each other, and new initiates to their remarkable fellowship. This is not, however, a matter that is fully settled. A 1973 study by the influential Rand Corporation concluded that social drinking is possible for a significant number of past alcohol abusers. A 1978 follow-up by the same group hedges that conclusion to a small degree. But most people who work with alcoholics hold to the conviction that it is the very exceptional person who can change from alcoholic to social drinker and that no one should be encouraged to try. Anyway, most alcoholics have already tried it a hundred times themselves and failed.

E. P. Noble, who headed the National Institute on Alcohol Abuse and Alcoholism from 1976 to 1978, calls alcoholism the most untreated of the treatable illnesses. He feels that much better results will occur when families and the medical profession overcome prejudice and ignorance so that treatment could begin at an earlier stage.[10] Individualizing the approach in alcoholism, as everywhere, should prove helpful. AA is a remarkable resource for many, many people, but not for everyone. Its religious emphasis turns off some people. Still, whatever approach is finally accepted needs the same enthusiasm and tenacity that people in AA bring to their efforts. By now, doctors, nurses, psychologists, social workers, ministers, and alcohol rehabilitation counselors do have a wide array of therapeutic approaches from which to choose. They include couple and family therapy, aversive and tranquilizing chemicals, and well-thought-out behavioral approaches that condition against not only alcohol but the environments that seem to suggest "it's time for a drink." Other therapists are prescribing transcendental meditation, biofeedback training, stimulus deprivation, and running. Hospitalization is sometimes useful, though non-hospital living settings may better suffice for detoxification and spiritual restoration after a period of intoxication.

In working with people who have an alcohol problem, a therapist's strategy is the same as in the treatment of people with other kinds of severe problems. First, you need really to want to help whoever it is who is under your care. It has to matter to *you*. You have to want your patient to be able to make a living, to be on good terms with his loved ones, to be hopeful about his life, to have people respect him and look up to him. You may have to help your patient deal with his practical everyday problems. Sometimes, you may need to talk to his boss. Second, you need to know the full range of potentially helpful therapeutic programs. Starting with the least expensive and least disruptive, you make those therapeutic resources available. In the case of the man or woman with a severe drinking problem, and the family whose assistance you regularly enlist, the full repertoire of techniques is sometimes none too many.

DUST AND JUNK ON THE STREET

Much of what follows in this chapter is a description of casualties among users of the various roots, leaves, flowers, plants, and synthesized chemicals taken to produce altered states of consciousness. Yet I know that the casualties psychiatrists see are only a fraction of the people who sustain injury from drugs and that the casualties are but an unknown small percentage of those who smoke, sniff, snort, or inject street drugs. Among 50 million Americans who have had experiences with mind-altering drugs (in addition to alcohol), there are many who would say on behalf of drugs what I say about having a drink or two of alcohol, "It's a bonus. I'm glad it's here to enjoy." Those who favor (other) drugs would say, "Drugs are better than alcohol and, in addition, they don't make you fat." If I protest the comparison and talk about heroin addiction and PCP casualties in the psychiatric emergency room, I'm told about alcohol skid row and the trauma centers where auto accident victims are brought.

Some of the people who use drugs do so, they say, not only for the sense of relaxation and euphoria, but to discover a new world of pulsating and vibrant color, rich textures, harmonious movement, a sense of the "universality of time and space," and, ultimately, a deeper personal understanding. This viewpoint has been put forward by a number of influential artists, writers, musicians, and an occasional defector from the academic establishment. One of the more persuasive proponents of the good possibilities that could come from drug ingestion has been Carlos Castaneda, a UCLA graduate student in anthropology at the time his influential first books were published, 1968 and 1971. Don Juan, the Yaqui Indian healer in Castaneda's *The Teachings of Don Juan* and *A Separate Reality*, exhorts his young "square" apprentice to "loosen up," to give up his conventional mode of thinking, to enter into the "other worlds." Don Juan insists that his protégé take a series of psychedelic drugs in order to learn how to "stop the world." When the world "stops," the person hears the language of animals, sees the life of vegetation, knows the links between the sky and earth. Everything that is "there" comes to consciousness. In a third Castaneda book, *Journey to Ixtlan*, however, Don Juan calls upon his student to forget the drugs and go on to experience the ambiguity, the mysteries, the dangers, and the sadness of life.[11] In the books—though not necessarily in real life—the drug experience removed blindfolds and made it necessary for the student (Carlos Castaneda himself) to assume more personal—rather than conventional—responsibility for his life. Ideally it would work like that.

I practiced psychiatry and managed outpatient and inpatient programs at the University of Wisconsin in the decade between 1955 and 1965 without having much occasion to think about street drugs either in the student population or the general Madison community. Until the early 1960s, "drug abuse" meant primarily the frequent overdoses of barbiturates by suicidally intent individuals, occasional hospital admissions of a confused patient suffering an accidental build-up in the blood of bromides or barbiturates, or the occasional appearance in the emergency room of an addicted patient seeking narcotics for alleged pain of kidney stones. Sometimes, I saw tense, thin women in their thirties referred by their doctors because they were taking enormous doses of amphetamines prescribed in the first place by doctors for weight control. I knew chiefly by reputation of the existence of a small and tragic subculture addicted to heroin living on the fringe of the society. They were thought to turn to criminality to support their habit. They were a "group apart," hopeless and incurable, latter-day lepers who were 1 percent sick and 99 percent depraved. When I consulted at the state prisons I heard a good deal about drug traffic inside the walls. But in those years, I was naive enough to think that prison walls would pose a barrier to drug trafficking. I didn't have any idea then that the unwritten constitution of many prisons begins with a preamble that says, "Let the prisoners' friends or a small number of crooked guards bring in drugs and then all the violence will stay between prisoners. Otherwise the prison will explode!"

In the early 1960s, when so many young people began to take drugs—marijuana, LSD, and cocaine—public attention became fixed on the subject. People asked the specialists in medicine, pharmacology, and psychology to explain what was happening and, particularly, how to put an end to parental concern. It soon became clear that laymen, lawmakers, and doctors alike knew little or nothing at all about the drugs in the streets and in the schoolyards. Indeed, much of their (our) knowledge was false information. They were very painful years and it has taken the whole decade and a half to clarify who are the victims and who are the survivors. There have been many of both.

By now, mostly without serious personal consequences, an estimated 25 to 30 percent or more Americans have used illegal drugs to produce transitory states of altered consciousness. Today a majority of the young people in their teens and early twenties have experimented with marijuana, and its regular use is now common. Some go on to try LSD, cocaine, or mescaline for brief periods. But most young people who are in school or who are gainfully employed find that they have little wish to make the heavier impact drugs a regular or important part of their lives. A small number of their peers find the drug-induced experience to be a worthwhile part of their lives and intend to smoke marijuana and sniff cocaine "at least on the weekends" for a long time. I worry a good deal about a small fraction of otherwise successful young people who count the drug experience as a most significant part of their lives and make all other matters subsidiary in importance. Drug intoxication becomes a daily ritual, coloring all life experiences. They are still young. Some are professionally successful. But, as with the chronic alcoholic, this kind of life, I feel sure, can only become a narrowing, repetitive, self-centered, and progressively less manageable existence. The counting of casualties from this group will require another decade.

Drug use among poor, unemployed ghetto dwellers is a profound problem. Some studies show poverty communities with heroin use rates of 20 percent of the young male population.[12] These figures would not include the many others who "only" use PCP, cocaine, LSD, and amphetamines. In one way or another, everyone who lives in or near these racially segregated ghettos is victim to addiction and addicts. The cause: racism in America.

I've tried a number of different approaches in an effort to be helpful to patients who suffered severe drug abuse or addiction problems. I've committed people to locked wards in psychiatric hospitals, placed patients in a dozen public and private "drug rehab centers" (in three states and two countries), treated patients in individual, family, and couple therapy, arranged for hired living companions who would attempt to provide day-by-day stability in a drug abuser's life, and a few times passively have gone along with a district attorney's decision to "throw the book" at a given offender to "let him cool down by doing some time." But all in all, I've learned little from those experiences other than that you need every conceivable break and every possible support if you are to have any hope that the severely impaired drug abuser or addict will have a chance for another kind of life. Even then, I've seen young people from the highest as well as the lowest social strata die from their afflictions.

A psychiatrist's office isn't the ideal place to develop a treatment plan for a seriously impaired drug user. But I'm not sure where that best place is. I've seen too many failures and disappointments when people trusted some "institution" to provide a level of *love and care* sufficient to cure their addicted relative. That is an almost impossible expectation. There are exceptions, but "institutions" mostly provide some protection, technical skills, and a certain degree of encouragement and support. *Love and care* are harder to come by than the technical information. Once or twice I've asked people to consider giving up hope that an "institution" will cure their family member and proposed that I would personally provide the technical consultation if they would provide the *love and care.*

Case Study 3: *Is There an Institution that Will Do Your Family's Job?*

I don't think so.
I didn't really believe in the devil until I came to

California and saw what the drug Phencyclidine, PCP, "angel dust," does to people. In these several years, I've seen hundreds of fiercely violent and profoundly psychotic men, women, and children brought in restraints by the police to my hospital's emergency room, where an often wild PCP episode might continue for hours, weeks, or beyond. Of course, I see only the casualties and I'm sure there are thousands of people who experience the "high" without going mad. But the victims are many and their responses are belligerent and tortured. PCP use is epidemic in Los Angeles. Originally used as an animal tranquilizer, it is easily made, not very expensive, and very powerful. There is a strong subculture in Los Angeles that supports its use. PCP is often mixed with other street drugs, guaranteeing an effect from whatever is taken.

I was receiving the morning report from the doctors who had worked through the night at the Harbor-UCLA Medical Center Psychiatric Emergency. Twenty patients had been seen. One of the patients described was Denise, a twenty-three-year-old black woman brought by the police because she had slashed her wrist while intoxicated after smoking PCP and marijuana. This was the eighth time she had been brought to our emergency room in the last twelve months, each time with a PCP episode. Six times before, the psychotic episode had continued beyond the twenty-four hours we kept patients in our emergency room and she had been sent on to the State Hospital. However, California law requires that patients be released from hospitalization, if they insist, as soon as they are no longer—for the moment—an urgent threat to themselves. All six times she demanded immediate release and was back on the street in a matter of days or a week. I talked with her that morning. Denise was an attractive, slight young woman. She was no longer belligerent, striking out, spitting, and shouting. She was, instead, quiet, dazed, inappropriately laughing. A note in the chart from an earlier admission indicated that she had a very responsible working mother. I called her. This was a Friday and I was going to be away for four days, but I asked the mother to come to see me on my return Tuesday and to bring Denise if she was released from our hospital over the weekend. Denise's mother, stepfather, and Denise herself did come at the scheduled time. Denise had been released on Saturday and had become re-intoxicated with PCP on Sunday. She was once again in a dazed, semicoherent state when they arrived in my office. Her mother and stepfather were seriously concerned. However, they were without ideas except to wonder if there wasn't "some institution" they hadn't already tried that would keep their daughter till she was "well."

I told them and they told me . . . there was no way their daughter could long survive. While intoxicated, she jumped from cars, had burned herself, received all kinds of beatings from all kinds of men on the street. In the brief days between intoxications, she was gentle, full of plans to get a job or go back to school. But then, she would intoxicate herself. She had been in both our local state hospitals, in three private psychiatric facilities, and in four separate drug treatment programs. Her stays were brief. Her promises were quickly broken.

Denise had finished the eleventh grade before becoming pregnant with a baby girl, who was now cared for by Denise's aunt and mother in the family home where Denise still lived. Her mother told me that Denise had been, essentially, incapacitated for more than two and a half years. The other members of the family were much more successful. She had three older brothers. One had a good painting business, one was a policeman, and one owned a small restaurant. The stepfather worked as custodian in a school and the mother was a nursing aide in a local hospital.

I looked at this twenty-three-year-old from the Los Angeles streets, her wrist still bandaged from her suicide attempt five days before. She was a wounded and bleeding quarry in a jungle, moving toward a sentence of death. I realized that no one, at least no stranger, could love her enough to do what would have to be done to give her even the slightest chance.

"Maybe you've got a week, maybe a month, maybe a year," I told them. "But you don't have long with this one. And nobody will do it for you."

I asked the family to consider taking the problem head-on themselves, finding a place far from the streets of Los Angeles where family members and Denise would live for the next three or four months. I had in mind a cabin in the mountains, a cottage on the prairies, a place to walk for miles and miles together. At that moment, the biggest truth, the only truth in Denise's life was the power of PCP. I hoped that family intervention might possibly create a new reality, another truth.

The parents listened quietly to my proposals. Denise woke up long enough to offer a puzzled look but drifted quickly back into her reverie. Her mother and step-father talked about their vacation schedules at work and about a leave of absence from one or another of their jobs. They didn't say no but asked me to think about an alternate plan while they talked with the three sons. We agreed to meet in one week. I said that by that time, I would have talked with the most knowledgeable people I could find to seek some less disruptive plan.

I made my calls, half a dozen of them. Several of the people with whom I talked knew Denise from earlier efforts to work with her. Nobody thought my plan was practical. After all, Denise's family were working people and, anyway, Denise could find PCP on the moon if she had to. I told them all I didn't want their opinion about my sense of practicality. I wanted to know if there was a plan they could propose that offered that stricken young woman a better chance to start back toward survival. None of them thought she had much chance. Worse, they all said they might do something like what I had suggested if the patient was their own sister, wife, daughter.

Of course, Denise was unique in terms of the magnitude of her problem. Our society pays a good price to train and support health professionals and health institutions. Many people receive wonderful institutional care for mental illnesses and alcohol and drug problems. But there are times when those professional systems just won't work. And I'm afraid professionals sometimes don't have the courage to tell patients and families to look more to themselves and to each other. They frequently are each other's only hope. I've found that all too often, no one will really do your dirty work for you.

A final word about PCP. I mentioned that the drug has attained epidemic proportions in some of the poorer communities in Los Angeles, in Detroit, and in other large cities in the United States. In the public hospital psychiatric emergencies in Los Angeles, we have at times treated more patients suffering acute PCP psychotic episodes than schizophrenic or alcoholic patients.

I had never heard of PCP until four years ago.[13,14] Hopefully, its use will abate when its consequences are more widely known.

HEROIN

I wrote earlier in this chapter about the extraordinary scientific breakthroughs that accompanied the localization of areas of the brain with specific affinity for morphine and heroin and the normally occurring morphine-like substances that have been called endorphins. This research has led to the development of drugs some of which appear to counteract the ordinary effects of opiates and others that prevent the very severe withdrawal symptoms that have heretofore been terrifying to addicts. They include agitation, a sense of imminent doom, nausea and vomiting, at times outright delirium.

For the addict faced with having to pay $100 daily to support a heroin addiction, robbery, mugging, and prostitution are usually the only "hope." An estimated 50 percent of those passing through the large city jails have been heroin addicts. The cities have been prey to the addict predators who were in turn prey to the billion-dollar criminal drug trade. It is a miserable, miserable life. But in the end, it is estimated that fewer than 10 percent of those offered treatment manage to get rid of the addiction.

Case Study 4: *Poor Baby*

I talked one day recently with a heroin addict, an eighteen-year-old young woman, seven months pregnant, three years away from her middle-class home. She'd actually come to my office as company for a non-addict friend. She was hoping, vaguely, to break her addiction soon because she did not wish to (further) endanger her unborn, first baby. But at the same time, she had grave doubts that she could ever live without heroin. She summarized her feelings this way:

"It's really lousy that something as unbelievably good as heroin has to screw up your life. People who aren't users don't have any way to know. I guess I have to quit—maybe about a month from now, not before. It's velvet. I will quit, about six weeks before the baby comes. My boy friend says he might quit with me. After the baby comes, I'll try but I'm not sure. Heroin is Saturday under a warm quilt."

Case Study 5: *The Prisoner Who Stayed Drugged for Twenty Years*

The public defender called me to ask if I could come the next day to testify on behalf of his client, who was a prisoner well known to me. He thought my testimony might help to lessen the length of sentence from a threatened "life" to "only" ten to fifteen years. I was irritated about the short notice but didn't bother to complain. In the life of people like Farrell, the prisoner, all things happen in the same casual, as if by chance, manner.

Farrell was actually a very unusual person. He was intelligent, had a sense of humor, knew everything about prison life. I had known him to befriend and protect prisoners new to the system, and once he bravely acted to help a new security guard who didn't know the rules and had invited retaliation. The other prisoners liked him and the security force left him alone. He was forty-two years old and a kind of senior citizen in prison. He had been on the street only six weeks in twenty years! He had spent 1,034 of 1,040 weeks behind bars! While in prison, on seven days of each of the 1,034 weeks he took street drugs, illegal drugs smuggled inside. There were always barbiturates, marijuana, LSD, tranquilizers, and once or twice each week heroin would arrive in the prison. Whatever was around, Farrell managed to take a share. His parents were living and, though they didn't visit anymore, they sent their son $50 to $100 every month.

The court hearing was for sentencing as the result of his participation in an unsuccessful group prison escape. That unhappy event had been an impulsive, last-minute "joining in" for him. He was serving the last months of a very long sentence. But someone yelled, "Come on, Farrell, let's go," and he was on his way. That morning, a few hours earlier, he had taken three or four LSD tablets and his memory for details was a bit clouded. However, he dimly remembered thinking there was less to be feared from the guards than there was to be feared if he refused to join in the escape. He understood that everybody would be back together in prison sooner or later. The escape went as far as the street, but no farther. It lasted only nine minutes. Someone had shot a bystander, and someone had cut a guard. Farrell was soon in solitary confinement and obsessed with the fact that he would return to court to face the victim, the prosecuting attorney, and the judge. Of all events in his life, this was the most feared.

I wanted in my testimony to describe the way in which Farrell lived his life and to point out that intoxication was a part of everything he did. I hoped to say that Farrell was probably dazed and confused with LSD. I also wanted to ask this question: Is this vulnerable man, who has been locked in a drug environment called prison, fully responsible for drug-related behavior?

I gave measured, careful, honest testimony. The judge gave twelve years.

Mercifully, the new scientific discoveries making withdrawal easier and raising the possibility of non-addictive chemicals as alternatives to heroin will improve the outlook. Presently, methadone, also an addicting drug but a more manageable one, is the only drug acceptable to addicts as a substitute for heroin use. There are a number of methadone maintenance clinics which serve at least to diminish the addict's need to commit crimes to support his addiction. Estimates of the number of American heroin addicts vary from 500,000 to 4,000,000 people.[15]

VALIUM AND LIBRIUM AND THE OTHER DRUGS

The "older" drug intoxication problems of excessive use of barbiturates and stimulant drugs such as amphetamines have been overshadowed by the widespread use of marijuana, cocaine, heroin, PCP, Valium, and Librium. However, they do remain as considerable substance abuse agents today. The barbiturates, though much less widely prescribed now, are a vexing problem because they are so often used in suicide attempts. Prolonged use of the stimulant drugs such as amphetamines has led to disastrous periods of "disinhibition" with many instances of confused, angry episodes in which all varieties of aggressive behavior, including murder and suicide, have occurred. And instances of permanent brain damage with amphetamines have been well documented. The barbiturates and the various stimulants have somewhat opposite mood effects. But there are many individuals who use them and other drugs interchangeably! In their flight from the nonintoxicated moments of their lives, they have discovered that "it doesn't make too much difference which road you travel, just as long as you can get out of *there* as fast as you can!" "Up" and "down" are both "out."

Valium and Librium are now the most widely prescribed drugs and they are, of course, widely abused. They have some good qualities, one being that it is relatively hard to commit suicide with these drugs taken alone. Valium overdoses are considerably less dangerous than overdoses of barbiturates, major tranquilizers or the anti-depression medications (which often produce a cardiac death). Valium and related compounds are effective muscle-relaxing drugs and they do help people through stressful moments. They start out as an aid in a stressful "way of life." After a while, they are the "way of life" usually along with a growing social and business alcoholism.

SUMMARY

Why do people drug themselves? And why don't people who are intelligent and who realize the damage they suffer from alcohol or other drugs stop? There are many reasons. Drugging oneself is above all a way of changing one's world. It is a mysterious event, uncanny. I am "a certain way" now. Yet I know that if I drink four ounces of gin, within an hour my world will be changed. For a while, things seem better. The same with smoking a cigarette of marijuana or swallowing two amphetamine tabs. My world would be even more drastically changed by my own act if I took PCP or if I injected a narcotic such as heroin into my body. This ability to make one's world change is a power, a dependable if not effective tool for the person in dealing with the joys, the fears, the sadness, and the boredom of life. Taking a drug is something to do that will have an effect. Even the most resourceless, most impotent, most ineffective individual acquires a mastery of sorts through a constant resorting to intoxicants. With experience, one could even acquire a kind of expert status in drug self-dosing: "No matter what they say or do, no matter how frightening the world, I have the ability to change it all for a while." Many who drug themselves have few areas of functioning in which they retain the ability to change much about their lives.

Thus, "getting off" an alcoholic or drug habit requires the decision to surrender a dependable and frequently utilized "emergency exit" from life's stressful moments. If the individual has other possibilities (loving, working, learning, meditating, praying, reading, playing, talking, hobbying), the process is as much trading and substituting as "giving up." Anything that rewards this act of substituting makes the trade a more likely success. It is usually easier to believe in something along with key others who believe in you. Therefore, the endorsement of family, friends, and/or therapist are always important and sometimes decisive in determining whether a person is able to break or modify patterns of intoxication. "Kicking a habit" means *believing* in something or somebody. Obviously, if that habit is accompanied by the intense craving of a physiological and psychological addiction and great discomfort accompanies the surrendering, the necessity for *believing* is even greater. However, those who have long been committed to a life dominated by alcohol or drugs are often the very ones who have stopped believing in self, in love, in work, in worship, and, sometimes, in the value of their own lives. When an individual is first beginning to drink to excess, something very important is taking place. That which he or she has been is in doubt and in jeopardy.

SMOKING AND OVEREATING

The bad news has been in on smoking and overeating for quite a while. It is worse than we thought, probably worse than we know.[16,17,18] Of every three or four American adults, at least one is currently trying to stop smoking and/or to lose weight. And with good reason. Between 25 and 45 percent of Americans over thirty are at least 20 percent overweight. And to be 30 percent overweight is to incur a 30 percent greater risk of mortality. Beyond 30 percent overweight, the risk is much greater. Data are equivocal for people less than 30 percent over the norm.

And for cigarette smokers, there is very little encouragement. New medical data demonstrate that newborns of mothers who smoke may suffer severe damage to brain and body similar to that described in the fetal alcohol syndrome. Smoking may cut blood supply to the uterus. This is the newest of the very bad news to be added to the documented facts about smoking, lung and heart disease, and cancer. There is probably more to come.

Not reassuring either are statistics about the results of people's efforts to lose weight or to stop smoking. Only 15 to 25 percent achieve a lasting degree of success.[19] A significantly larger number start out strongly, but it doesn't hold. From 75 to 85 percent of those who try to lose a significant amount of weight or try to stop smoking fail in the effort. For the obese, even the treatments are sometimes dangerous. Food is the fuel of an extraordinarily intricate body that evolved through millions of years of precise development. We are discovering that we have less freedom to make stark revisions in food intake patterns. When we try, unexpected consequences seem to take place. The liquid protein diet supplements are a current case in point. More than 1.5 million copies of *The Last Chance Diet* were sold after its publication in 1976. The book detailed the great hope that this appealing, less painful way of losing weight by drinking the protein "milk shakes" could help "avid eaters" who had failed with other systems. But reports of sudden death due to cardiac arrhythmias raise serious doubts about the long-term use of such methods. This is not the first time that the hope of losing weight painlessly proved short lived.[20]

It is very difficult to lose weight. It is very difficult to stop smoking.

I had the good fortune to visit the People's Republic of China in October 1976. The "Gang of Four" had just been removed from power at the time of my visit. The China I saw was the zealous hard-line China with the morality and discipline imposed at the time of the Cultural Revolution in the late 1960s still in force. Sustaining health was equated with patriotism. One couldn't "serve China" unless health was protected. Everywhere I visited, the people talked about their personal efforts through exercise, good nutrition, health checks, and so forth, to keep themselves in good condition. I saw very few obese people.

But everyone smoked!

I thought that one possible explanation was that all over the country there were pictures of Mao with a cigarette. For a while, I accepted that theory as the best explanation of a superzealous medical establishment ignoring the long-known public health dangers of smoking. If the beloved leader smoked, who could say it is bad?

But as I thought about it, I came to favor a different theory. I decided that the Chinese government didn't want to start a campaign with their people that they would lose. Admittedly, they had had many health campaigns with good luck and perhaps my analysis is faulty. But I'm not sure that even the Chinese government could win a campaign against smoking. Of course, someday they, like us, will have to try.

I have little to add to what everyone knows about the problems of discontinuing smoking and moderating eating. There are a number of behavior therapy programs advertised on the radio, television, and in the newspapers. Most of them report that they obtain good results, but, as indicated, impartial studies show that longer-term effectiveness is considerably less than claimed.

The key appears to be motivation. *After* heart attacks, *after* the start of diabetes, and so on, people discover they have the will to do what before had seemed almost impossible. But *before* the damage is done, the present pleasures are just too compelling.

The "behavior therapy" techniques available to discourage continuation of the unwanted behavior(s) vary with the condition being treated. But in each instance, the goal is to firmly fix in the individual's thinking a message to abstain. Many programs are modeled after one designed by Spiegel as a simple hypnotic treatment method to stop smoking.[21] The messages imparted to the hypnotized subject are these:

- For your body, smoking (alcohol, overeating, and so forth) is poison.
- You need your body to live.
- You owe your body this respect and protection.
- You must not smoke.

Sometimes behavioral techniques employ averse stimuli as a way of discouraging a specific behavior and making noxious anything associated with the behavior. Antabuse, an averse drug used in the treatment of alcoholism, is frequently introduced in such a way as to make unpleasant any association not only with alcohol but with the entire environment in which the individual has habitually done his or her drinking. The same general approach can be structured in the treatment of overeating, smoking, and so on.

How do you succeed in "persuading," "teaching," or "conditioning" an individual to remember the lesson? You can, of course, repeat the lesson, make it more emphatic, or make it very personal and individualized. Or, you can attempt to present the message at a time when the individual is uniquely prepared to listen. The latter approach, that is, making people prepared to listen, is the specialty of University of British Columbia psychologist Peter Suedfeld, an exponent of restricted environmental stimulation programs (REST) in the management of pleasure-linked behavior.[22] Suedfeld uses "stimulus deprived settings" in which there is neither light, sound, nor the motion of air. Subjects remain in these darkened, quiet rooms for as many as twenty-four hours. Long hours with no sensory input create a hungering for information and an eagerness to hear any message, any message at all. When a message is finally provided, it is remembered. At least, that is the theory. The message that comes is: for your body, smoking is a poison . . . eating, eating, eating is a poison. . . . Why is it so difficult? In part, it's not only that people enjoy their habits, we "are" our habits to a significant degree. One person who helped me understand that fact more clearly was the woman I will next describe.

Case Study 6: *A Low Roller at Vegas in a High-Stakes Life*

Sue Osborne and her two girl friends flew from London, Ontario, to Las Vegas in April 1971 for a fling. Sue was twenty-one. Her plane ticket, hotel, three show tickets, and meals were paid for and she had an extra $93 for gambling and treats. The plane was late, arriving after 10:00 P.M., but Sue and her friends went wandering. They found a restaurant-casino with large (water-glass size) shrimp cocktails for 49¢. Sue lost $7 in one of the restaurant's 25-cent slot machines and for revenge had a second shrimp cocktail. The next day, Sue had six shrimp cocktails, seven the following day, and four on the last day prior to a 2:30 P.M. departure to return to Canada. Her two friends had met some boys on the trip, but Sue's great moments were brief instants when she was "ahead for the day" with the slots and in the moments when she engaged with the "bargain shrimp."

Then back on the airplane, and for Sue a date the next week with a surgeon. She had arranged "intestinal bypass surgery" for the treatment of her obesity. She weighed 290 pounds. She was 5 feet 6 inches tall. She made a little joke to the stewardess as she entered the plane: "The blimp is boarding the plane."

The surgery resulted in a miracle. She was incredibly lucky. It is a dangerous operation and many patients fare badly. She had talked the surgeon into the procedure. He'd never done the operation before. Technically, she had a jejunoileostomy. That meant that most of her small intestine had been bypassed and could no longer digest the food she ate. The surgery itself went well. She escaped the 2 to 5 percent immediate mortality rate of surgery and avoided the complications of pulmonary embolism, wound infection, gastrointestinal hemorrhage, renal failure, and pancreatitis. In the process of losing 170 pounds in two years, she did not fall victim to kidney stones, gall bladder disease, progressive liver failure, peptic ulcer, intestinal obstruction, or decalcification of bones. She even avoided the psychiatrist for five years after the surgery—and two years after writing in her diary, "A sex object . . . at last! She did have an operation to remove excess skin (lipectomy) several years after the bypass.

I found Sue to be a very strong, competent, funny, and most attractive twenty-six-year-old woman. She worked for a major newspaper handling advertising contracts that totaled hundreds of thousands of dollars each year. There were three immediate events that had been very stressful to her which caused her to come to talk over her problems. There had been a disappointing experience with a boy friend. She was discouraged about her continuing problems with her parents and sister. Finally, she felt very guilty about the suicide of a thirty-four-year-old male intestinal bypass patient whom she had encouraged to undergo the procedure.

But beyond those immediate stressful events, she felt she needed to mourn her death as a fat person and to reconcile herself to a life without excuses. "All those years I could absorb insult and explain being passed over and my plans not working out because I'd say it's because I'm fat. When you're fat, there is nothing that takes place that you don't interpret as kind of out of your hands. After everything, you add, 'But I'm fat.' I mean everything. I feel tricked in a way by life. I'm glad I'm thin. I thank God every day. But after five years, I just can't get over that I'm not fat."

Sue was the older of two sisters in a middle-class Canadian family. Her mother was French Canadian, her father had been born in England. The father's

family were large people and there had been super-
obese women among family members for several
generations. Sue's mother was haunted by the possibility
that Sue would be obese, from the time she was born
with a birth weight of nine pounds, perhaps before.
Sue was in a pitched battle with her mother throughout
adolescence, starting on diet pills when she was twelve
years old. She was very ashamed of herself, miserable
about the anguish she caused her family. She felt helpless in her efforts to stop overeating. Her babysitting
jobs with access to other family refrigerators were her
main sources of excitement and shame. She weighed
165 pounds when she was sixteen, 200 pounds at
eighteen, 250 pounds at twenty.

I told Sue that one best mourns the deceased by
living well and living proudly and I did everything I
could do to encourage her to bring an expanded cast
of characters into her life. I saw her for almost one
year, once a week. I also saw her with her sister and
her parents a dozen times. I was impressed (depressed)
by how hard it was for everyone in the family to sit
back and enjoy the miracle. Perhaps it is understandable. Few humans in history had successfully under-
gone a comparable body change! Her mother feared
for Sue's health and thought putting on a few pounds,
going from 125 to 135, wouldn't hurt. Her father felt
she should marry as soon as possible. Her sister was
very threatened by Sue's modified status in the family
and, in particular, by her feeling that Sue was now
more remote and inaccessible, something that Sue
acknowledged. Before, when she was fat, Sue had done
a good deal of living vicariously through others. The
surgery had made her one of life's full-time contestant-
participants.

I identified strongly with Sue, and was more than a
little in awe of her having survived so much alteration
of her person while preserving so much that was special
about her personality. I'm afraid that in my younger
years as a therapist I'd have been very defensive for
her, perhaps critical of her family. That criticism would

have gone something like, "You seem threatened by your daughter and sister's thinness. Don't you want her to have a life of her own, independent of you?" But that stance would have been wrong, very wrong. Assured that they were not in store for unfair criticism by Sue's psychiatrist, the parents and sister were happy to use part of our times together to talk about matters that were important in their individual lives. Our therapy was not a monotonous fat-thin-fat-thin-fat-thin (sex?) rerun.

Sue had great difficulty in allowing herself to enter fully into her world. She was not a passionless person. But most of her intense involvements had been narrowly focused around food and the danger of insult. Otherwise, she was something of a voyeur, a person watching other people. The need to redirect her considerable capacity for intense caring, acceptance of a life more free of shame and guilt than she had known before, and recognition that her prior experiences had been somewhat restricted and artificial were the matters we talked about a great deal. Sue formulated her life as "delayed" teen years, and that is probably not far off.

What I wanted most for Sue was further experiencing of life, new friends, mistakes, retention of her strengths, and changes for the good between herself and her family. We didn't talk too much about it, but, like her, I looked forward to her white-dress wedding in the family church. She was rather old-fashioned underneath.

A final word about this seeming testimony for surgery. Very, very few people had Sue's good luck. I'm happy about Sue and happy to write about her. I'd hate for my book to raise dangerous hopes for people with superobesity. If such surgery is to take place, it should be done only in major institutions and only after any and every other approach has been tried.[23]

The problems of smokers and people who are overweight are very serious. How much the adult generations will be able to modify existing behavior isn't clear. I feel sure that public education will be one very important factor. Our government is ambivalent about tobacco (and the industry), so the big government-sponsored television campaigns have yet to come. Whatever campaigns there are seem to start and quickly stop. Certainly, while finding such help for ourselves as we can, we need to devote every bit of energy to helping young people avoid the habits that are so desperately hard to unlearn. Perhaps we should give a tax credit to parents whose kids don't smoke.

PART FOUR

NEUROTIC AND PSYCHOTIC PATTERNS OF LIVING

8

Hysterical Living

One of the most fascinating areas for study in medicine, psychology, or the social sciences is that way of living, thinking, and reacting to oneself and one's world which I will refer to as "hysterical living." As early as the 1700s it was noted that some persons when worried or frightened could describe or demonstrate symptoms related to every bodily system and suggestive of almost every disease. The pioneers of modern psychiatry, Kraepelin, Charcot, Freud, and Breuer, were each in turn mystified and challenged by the extraordinary diversity and intensity of symptoms described by patients they diagnosed as "hysterical."[1,2,3]

Freud theorized that the appearance of "hysterical" symptoms in childhood and adult life resulted from unresolved conflicts originating in very early childhood.[4] Specifically, he hypothesized the existence of early childhood "sexual" impulses directed toward the parent of the opposite sex that threatened the equilibrium between the two parents and the child. These are the famed Oedipal and Electra complexes. Optimally, in the Freudian view, the "sexual" impulse directed toward the parent of the opposite sex is worked out in an affectionate parent–child growing-up relationship until it is ultimately redirected and more sharply focused to an appropriate heterosexual partner. At the same time, in a mature family, the rivalry with the parent of the same sex is overshadowed by a basic affection and acceptance. This process also serves to facilitate the child's own sexual orientation and confidence about the integrity of his or her body and the essential friendliness of other people. However, when the maturational process does not go well, the unresolved drives that energized the early childhood phases of development cause the individual to be fearful, troubled by somatic concerns, and lacking self-assurance in personal relations. Much of the process is "unconscious," that is, it is not in the person's awareness that he behaves toward adult friends, mate, and working companions as if they were heir to the unresolved conflicts of the parent–child life. His way of experiencing day-to-day events is fixed in a context of parent–child, strong–weak, and the dangers of dependency on "unreliable people."

Over the years, there have been many different kinds of people grouped together under this diagnostic catchall of "hysteria," and many efforts have been made to better classify what is wrong and more accurately predict therapeutic outcome.[5] For some twenty years, clinicians have used as diagnoses the categories of "hysteria," "hysterical personality," "phobias," and "conversion." In the new psychiatric diagnostic system, DSM-III, disorders that suggest physical illness but are basically psychological conflicts, formerly called "conversion," are called somatoform disorders. These will be contrasted with "factitious disorders" (those that seem troubling to the patient yet are very contrived) and "malingering," the deliberate effort to deceive. There also will be new diagnostic divisions of the category of "phobias." Some have been discovered to respond rather well to medication; others do not.[6] "Hysterical personality disorder" as a diagnosis will be supplanted by "histrionic personality disorder." Hopefully, these new diagnostic divisions will be of some help in selecting appropriate therapies for people who suffer the thousand and more symptoms that have been grouped together under the general heading of "hysteria." I suspect there will be still other diagnostic systems that will emerge in future years.

Symptoms run the gamut from total bodily paralysis and complete loss of sensation to an uncounted number of unexplained physical complaints and/or psychological uncertainties and to dependency resulting at times in lifelong invalidism. Other symptoms have included abnormal movements such as tremors (shaking) of the head, arms, and legs; a variety of tics and jerks; convulsive movements of the entire body; disturbances of gait; paralysis of the extremities suggestive of strokes; and paralysis of the muscles affecting the vocal cords, which leads to an inability to speak. Such a list would also include disturbances in the ability to feel, including loss of sensation in one part of the body or in the entire body; disorders of the organs of sense including hearing, vision, and swallowing; and pains of all varieties and in all locations including, not infrequently, pains of such magnitude and persistence that they lead to surgical intervention. And what is sometimes called "hysterical overlay" can produce a substantial exaggeration of symptoms of any and every organic illness. In short, the physical symptoms that may be experienced in hysterical living are many and varied, either reasonable facsimiles or grotesque caricatures of symptoms ordinarily referable to organic disease.

No less complex are the dependency, tears, anger, childish temper, fainting, periods of confusion, sexual difficulties, and fears that are beyond all reason (phobias) that are also frequently a part of this condition.

Who is this individual who may come to the doctor with any of the hundred symptoms listed above? Why would anyone view himself as so fragile and vulnerable? Is it possible to understand this fearful approach to life? Hysterical living patterns in contemporary Western culture are more characteristic of women than men. This is because social roles based on dependency status have been regularly assigned to women, and the rearing of girls pointed the way to such assignments. The term "hysteria" is derived from the Greek word *hystera*— meaning "uterus"—and reflected the belief that uterine displacement or malfunction was involved in the symptoms and life-style of unhappy or physically ill women.

OBSERVATIONS ON
HYSTERICAL LIVING

Every person is, from time to time, given to a view of self or of self in relation to others which is characteristic of hysterical living. It may follow a sudden telephone call from one's boss with the crisp message, "I want to see you immediately." Or it may be when a woman is about to break her engagement and reveal that there is someone else she prefers. Or it may follow a call from a banker or from a bill collector or an unexpected message from the children's pediatrician. The sudden awareness of personal impotence or danger, the acute sense of being junior to another person, and the overwhelming inclination to dependency are characteristic of the way life has been discovered to be in hysterical living. To defend oneself against the ever-present danger of anxiety, the individual may try to establish some kind of symbiotic allegiance with a stronger person or group of individuals. For example, a woman may behave as if she believes that "so long as Mr. lover stands beside me, immortal giant that he is, I am safe." Most of her life's problems recede or disappear when she is "tied in" with him. In turning herself over to him she must learn to suppress her own feelings about many things. This is compensated for, however, by the fact that she is not afraid while he is there. In the most intense and pathological form, her surrender of herself and her total trust in the other person's solutions represent a great personal delusion about the nature of the world. Hysterical living cuts her off from important aspects of her own life. She tries to feel and say and do those things that she hopes will win his approval. She seeks a kind of safe, neutral ground, always watching him rather attentively for clues as to how he feels and, in particular, how he feels about her. It is not only that she is dependent upon him; rather, she structures her very existence in order to remain with him. She has a well-developed radar system to learn what he is thinking and feeling almost before he knows himself. She remains constantly on the alert. She is always "running scared" and in stressful periods may resemble a new member of a dance team, unfamiliar with the routine, hoping to bluff along by watching carefully what the other members of the troupe are doing. This dependency and turning to another makes her like Blanche, who in the final scene of Tennessee Williams's *A Streetcar Named Desire* places herself and her destiny in the "hands of the gentleman."[7] (In that instance, as in most, the trust was misplaced. The gentleman was taking her away to a mental asylum.)

The same penalties exist for the man who establishes himself symbiotically and in denial of his own strengths in a relationship with spouse, parent, or employer. Not only are such relationships costly, they are inherently unstable. In real life, the attempt to achieve a sustaining dependent relationship leads not only to loss of genuineness and surrender of personal destiny but also to disappointment, humiliation, and betrayal. There is a fraudulence inherent in any person who claims that his destiny is in another's hands. It requires a great deal of pretending on everybody's part. Her destiny is uncertain, but no more so than his. She is essentially as rich as he in terms of the potential for experiencing her life. If they are the same age, she is likely to outlive him! The hysterical living adaptation is her way of hiding or losing herself by using him to obscure her unwillingness to be responsible for her own life. His acceptance of that role accomplishes the same self-deceit in his life. Sooner or later, the pretending gives way. He may desert her despite years and years of promising, in essence, "Trust me. You need not concern yourself with responsibility for your life since I am here and I will always be here to care for you. I am immortal." The facts of life will make him fail to fulfill this commitment. He may die and in that way desert her. Or he may tire of the awesome burden of her trust and betray her or abuse her in such a fashion that she simply cannot pretend that he is taking care of her. She may find herself caught between two strong men (or, occasionally, between a strong man and an equally strong mother) and be in great conflict as to where to entrust her own destiny. In this moment, when hysterical living no longer works and she experiences her shield falling away, she may be flooded with anxiety. Or, following a brief interval of anxiety she may feel absolutely helpless and demonstrate her sense of inadequacy through the emergence of one or another of a thousand complaints about her body.

Even when her relationship with him remains more or less intact, there is inevitable dissatisfaction because of the limitations imposed by the role-playing in her life. At such moments, she may turn to the person who is to provide solutions to her problems and angrily declare that the world (for which he is responsible) is not perfect. Garbage is not collected. Mice abound. Bodily parts ache. Yet he seems powerless. She experiences a kind of smoldering resentment, pouts, complains, and accuses him of failing in his promises. Then he may come to resent her demands, and the time comes for him to opt out of the impossible contract. The game of "let's pretend" no longer meets his needs.

In gross form, hysterical living represents a great loss of human potential. Its basic pretense that "he or she is immortal," "I am more fragile than others," "he or she can stand between life's problems and me," gives way and reveals an overwhelming sense of being a child in an adult world and of living within a body one cannot trust. She must then move frantically in a chaotic search for how she feels, who she is, and where she is going.

As I noted previously, in Western culture symptoms associated with hysterical living have appeared more frequently in girls and women. However, the essential attitudes toward life and developmental circumstances that predispose to such symptomatology can exist for a man as well.

Case Study 1: *A Man with Chest Pain and Two Women*

Arthur Reynolds, a thirty-three-year-old unmarried schoolteacher, was seen in psychiatric consultation in April 1973 because of mounting anxiety about his heart. He had been repeatedly examined and had several normal electrocardiograms in the preceding six months. But he was not reassured. His internist decided to refer him to a psychiatrist. The interview revealed a friendly, somewhat passive man who was very anxious as he offered details about chest pains and other bodily sensations he was experiencing.

He had been teaching in the same school system for eight years, seemed to be an appreciated teacher, and appeared to have a good attitude with regard both to the importance of his work and to his ability to perform adequately. His initial response to questions about his social life was that "everything is okay." Closer questioning, however, revealed the following information: His father had died some seven years earlier and he had moved into the mother's home, where he was living at the time of the interview. His father's death had followed a series of heart attacks that continued over a number of years. The mother was in generally good health but did suffer from "spells" at times of great pressure. During these periods she would withdraw to her bed for several days and her son assumed minor nursing duties as well as the tasks of straightening up the house, cooking, and preparing a good deal of tea.

There was another woman in his life. For two and a half years he had been dating a woman six years younger than himself. She was also a teacher. He felt that he loved her but was cautious about marriage. He had found it necessary to return to his mother's home each night, preferably before midnight, even though his relationship with the other teacher was an intimate one. Understandably, there was little love lost between the two women despite the patient's strenuous efforts to maintain a peaceful status quo. A showdown loomed. Christmas was coming and his friend was anticipating an engagement ring while his mother was making holiday plans for her son to drive her 800 miles to the south so that they could visit her old friends.

Throughout his life, Arthur Reynolds had been a shy and uncertain person, the only boy in a family with three older sisters. He had been particularly close to his mother because his father had worked as a railroad conductor and was away from the family a good deal of the time. After graduation from a state teacher's college he had lived in another part of the country, but his father's illness and his mother's wish that her son return proved too strong for him to resist.

The patient was seen for eight hours of psychotherapy. His mother was present for two hours and his friend (who considered herself his fiancée) was also present with him for two hours. I had proposed a session with both women present but the patient had asked to postpone such a meeting.

Both women seemed to have a similar effect on Arthur Reynolds. In their presence (in the consultation room at least) he was quiet, appeasing, and inhibited. He appeared fearful of being asked a direct question and was very defensive when it was his turn to speak. He was frightened of provoking either of them. He was trapped between two strong women, both of whom had the capacity to make him feel anxious and guilty.

I tried to be carefuly not to become a third strong person in the life of Arthur Reynolds. Instead, I encouraged this very intelligent man to look at his obligations to other people and to try to understand the reason for his fear of provoking an angry response from anyone. At times the focus was upon the psychological problems; at times the patient talked of his physical complaints. On occasion, the areas coincided:

PATIENT: "I've worried about mother's health for years. She's getting up there, you know."
THERAPIST: "She looks pretty robust to me. I figure she might outlive all of us."
PATIENT: "Well, fifty-seven is up there. And if anything happens to her, I'd never forgive myself."
THERAPIST: "Pretty well preserved for fifty-seven. Looks pretty good. Maybe if you'd get off her back, she could get married again."

PATIENT: (Pauses) "My God! I just had that pain again in my chest."
THERAPIST: "That would really be cool. A double wedding. You could give each other away."
PATIENT: "Then you think my pains are. . . ."
THERAPIST: "I'm rooting for growing pains."

There was something not true to life about it all, and in our sixth hour, when we were by ourselves, I told that to Arthur Reynolds. "You know, Arthur, there's something crazy about all this. You handle five classes of twenty-five kids, that's 200 extra parents in your life. Why would one be such a problem. And what's more, you just seem more competent to me than the way you come on. Is there something missing?" Arthur said that there was something he wanted to talk over with me. It had to do with homosexuality. He didn't think he was primarily homosexual but he'd had a series of experiences in that interval immediately before his father's death and the move back to live with his mother. He felt that one of the reasons he had returned home was to end decisively that part of his life. But even now, sometimes, he would meet a man who was attractive to him and that made him very uncomfortable. He went on to give me a percentage estimate of his sexual tendencies. He said, "I think I'm 80 percent heterosexually inclined, 20 percent homosexually inclined." I asked whether he had wanted to share any of his concern about himself with his fiancée. He said he had come close on many occasions to telling her but was sure it would be very painful. He said he was afraid he would lose her. But he told her that night and nothing happened. He was touched and grateful. She told him she thought 90 percent.

One pattern of hysterical living, "the grand hysteria," has always called forth much interest. It was more commonly encountered several generations ago. It is a condition that arises as if by magic or in response to the thunderous wrath of the gods: "And she was stricken with blindness"; "And suddenly, all the power left his legs and he could not move them"; "And as the train on which he was riding disappeared in the distance, she fell into a faint. When she revived, all memory of who she was had disappeared." Several of the patients with whom Sigmund Freud initially worked and who served as the sources for his original theories presented these colorful symptom patterns.

Bearing in mind that the hysterical symptom is most likely to appear and persist in an individual whose life experiences and sense of self are congruent with hysterical living, the following case of "hysterical aphonia" (loss of voice), though less often seen in the contemporary Western world than was the case thirty years ago, may be illustrative of the kind of environment that allows or encourages the denial of self in a "grand hysteria."

Case Study 2: *A Disease that Magic Alone Could Cure*

Barbara Williams, aged sixteen, was admitted to the hospital on November 9, 1973, because of a loss of voice that had persisted for two and a half months. All medical examinations of her throat were negative. A variety of therapeutic efforts had failed to restore her ability to speak above a whisper. She presented the picture of a calm and unconcerned, somewhat immature sixteen-year-old girl. She whispered answers to all questions but demonstrated little concern over her difficulty. She resembled closely the classical picture of "la belle indifférence" described one hundred years ago by Pierre Janet as characteristic of patients with "grand hysteria."

The patient's difficulties had begun at a high school dance when her eighteen-year-old boy friend pulled and broke a necklace that she was wearing. She complained that he had hurt her neck at the time and gradually, over a period of three days, developed an "aphonia" of sorts, characterized by whispering and moving her lips without making sounds. In the succeeding weeks, she received a great deal of attention from her family, teachers, and classmates. The doctors were initially puzzled, then increasingly frustrated as the symptom resisted all treatments.

Although the patient and her family were products of a lower-class background, she was taken to the hospital in a chauffeur-driven limousine owned by a well-known Mr. Green, the seventy-eight-year-old retired industrialist on whose estate the Williams family lived. The patient's father worked as a custodian. At the time of admission to the hospital, Barbara's mother proudly explained that Mr. Green was underwriting Barbara's expenses. The Williams family—mother, father, and six children—had come north from Texas as migrant workers eight years earlier. The family had been more or less adopted en masse by Mr. Green in the aftermath of a workers' strike against Mr. Green during which Barbara's father had sided with the old man and against the other workers. As a result, the Williams family was moved into a custodian's house on the Green estate, and the old industrialist, turned philanthropist to this family, assumed a kind of distant parental interest in them. Although actual contacts between the family and Mr. Green were formal and infrequent, the relationship was of overpowering significance within the family. The mother talked continuously about his occasional visits and what he had said to each child. Her chief technique in disciplining the children was to threaten to notify Mr. Green of their misbehavior, so that he would withdraw their Christmas privileges and other favors. The family was committed to the idea that "so long as he lives, we are safe."

Barbara was, recognizably, a child who had emerged from a family with this kind of perspective. She viewed herself as a child in a world where "things happen to you." She shared unquestioningly the family's superstitious commitment to a fundamentalist faith; the notion of the hand from above reaching down was quite plausible to her. Her view of the world was one that seemed to say, "Of course, when your throat gets hit, you can't talk."

As a patient, Barbara repudiated the possibility of a psychotherapeutic encounter based on any idea of parity among the participants. The initial intention of the psychiatric staff was to avoid dealing with Barbara in a manner suggesting that "big and powerful people were acting on little, passive, and helpless people." That effort was not successful, however. In the end, after six weeks of hospitalization, to the disappointment of the staff but well within the frame of reference of Barbara and her family, Barbara was induced to speak through the use of an intravenous chemical, sodium amytal, a kind of "truth serum." The following day, in the presence of her family, again with sodium amytal, she was induced to sing a Christmas carol (it was that time of year). That afternoon, talking cheerfully, Barbara returned triumphantly home in Mr. Green's chauffeured limousine, prepared to join her mother in telling to all who would hear the tales of the miracles wrought by Mr. Green and his hirelings.

Some individuals present their complaints in a vivid and colorful fashion, demonstrate a broad range of emotions, and with great conviction demand immediate attention by presenting all symptoms as if they were desperate indeed. Posturing of this kind tends to make the clinician excessively reassuring, more willing to prescribe medications, freer with gratuitous advice, and so forth. But when this happens, the clinician has assumed a role facilitating the patient's dependency. This is a mistake, as may be surmised in the following case study.

Case Study 3: *A Woman, Abandoned, Goes in Search of a Doctor*

The patient, a twenty-one-year-old woman, a former student at the university, sought treatment because of very profound anxiety, a fear of being alone, and specific concern that she might harm herself. Her symptoms developed after she had been abandoned by a rather dominating fiancé, upon whom she had been quite dependent for two years. Symbolic of their relationship was the fact that she had given up her own schooling in order to live with him, had allowed her driver's license to lapse because he was critical of her driving skill, and had taken on his political activism although she had little personal interest in such matters. In general, she overlooked his domination and abuse because, in her words, "I wasn't afraid of anything when I was with Jack." However, her fiancé abandoned her in favor of another girl and suddenly she was thrown back upon herself. She was filled with a variety of self-deprecating thoughts and somber fears. Old doubts about herself that had been out of her mind for some years returned to torment her. She was easily startled, cried with little provocation, slept poorly, was fearful of a nighttime intruder, and, puzzlingly, for the first time since early childhood was afraid at night that a mouse or a rat would enter her room. At the same time she was fearful of herself—fearful that she might harm herself or that in some crisis situation she would be paralyzed by fear and unable to seek safety.

She appealed to the doctor for immediate help, medicine, and reassurance. But the doctor pressed on and asked for more details about her feelings about the change in her life. He learned that she had, to her surprise, experienced some good moments in recent days, moments in which she realized that her fiancé had treated her shabbily. She reported that there was a part of her that was glad he was gone. She spoke of having felt dominated by him and wondered whether she might in the future have a greater chance at self-expression. She recalled her parents' disapproval of their relationship and the general disdain with which her fiancé's dominating behavior had been regarded by all of her friends. She tearfully asked herself why she involved herself with him in the first place, asked why she was "so weak and willing to be taken over."

Then, in almost the same breath, she said to the doctor, "I'll do anything you tell me. I'll take anything you'll give me. Perhaps you will want to put me in the hospital. You have got to do something."

The doctor viewed her symptoms and the pull they exerted upon him with very mixed feelings. He could reassure her, could offer medicines that would likely reduce the level of her anxiety, or could hospitalize her, thereby guaranteeing that there would be no mice and that she would not be alone. At the same time, he did not want to reinforce the patient's tendency to escape from herself by pretending that "so long as he lives, I need not concern myself about the meaning of my being."

In making the decision as to how to respond to the requests of his patient, the doctor tried to sort out in his own mind what he hoped would result from this stressful and unhappy time in her life. Freedom from anxiety was certainly an important goal, but she had been relatively free of fears while she was with her fiancé. Yet freedom from anxiety on the same basis—substituting a doctor for the missing fiancé—was not a sound approach. Therapy would have to go a different way.

In the subsequent months of working with this patient (outside of a hospital), the doctor often felt that she wanted him to assume total responsibility for her. Her message, disguised or otherwise, was, "You take care of me! You are bigger than I am!" She repeatedly presented to the doctor a series of complaints that added up to: "There's something wrong with my body. Do something!" Or, perhaps more fundamentally, she stated, "I've never really trusted my body. It's never been quite right. It requires attention and lots of it." In a way, the doctor's greatest contribution to this patient, by word and by act, by attitude and by manner, was to respond with the following message: "I trust your body. So can you. It's really okay. As a matter of fact, the same goes for the rest of you. You could really trust yourself if you'd give yourself a chance. I'm very curious how you will choose to live your life."

I am usually careful to avoid offering advice about personal matters that people might feel obliged to accept. But sometimes, I forget I'm a psychiatrist and become a man with an opinion.

Case Study 4: *Please, Doctor, See Me This Once*

John was 6 feet, 2 inches and weighed 220 pounds, but he felt as if he were the runt of the litter. He was thirty-six years old. He came from a California family well known because of the business achievements of his father and older brother. He was the manager of the smaller of two family-owned hardware stores. His father had died several years earlier and he lived with his mother in the home in which he had grown up. His brother was married and had children but John had never married. He consulted me because he had recently failed, as he had always failed, when he tried to make love with a woman. He was painfully shy, had been haunted from childhood with the feeling that he was a weak person. That feeling was increased on the four or five occasions when he had attempted to make love with a woman friend and had been unsuccessful. He felt desire, could experience an erection, but then it would go and he was left with a sense of shame and defeat. He said he had no homosexual interests. He masturbated regularly. He was ashamed of that.

He was overwhelmingly intimidated by his mother and brother, both of whom seemed to be judgmental and critical. His mother told him frequently that she was embarrassed that he had not married. His most painful memory was the day of his father's death, when his mother asked him if he was all right sexually.

I told him that I'd be glad to work with him on condition that his family share in some of our initial sessions. He was both tempted and frightened by my request. He did ask his brother and mother to come to the second appointment. They were infuriated and told John that his seeing a psychiatrist was dirt on the family name and they wouldn't have it. There was no further appointment at the time. John called me apologetically to say he had decided to wait awhile before he had treatment.

Almost two years later, John called me to ask that I see him that day. He said he was very desperate. I believed him and changed my schedule to make time for a meeting. He arrived with a woman he had known for several years. Her name was Martha. They had spent two days together in a motel (his mother was away but he was afraid to go to his home with his friend). He had been unsuccessful in his attempts to make physical love. Martha had felt as defeated as he. She was an administrative assistant at a college in another state and due to report back to her job the next morning. She was to leave on a late evening plane. John was very upset, was crying, and wanted me to explain to her that it was not her fault. She was baffled, very uncomfortable, and said that John was the nicest man she had ever known. She had never married. Like John, she was very involved with her parents. She was, like he, thirty-eight years old.

I listened to their conversation and commented out loud that they seemed to like each other. She repeated that John was the nicest man she'd ever known and that she would write to him and perhaps sometime they might see each other again. I asked John if he'd thought of asking her to stay. He said he had. I asked him why he hadn't done it. He turned to her and asked her to stay. Martha was very surprised. She said she wasn't sure the college would give her a leave. Then she said she'd stay if he really wanted her to stay. He said he did. And he meant it.

They asked if they could come back to talk with me. I told them they didn't need me.

He was cured that night.*

* I should add the kind of sexual problem that John suffered, that is, no lack of desire and no impairment in arousal but inability to sustain erection, is very often successfully treated by the programs pioneered by Masters and Johnson.[8] Less success is achieved with patients who have sexual interest but do not experience physical arousal. Relatively little success is achieved in work with individuals who have problems in the desire phase of sexuality. A very fine review of the remarkable development of the field of sexual therapy has been written by Dr. Helen Kaplan. It is called *The New Sex Therapy: Active Treatment of Sexual Dysfunction.*[9]

9

Obsessive and Compulsive Living

A diagnosis of an emotional disorder can never be more than an approximating generalization that designates past ways of experiencing and behaving. And since life allows at least the possibility of feeling or behaving differently in the next moment, a certain or total description of any living being by a diagnosis is impossible. Only with death and the loss of possibilities can a diagnosis be in any measure complete. No person is ever simply "a hysteric," "a compulsive," or "a schizophrenic." Nor can anyone predict with certainty that the mannerisms, attitudes, and ways of behaving previously characteristic of a person will be descriptive of him in the minutes, hours, days, or weeks ahead. The cowardly man may come to live the life of a hero; the suspicious person may become trusting and relaxed; the girl who lived dependently and seemed so much a child may one day demonstrate conclusively that she is indeed a woman in the fullest sense. Unpredictability is an inevitable characteristic of human beings. It's one of the best parts.

However, there is a kind of person who experiences the uncertainties of human life as bothersome and as a source of sustaining discomfort. As a result, he often structures his life as if to deny as much as he can of such uncertainty. He seems to have a *modus vivendi*, a motto for his life, that says, "So long as I keep in scrupulous order all of the people, all of the circumstances, and all of the personal feelings that are important in my life, I will be happy and safe." He or she cautiously and carefully maintains a continual perusal of the carefully ordered and often narrow set of potentialities in life that have been staked out as important. He is not a person who is open to the full experience of life. Instead, the range of his meaningful personal engagement is sharply restricted. If the world of feelings, ideas, possibilities, and relationships is a full field up to 360 degrees, this person may limit his range of concern to an area that is simply "that which is ahead." Certain activities are lifted out and placed above, assigned primary significance, and faithfully attended to. These possibilities may include earning approval, recruiting money or goods, maintaining a clean house, achieving a perfect record in something, living precisely as "they" would have one live, keeping perfect records, and such. Other matters are assigned a subsidiary place in his life.

He may be a person who comes to a sixty-page newspaper day after day and, ignoring all else, turns to the page listing stocks on the New York Stock Exchange. On that page, of the thousand items listed, he concerns himself with two or three. These he studies, restudies, orders, tends to, and then reorders again. In his life all other matters are subsidiary. Indeed, he may be remarkably free of the ordinary anxieties that beset other men because he is unmoved by forces and events outside the narrow area of his concern: Money is life, money alone.

Or, she may be a wife and mother, living in a home with agile, growing, changing children, who savors little of her day-to-day living because there is no time left after scrupulously attending to the tasks of tidying, cooking, counting, washing, saving, disciplining, and worrying. Her life may be completely filled with the urgency of "things to do," responsibilities that are the first priority, deeds that must be performed. A departure from the regularity of her schedule makes her feel guilty and apprehensive. She is living the kind of life of which

Sartre wrote, "She makes herself such that she is waited for by all the tasks placed along her way. Objects are mute demands and she is nothing in herself but the passive obedience to these demands."[1]

Or, he may be a serious, essentially friendless person of high school age who postpones having fun because of the urgency of doing well in high school in order to earn good grades, which would allow him to gain entrance to a fine college. There, still postponing, he will earn good grades, which will allow him entrance into a good graduate school. Once in graduate school, rigorous discipline, commitment, and further postponing will allow him to establish a good record so that he may....

Obviously, it is not a simple matter to sustain this kind of narrow world view. Other matters keep pressing in. Keeping one's attention locked in on a designated area of life and putting aside everything else requires much effort. Threat to order must be put down. The irrelevant must be fitted in or extruded. The suppression of "irrelevant" experience may require denial, compromise, pretense, isolation, detachment, repression, turning away from or, finally, cutting down even more sharply the total area of life to which one is attentive. He says, over and over again: "There really is no problem, no basis for uncertainty. There will be no danger unless one loses one's head. The secret is to stick to business, keep in order what is important." Thus, openness to the new, the unexpected, the unpredictable, or recognition of the fact that potentials diminish and time slips away are all matters somehow overlooked, obscured from view, or discounted. He tends his small garden, almost never leaving it. Occasionally, he must narrow its dimensions in the face of insistent pressure from the outside or in the face of his own diminishing physical strength. Death, a matter that makes all planning irrelevant, must be dealt with in a way that denies its reality.

Case Study 1: *The Physician Who Planned Everything*

A thirty-nine-year-old married physician who worked on a geriatrics ward in a large university hospital was extraordinarily attentive to his work, meticulously organizing a myriad of small details related to the management of his patients. He had prepared a daily "checklist" with forty items for each patient, and the nursing staff were asked to submit a list to him for each patient each day. He was, without question, remarkably dedicated to his ward and to his patients. The doctor who had preceded him was by no means as committed to the work. And the same was true of the doctor who preceded his predecessor.

In this aging population, there were many who were mortally ill. The doctor was constantly in attendance, grimly battling to postpone, to head off, death. The oldest, most incapacitated, most hopelessly ill of his patients received every possible medical assistance. When necessary, he introduced heroic efforts to win or prolong the battle with death. Yet, surprisingly, he was never known to lose his composure when the battle to sustain life was lost. Instead, he would retreat at once to his office, the patient's chart in his hand. Once there, he would unlock a file drawer, extract a large group of cards, and begin to make out a new card, one containing a compilation of all facts and figures about the patient who had just died. He would comment about this activity, "You see, in a way, he is not really gone. I have him here."

For the obsessive person, the need for structure, predictability, and stability is very great. The journey through life is not a casual wandering. It is not a free-form dance. It is instead a series of planned, strategic, and logical steps. Vagueness is poorly tolerated. Human events are judged in terms of their potential for disruption of the previously structured plans. The spontaneous nature of emotions makes them a potentially disruptive force, and so they must be discounted, underplayed, or even "disowned."

In a discussion about a young couple who had terminated their engagement on the afternoon of December 31, the doctor in the previous example stated, "I can't understand why they didn't wait until after New Year's Eve."

The need this kind of person feels to establish consensus, order, and certainty in his own life often governs his expectations of relationships with friends, mate, and children. And, from time to time, he or she may be deserted by the spouse, who is always a little bewildered as to why it is necessary to flee. The wife of the doctor was one such person.

> Of course, materially, we do have most everything I want. And he's not mean to me. He does remember our anniversary, birthdays, and the like. But living with him is like living by the numbers. It's a long, dark, monotonous cave. It's no fun. Nothing is spontaneous. There are no surprises. It's like living trapped in ten feet of space. Walk three steps one way and the wall is there, three steps the other way and there is another wall. I have to get out.

Her husband expressed great puzzlement as to what was troubling his wife.

> I guess I have a lot of trouble letting go. I like to be sure, I try to think it out, sometimes write the pros on one side and the cons on the other. You wouldn't want to make a mistake if you could avoid it. Not that one mistake would be so bad, of course. Everyone makes a mistake sometime, but if you just go on making mistakes, then sooner or later you're going to get into trouble. But I started to talk about how hard it is sometimes for me to let go. My wife went out last week and bought a toaster and I was very upset with her. She just went out and bought it. I like to, well, to begin with, make sure that we need it. And then, I try to figure out the money for it. We do have a good income since both of us work. So it's not exactly that we need the money. But I like to know that if we are going to spend money for a toaster that we'll get it back and save it by not spending for something else. Then, I like to be sure that we get it for the right price. I usually call one or two stores and look in the newspapers to see if there

is a sale. Sometimes I look in the want ads of the newspaper under used items. Of course, we've never bought anything like that that's used, but just to be sure. Then, I'll go over to the library and look up what the consumer magazine recommends. And, I guess, if I feel we have bought the right machine, and at the right place, I feel, "A job well done. It's as it should be."

It remains a speculative matter to attempt to correlate early life experience with the development of overriding obsessive and compulsive approaches to later living. Many of these individuals in early childhood were taught that life itself is a long series of instructions as to "how things should be," what is good and what is bad, proper and improper, safe and unsafe. Instead of being encouraged to trust his own instincts and impulses, the child learns to seek comfort in ritualized behavior. Symmetry, counting, ordering, and categorizing come to be the ordinary ways of reacting in the face of stress, vagueness, or doubt. These kinds of responses are usually reinforced positively by "good grades." In school, the obsessively organized child may do quite well. But, of course, the child who is devoted to learning and participating flawlessly in adult-created behavior is somewhat less the child and is instead a small replica of an adult. And many obsessive adults have difficulty recalling much difference between their spirit and frame of mind as children and that which characterizes them as adults. They never really had much of a childhood. There is a kind of sadness in hearing such an adult describe his efforts to understand spontaneous behavior in his or her own children.

Those with obsessive living patterns tend to resist change, and their patterns tend to be rather durable. They often persist through an entire lifetime without disruption. However, this is not always the case. Certain circumstances seem to promote a breaking down of obsessive living with a resulting anxiety that may be very intense. The very individual who had lived his life as if he were being graded each hour on a Sunday school behavior checklist becomes pervasively preoccupied with fears about obscene, aggressive, or shameful deeds (obsessions). As if to divert himself, the individual may undertake some ritualized (compulsive) act such as hand washing, counting, or listing which becomes his total preoccupation. The greater the sense of threat, the more frantic are the efforts to reestablish order, perhaps by cutting down even more sharply on the dimensions of his or her life. Under stress he may ultimately retreat to a preoccupation with the thinnest conceivable aspects of human experience. The possibility of having done something wrong or incorrectly is constantly reviewed, relived, weighed, pondered. All other considerations recede in importance. Concern may center on some past sin, real or imagined, some past oversight, or he or she may be totally preoccupied with keeping clean. In the most severe instance, life's concerns may be reduced to the space between hospital bed and wash basin; life becomes only a ritualized treading back and forth. In this desperate way, the obsessive person continues the struggle to sustain some order so that life may be lived out. The events that seem to precipitate this kind of "decompensation" hint at the dangerous elements which had always resided immediately outside the narrow areas of concern that had previously been the "life" of the obsessive person. The characteristics of this outer world, the weeds from next door, which, with decompensation, overrun the well-tended garden, are dirt, shame, disease, disapproval, chaos, hate, failure, and finally "my own death." With the collapse of the long-standing, defensive way of living, all of these matters confront and terrify the person who for so long had evaded them.

In a general way, three kinds of circumstances appear to lay the groundwork for a breaking down of an obsessive and compulsive pattern of living. They are: the occurrence of an overwhelming life event such as desertion or death of a spouse or severe illness or death of a child; promotion to a position at work too complex to manage with a tight, obsessive plan; physical illness or forced retirement.

Occasions do arise when even the most strenuous efforts at denial cannot remove pervasive anger, resentment, disappointment, or fear. Grievous personal insult, terrible troubles with children, the threat of divorce, death of a family member, dislocation from a position of honor, any of the overwhelming circumstances that life can allow call for the expression of profound emotion. Yet there is no place in the life of the obsessive individual for direct expression of such emotion. In this kind of circumstance, the individual may flee from his despair (resentment, fear). At the same time, he is fleeing from himself.

One of the events that may produce a breaking down or decompensation of a previously stable obsessive pattern is, paradoxically, a promotion to a more responsible position. Because ordering, maintaining stability, tidiness, careful attention to paperwork, and good office management are, in a general way, business virtues, a person who has performed every act methodically is often promoted. Success in maintaining rigid schedules, precise timetables, and the like sees the obsessive individual promoted to an executive position calling for flexibility, the ability to tolerate uncertainty, skill in interpersonal relationships, and, above all, the capacity to sort out the important from the trivial. A promotion from secretary-treasurer to president of the company, from teacher of introductory science to school principal, from physician on the ward to superintendent of the hospital are all cases in point.

Another cause of decompensation in obsessive and compulsive living patterns is failing physical health or forced retirement from duty. The person who avoids anxiety by keeping busy, keeping organized, working hard, and keeping up a schedule faces an impossible problem as he or she grows older. Physical illness, in particular, poses an extreme threat to psychological equilibrium. The individual who feels that "what I am is what I do," on being deprived of the ability to do, may experience a severe sense of depression and worthlessness. This is what happens to the woman whose whole life is devoted to husband and children and to "doing" for them, only to have this role taken from her by death or divorce from the husband and the departure of the maturing children. The man or woman whose "whole life" has been his or her working career faces a similar threat when age, company reorganization, or failing health necessitate retirement. When this happens, depression, self-deprecation, and anxiety occur along with an increasingly frantic preoccupation with obsessive or compulsive acts.

The way in which therapists attempt to help individuals who have grown dissatisfied with all that doesn't happen in their lives or who are suffering anxiety because their defenses are coming apart will be considered in more detail in a subsequent chapter. However, some general observations are appropriate at this time.

First of all, no theory can be allowed to stand in the way of offering relief to someone in pain. And since no theory is assuredly correct when it comes to a given individual, a clinician needs to listen very carefully to what a patient and the patient's family have to say both at the start of therapy and as the treatment continues. Sometimes, from the underlying life-style, you can predict the direction and nature of decompensation. Often that is not the case. The obsessive person under great stress may become more tightly restricted and stubborn. He may develop a depression that can be of great severity. On occasion, decompensation may be in the form of a paranoid and/or schizophrenic episode. Alcohol and sometimes drugs may become the unstable source of relief for the obsessive man or woman whose usual control-oriented approach to life isn't working. So there can be no blanket prescription for the appropriate therapeutic response to a decompensating obsessive patient.

When severe anxiety and/or depression are prominent features, there is every reason in the world to try to offer relief with medication. Depression is a common occurrence in individuals under stress who have unbending and rigid personality structures, and I have often used anti-depression medications with considerable success in such patients. Sometimes, other types of medications are more useful. Very often, you have to initiate a drug trial to find out. It is also helpful to explore with your patient activities he can undertake in times when he experiences intense need for compulsive activity. I've known many individuals who made great use of relaxation procedures, learning to relax sequentially one after another of their muscle groups and simultaneously fixing their thoughts on a friendly and happy memory. Simply, it is difficult to be tense if one's body is relaxed. Relaxation exercises rarely suffice to fully solve severe anxiety and depression, but they are tools that the patient can use when he feels particularly tense and anxious. Learning to relax as an alternative to anxious action can also be very useful later on. Some people have found meditation rituals such as transcendental meditation helpful in controlling anxiety and agitation. For others, prayer is a source of strength and encouragement. I've known couples who have developed an agreement that when he or she felt overwhelmed, the two of them would take a twenty-minute break (sometimes, if needed, by phone) to establish a pattern of respite. If all this sounds amateurish, it's not. In working with any patient and family on any problem, one of the clinician's major tasks is to help people find ways to overcome their discomfort.

At the same time, I almost always try to work psychotherapeutically to encourage the patient to look for new ways to make the most of his opportunities. In many instances, however, the basic obsessive defenses are more easily described than effectively changed by known treatment methods. The lack of spontaneity, the patient's inability to express his own feelings, and his continual search for instructions as to "exactly what am I supposed to do now" are very discouraging. The tendency of the obsessive patient to create strict routines and remove spontaneity in life applies to therapy as well. He attempts at all costs and at all times to eliminate vagueness, urging the therapist to outline areas that should be carefully explored, turning to other resource persons, reading articles in periodicals or in texts in order to discover what he should take up with his doctor. The possibility that useful discovery could come spontaneously in the relationship is ignored. Instead, he hopes the therapy will represent a safe and planned journey up a familiar, well-marked road. But that is precisely his problem!

The therapist, exasperated, tired of tugging at his patient in the attempt to divert him from ritualistic, relentlessly narrowing efforts, says, "Your estrangement from real human emotions and your refusal to look at your life deceives only you.

Your blind search to find meaningless rules alters nothing. Your making of lists is absurd. You are mortal like the rest of us and while you are counting, your life recedes and disappears." There are times when the patient will reply, "Can't you see by the feverishness with which I work, by how much I surrender, by the heavy demands that I place upon myself that I know all of the things that you say about me even better than you?"

10

Depressive Living, Mania, and Suicide

What is it like to be severely depressed? The average person's memory of transient moments of being "blue," disappointed, or unhappy is a misleading guide in answering this question. Mild or even moderate depression occurring as a now-and-again episode in the life of almost every person is many levels removed from the experience of severe mental depression. The average reader would need to recall the period of greatest unhappiness and hopelessness in life, multiply its intensity by some factor of ten, stretch the interval of despair over time, not simply hours or days, but weeks, months, even years. Then, compound such experience by a relentless, every-night interruption of sleep beginning at 2 or 3 A.M. and continuing till dawn. There is no respite, no interruption. The depressed person's existence becomes a timeless ordeal. Each year, thousands of persons take their own lives in order to escape the anguish of depressive living. Many others contemplate and attempt suicide. Profound depression is among the most catastrophic of all human afflictions. Yet, paradoxically, there is no tangible injury. There is nothing to show to enable another person to comprehend. There is only suffering without clearly evident reason. The sentence most commonly spoken by depressed individuals in this one: "No one knows how bad I feel. No one could possibly understand."

DEPRESSION

Episodes of depression are very common. As many as 10 percent of all people will have at least one period in life when they are significantly limited in their ability to function because of the symptoms of depression. Those intervals, though sometimes quite severe, are ordinarily of brief duration. However, an estimated 1½ to 2½ percent of the population suffer serious depressive or manic episodes in which life itself may be threatened.[1] For reasons that are not well understood, more women than men suffer these illnesses.

From a diagnostic standpoint, depressive disorders are now divided into three categories. There are, first, acute reactive depressions precipitated by an overwhelming environmental stress such as death of a close relative, divorce, sudden job loss, or serious physical illness. They can occur in anyone but are usually self-limiting, often improving in a month or two. Of course, even the best adjustment to the loss of a spouse leaves a terrible void and vulnerability to illness and death, as many studies of widows and widowers attest. While most people survive and heal even after serious loss or injury, there are others who develop sustaining depression and incapacity. Perhaps some of them were already vulnerable to what will be described below as endogenous depression. The second category of depression is a somewhat broader classification and includes individuals with life-styles that are governed by feelings of inadequacy, chronic depression, chronic disappointment. The depression is "characterological," often of long duration, and with varying degrees of disabling impact. Many such patients were formerly diagnosed as suffering "neurotic depressions," but because of the vagueness of the term, it has been replaced in the new psychiatric nomenclature of DSM-III. It seems probable that this group of patients is made up of several subgroups, some of whose depression is the result of sociocultural factors, others who have developed a depressive life-style because of discouraging family relationships, both early and late, and others in whom genetic predisposition may be an important matter.

The third category, endogenous depression, is believed to occur almost always in individuals genetically at risk. These depressions are classified as unipolar or bipolar affective disorder depending on whether the patient experiences only depressions (unipolar) or depressions interspersed with bouts of mania (bipolar). Though they may respond to drug therapy or electrical convulsive treatment, these depressions are often very pervasive. I hope to convey some sense of the disastrous impact of such illnesses in the pages that immediately follow.

Many severe endogenous depressions begin subtly, and it proves difficult to date their onset. Insidiously, over a period of weeks or months, persons, places, and activities that had earlier possessed an aura of friendliness and pleasure become instead burdensome and to be avoided. Life begins to lose its flavor. At the same time, episodes of anxiety and despair, unexpected and without apparent cause, occur in situations that were formerly routine. The individual starts to withdraw, to hold back, to avoid, and there is a consequent narrowing of openness to life experience. Old friends are avoided, work is postponed, and religious services are shunned, even if each of these have been part of the patient's way of life since early childhood. When obliged to attend some public occasion, on entering the meeting room, the depressed and anxious individual takes note of all possible modes of exit, planning to withdraw even as he or she arrives. Where before the individual lived in relative comfort in his or her world, he now feels estranged and made restless by it. There is a loss of harmony with things, with others, and with oneself. Progression of the state of depression leads to extreme agitation and fearfulness, or, conversely, in some instances the individual may feel apathetic, tired, withdrawn, and uninterested. Or, as depression grows, the individual becomes both restless, impatient, and agitated and at the same time uninterested in matters that were formerly very important.

One such matter is sexuality. Many who are depressed progressively lose most or all interest in sex. If depression is developing in one member of the couple, he or she approaches the mate much less frequently. If the wife is depressed, she may seem remote, may refuse, or may participate perfunctorily. This is not to suggest, however, that the depressed person pulls away from the mate in all respects. He or she may become extremely dependent and prone to hang on and stay close. Sometimes this dependence is accompanied by a general reluctance to be alone and the mate is obliged to assume almost full-time "baby-sitter" responsibilities for a spouse who formerly had been confident and self-reliant.

By this time, a severe sleep disruption may exist and the patient dreads his nights as much as his days, ultimately more! The sleep disturbance characteristically is an early morning awakening. The day has been long and miserable and the individual is tired by bedtime and soon falls asleep. However, he or she awakens at 3:00 or 4:00 A.M. and is not able to fall asleep again. These early morning hours are a time of particular despair. She is tired, even exhausted, but her mind is beset with somber, ominous, hopeless thoughts about current problems or about difficult periods in the past. She may focus upon wrongs done to her or her family. Or at times she will brood about her unfriendly acts to others. In those dreadful early hours, the noises of the home and the sensation and sound of her own heartbeat come heavily together. Worries about personal health or the health of the mate, children, or grandchildren loom large; financial worries, real and imagined, are stark and overwhelming; the aggressive and ungrateful aspects of the world replace warmer and more tender sentiments. Everything is bad! Things are hopeless! There is no end to it! It is puzzling that some of these patients report that they do not cry. One woman, who in the face of an exquisite level of depression in which she had twice attempted suicide, explained, "I wish I could cry. I feel like crying often. But no tears come. It's as if I'm dried up."

The consequences of mental depression on general health may be very profound. Depressed individuals may appear to be suffering from serious disease with weight losses of twenty to thirty pounds in a matter of weeks. Quite often, physiological manifestations of anxiety in the form of blushing, sweaty palms, rapid heartbeat, headache, and tremors will also be present. Or some long-feared and ominous disease may seem to be developing. Because he or she feels so bad, only a diagnosis such as cancer, brain tumor, or heart attack seems a sufficient explanation. Since any one of a thousand bodily complaints may be offered by the individual as the source of despair, a false clue may come from one of the laboratory studies that are performed to clarify the confusing clinical picture. In this situation, it comes to pass that the severely depressed patient is told by his doctor:

> I've been over you carefully and you are in good shape. Except, you have a very, very slight anemia; that is, your blood is a little thin, only slightly, but a little. And also, your pulse is a little fast. Now neither of those problems is serious. I'm going to give you some iron pills for the blood problem and a little sedative to slow down the pulse. And in a month we'll see how you are.

The patient is misunderstood and the consequences are often serious. What is really wrong goes undetected. This happens often. It is a common medical error.

There has been a detailed search for possible biological alterations that might explain the physiological changes that often accompany and underlie the symptoms of severe depression. This search has uncovered a number of "biological markers" that appear to occur in many of the patients suffering endogenous depressions. For example, many of the patients with endogenous depressions seem to have altered brain wave patterns during sleep, specifically a shortened interval between the moment of falling asleep and the change in brain waves to a pattern called "dream sleep." There are also significant changes in endocrine secretion involving pituitary, adrenal, and gonadal activity that occur in endogenously depressed patients but not in other kinds of depression. At the moment, these biological correlates of severe depression are used in diagnosis and treatment of depression only in the advanced scientific centers. But within a few years, it is probable that psychiatrists and physicians in general practice will be able to use laboratory measures to verify their diagnoses and measure the progress of treatment of depression in the same way that physicians in other specialties use laboratory tests to aid in the management of disease of the liver, blood, or other body systems.[2,3]

Case Study 1: *Some Problems in the Treatment of Maria Hernandez*

Psychiatric treatment across a cultural barrier is very difficult. One of my Chinese colleagues makes that point in a paper he wrote and uses my attempt in Taiwan to treat a young schizophrenic boy in family therapy as an example. I had begun (and ended) that attempt at treatment with the request, "Tell me about family relationships" and the answer came back that the mother and father loved the boy very much, the boy loved the parents very much, the mother loved the husband and the boy very much, and the husband loved the mother and the boy very much. And they all loved and respected the ancestors (very much). It was something like John Mitchell's testimony in the Watergate hearings, except that they were all telling the truth.

I was invited to serve as a consultant to the treatment of Mrs. Maria Hernandez by a young, female resident psychiatrist who felt that after the passage of four therapy hours she hadn't accomplished very much. Her patient was a forty-seven-year-old mother of six children who herself had been the seventh of nine children. She had been born in Los Angeles in a closely knit Mexican-American family. Her parents and several of her brothers' and sisters' families still lived nearby and she saw them daily. Mrs. Hernandez had been referred from our hospital's Medical Clinic because they could find no basis for her many physical complaints. She said that she had been in good health and good spirits until six or seven months earlier and that possibly she had had the flu at that time. She had an assortment of complaints. Her back had painful areas that seemed to keep her from sleeping. Also, she could hear her heart beating when she went to bed and it was frightening. She felt weak much of the time, didn't enjoy her food, and in general felt that there must be some very serious disease present because she felt so bad.

The fact that she was subjecting herself to examination and treatment in our hospital was a testament to how poorly she felt. Through her life, she had avoided all contacts with doctors except at the time of her pregnancies. For difficulties at other times, she would go to a "non-medical healer" who also was "doctor" to other members of her family. She had consulted him several times before allowing her oldest daughter to bring her to our hospital.

I asked her doctor what she thought was wrong. She felt Mrs. Hernandez suffered mild-moderate depression, that she was also struggling with the changes taking place in her family as the children grew up, and she wondered whether her patient might feel oppressed by her husband. The young doctor and Mr. Hernandez didn't like each other too much. She had asked him to participate in the therapy hours and he did come to the first meeting. But for the second, third, and fourth hours he didn't come, but sent instead his sister and his daughter. The doctor didn't like what she felt were his "macho" attitudes.

I asked her to criticize her own theories and this is what she said:

"I'm not sure where I am with this lady. I'm an Anglo who speaks some Spanish but that's different from sharing her culture. I think, or assume, she must be feeling the need for 'emancipation' but maybe that's my need, not hers.

"Second, she won't offer any criticism of anyone in her family. She voices no concerns about her role as a woman. She isn't critical of the fact that her husband often stays after work for a drink with his friends.

"Third, I wonder if I'm underestimating this woman's depression."

I agreed with all three of her worries, that is, she didn't have much understanding of her patient's sociocultural values, didn't know her patient very well, and probably greatly underestimated the magnitude of the patient's depression. There is no such thing as psychiatric treatment without some cultural and value bias, but there are special problems when working across a substantial cultural gap. There is an increased risk of misunderstanding. This is one reason that patients from ethnic minority groups often avoid consulting a psychiatrist even in public clinics until their problems are more severe and long term than those of non-minority citizens seeking treatment.

The question that was most helpful in estimating the magnitude of the depression was asking Mrs. Hernandez to compare her present mood and health with her situation one year ago. She replied to her young doctor, "La noche y el dia [the night and the day]." There was one other matter that we looked into, though in this instance it proved to be without significance. A number of drugs prescribed for management of other medical problems can cause depression. This would include some of the drugs used for management of hypertension, drugs containing cortico steroids, oral contraceptives, and tranquilizers. Mrs. Hernandez was taking "medicines" for "her heart," but when we checked them out, they proved to be vitamins.

DEPRESSION AND MANIA: BIPOLAR DISEASE

A manic episode, in full force, unmodified by tranquilizer medications, is the most extraordinary aberration imaginable. It is a mixture of ultimate agitation, nonstop rapid speech, singing, shouting, laughing, constant motion, a torrent of gaiety and obscenity, and perhaps above all, the pathos of a frenzy without purpose or meaning. At the time of my training in psychiatry, there were moments when the only treatments that could save a patient from a level of agitation and hyperactivity that raised body temperatures to a lethal level were general anesthesia or repeated electrical shock. And the amount of anesthesia needed to induce sleep was sometimes near to a fatal dose. Death was not unknown in such moments. Then, as if to defy one's sense of reality, that same individual might, in days, a week, or a month later, be discovered in the most profound gloom, sodden with despair, mute, tortured. The depression might last for many months or years. Sometimes it continued through the life of the individual. Suicide was always a serious risk.

Manic and depressive illnesses have mystified people worldwide through the centuries. Little wonder. The lifetime course of the various illnesses is varied and the fact that frank manic episodes occurred less than one-tenth as often as severe depression was particularly puzzling. Most patients who suffered severe depressions never had a manic period. Among those who did, there were individuals who experienced one or two episodes in a lifetime with long periods free from all symptoms between recurrences. More often, the pattern of illness was more malignant. The first episode of mania or depression heralded years of frequent recurrences with prolonged hospitalization a necessity. Some entered the hospital early and never left.

It has been known for years that there were strong genetic factors in both depressive and manic-depressive illnesses. In many families, there were successive generations in which one, two, or three siblings were afflicted with severe episodes of depression and/or mania. Other family members, though never known to experience manic or depressive episodes, lived stormy lives with alcohol abuse a prominent characteristic. Many times, those same families were known as well for their collective drive, vigor, creativity, and success. In addition to the ultimate states of manic frenzy or profound depression, many patients also had lesser manic episodes, that is, hypomanic periods often marked by bad judgment, extravagant purchases, enthusiasm with little cause, extreme, garrulous behavior, sometimes alcoholic binges, and/or sexual activity well beyond the individual's ordinary patterns. From afar, it sounds easy to diagnose such episodes, but in the midst of an otherwise responsible and active life, things often were far out of hand before people knew that something was terribly wrong. Sometimes, it wasn't until ten years later, when a clear manic psychotic episode took place, that the earlier hypomanic period could be seen for what it had been.

Intense scientific study in the last decade in the fields of neurochemistry, genetics, neurophysiology, and clinical response to therapy has accomplished a great deal in sorting out complex and overlapping clinical manifestations into coherent groupings with relatively well-defined treatment implications. I cannot imagine a more remarkable worldwide partnership between basic scientists and scientist clinicians than that characterizing this work.[4,5]

One product of the last decade has been the establishment of bipolar patients as a relatively distinct group. In addition, as indicated in the book's earlier section on alcoholism, careful family studies of several generations of the relatives of bipolar patients revealed a significant over-representation of individuals suffering from alcoholism and, to a less certain degree, drug abuse, a tendency to become violent, and the self-starving illness anorexia nervosa. The better defined division of groups of patients whose clinical pictures are at times almost identical into distinct diagnostic and treatment categories that predict long-term outcome is extremely important for the individual patient and his or her family.

Case Study 2: *A Woman Whose Life Changed for the Better*

Mrs. Laurie Fisher had been hospitalized on a number of occasions because of recurring periods of depression and occasional periods of "elation and mania." I first saw her in 1971. She was forty-two years old, married, working as a legal secretary. Her difficulties had apparently begun quite early in her life. In 1940, just after her tenth birthday, there was an interval in which she was unable to go to school and instead remained home for about four months. At the time, the family doctor believed that she suffered some obscure physical illness, but on looking back at the episode Mrs. Fisher felt that it was the first of the recurring depressive cycles. The second came when she was sixteen years old. It was a very severe experience for her. At that point she felt so bad that she tried to hang herself. She was hospitalized. The doctors recommended shock treatments but her family refused permission. After approximately six months, the depression lifted. At the age of twenty-five, the first period of mania occurred. It began gradually with a several-month period of growing elation.

The patient described that episode in the following manner:

"That first time when I got high, it started slowly. I'm not sure just when or how it began. However, after three months of being more and more elated and enthusiastic, I began to buy all kinds of things I didn't need and couldn't afford. I also began to make long-distance telephone calls all over the country at early hours. I had always been very restrained when it came to men, but during that time, I'm embarrassed to say, I dropped my standards altogether and I guess I had three or four sexual affairs in less than three months. And I wasn't sad when I broke up with each one. I happily went on to the next. I try not to think of that part of it. I was married when the next severe manic episode came and I was really interested in sex again, but that time all with my husband. Was he surprised! But let me go back to describing that first manic episode.

"Finally, I drove eight hundred miles to see a friend who didn't even know I was coming. I arrived at 4 A.M. and woke her up and started talking and couldn't stop talking. After a while, she got the idea that something was wrong, and the next day she and another friend drove me back home. My folks met us and took me to the hospital. I don't remember too much about that except that I was singing and laughing and dancing in the ward."

This period of elation continued during hospitalization for another two months. Then, rather abruptly, it was followed by a very severe depression that lasted three months. Even after partial improvement, she was unable to return to work for an additional three months. The various cycles continued through most of her twenty-fifth year, then spontaneously went away. She subsequently married at twenty-eight, had two children without difficulty, worked on a reduced schedule, and was quite happy with her life. In 1966, at the age of thirty-six, again apparently without clear cause, she became very depressed and made a serious suicide attempt by cutting the blood vessels in her neck. She barely survived this attempt on her life, and when she regained consciousness she felt acutely disappointed that she was still alive. She believed that she was a sinful person and sat mute for hours, staring straight ahead. Her posture was frozen except for the continual wringing of her hands. She usually made no response when approached or spoken to. At that time, a long series of electrical shock treatments was given. They helped, but the tendency for depression remained to a greater or lesser degree over most of the succeeding year. She was not herself. While able to function in a superficial fashion, she derived little satisfaction or sense of continuity from her life.

During the succeeding four years from 1967 through 1971, there were two further episodes. One was a depressive period, the other a period of mania. Both were treated with electrical shock treatments. Following the period of depression, the newly developed anti-depression medications were given for a period of one year. I first saw her in a good period in 1971. She was generally content with her life, devoted to her family, and interested in her part-time job. She was concerned and guilty about the great financial burden her illness imposed on the family and she was grateful to her husband. The history that she provided indicated that at least several members of her mother's and maternal grandfather's family had suffered nervous difficulties and that one uncle and one great-aunt from that side of the family had committed suicide. At that time, early 1971, there were a number of reports beginning to appear in the psychiatric literature about the effects of lithium carbonate in the treatment of mania. But since she was a new person for me, and since at that time she felt that she was doing well, we agreed that she would return at the first signs of either mania or depression and that we could try the new medication at that time. Her husband was the third party to the agreement. Not much time passed before he called me to say that he was sure his wife was becoming "high" but that she was reluctant to come back to see me and she felt sure that things were going well. I told him to come with his wife in two hours and when they arrived she was indeed quite elated. She said she was feeling much better than on the last occasion that we had met, that she felt happy, creative, more successful in her work, and, to the embarrassment of her husband, reported that "last night he was terrific." She very reluctantly agreed to come into the hospital for a week of tests and the initiation of lithium treatment. To the wonder of her husband and my own cautious astonishment, she was in a good, but more restrained mood ten days later.

Mrs. Fisher has remained on lithium during eight of the last ten years. She has had no major recurrences of either mania or depression. She has had no major side effects from the medication. Twice with my agreement and once without my knowledge, she discontinued lithium, but on each occasion, after two months, seven months, and eight months, depressive symptoms began to appear and my patient was more than happy to start the lithium again. On two of those occasions I also treated her with anti-depression drugs.

My patient, her husband, and I all share in the sense of awe and gratitude that she has been privileged to be among the first to benefit from this major treatment advance. The Fishers read all they could find on the subject of lithium and they wrote a joint letter of thanks to Dr. John Cade in Australia, the first clinician who reported that lithium salts controlled the manic phase of the disease.[6] Cade's first publication on the subject appeared in 1949. Unfortunately, soon after, there were several cardiac deaths in the United States among patients who were using a lithium salt as a salt substitute in cooking, and lithium studies were few in number in the next fifteen years. The margin of safety with lithium is relatively narrow, and one continuing inconvenience in its use in treating mood problems is that blood levels need to be checked once a month (or a little less often in well-stabilized patients) to assure that there is a high enough blood level for the drug to be effective without being toxic. There is reason for concern about possible kidney damage and other side effects. But the effectiveness of the treatment in what has been among the most refractory of conditions makes lithium, on balance, an undoubted gift to mankind.

Of course, there has been a great deal of study in the last decade in all aspects of the treatment of mania, depression, and a number of potentially related disorders with lithium. Not every patient does as well as Mrs. Fisher. But many do. In a number of carefully controlled studies it has been demonstrated that lithium maintenance is very effective in preventing expected recurrences of mania and hypomania and at least of moderate effectiveness in preventing depressions. There is also evidence that the anti-depression drugs can be used prophylactically to prevent recurrences of depressions and that, on occasion, lithium and the anti-depression medications can be used in an overlapping manner to control the sometimes rapid shift between both mood extremes.[7]

I need to say that the ideal medications for management of mania and depression are not yet available. A significant number of patients are not responsive to either lithium, the tricyclic anti-depressants, or the monoamine oxidase inhibitor drugs. A larger number appear to be helped but only to a partial degree. Some patients suffer from toxic side effects, which, not infrequently, make it necessary to discontinue or at least reduce their use. However, a number of very promising drugs are now being developed in laboratories and tested in clinics in the United States, Canada, and Europe and without doubt, the future management of affective disorders will be accomplished in a still safer, more effective manner with greater freedom from troubling side effects. Electrical convulsive therapy is still of considerable value in the management of depressions that are not responsive to medications or in patients whose specific health problems contraindicate drug treatments. Electrical convulsive therapy is also the treatment of choice in situations where the likelihood of suicide is extremely high and the one- to three-week interval before the drug becomes effective is too long to wait.[8]

MANAGEMENT OF SEVERE ENDOGENOUS DEPRESSION AND MANIA

It should be evident that adequate management of unipolar and bipolar illnesses requires that an experienced and caring psychiatrist play a central role. *In the management of depression, hypomania, and mania, denial of a medical approach with full access to anti-depression medicines, lithium carbonate, repeated physical and laboratory examinations, and, when necessary, hospitalization in a psychiatric unit is an unforgivable mistake.* The therapeutic tasks call for the greatest personal and professional skill. The clinician's first and immediate need is to reach out and make contact with a person who has become very much out of touch. This first task of "touching down" and bridging the patient's isolation is highly important. The hypomanic patient ordinarily enjoys the elated experience and is often reluctant to come for therapy. The severely depressed person has difficulty trusting anyone because he or she is almost always convinced that no one is in a position to know what is wrong or to offer assistance. In depression, the relationship between doctor and patient may be the last barrier to suicide when the patient awakens at 3 A.M. and contemplates until dawn what to do next. Establishing that relationship is both difficult and absolutely essential. I repeat the following as often as necessary; it must be heard:

> I understand how bad you feel and how hopeless everything seems. I've cared for other people who had a similar depression. I will work with you until you've recovered completely. I am going to ask your spouse to help us.

Including the patient's mate, or if there is no mate another responsible adult from the family or a friend, is almost always a constructive and sometimes a life-saving step. The patient, mate, or friend should all be enlisted as allies and partners with the doctor in trying to find a remedy for the patient's difficulty. There are many times when you need all the help you can get!

It's best not to be vague about suicide and I bring up the question directly: "I wonder if you have felt so bad that you have thought of taking your own life?" If the answer is an affirmative one, which it is with surprising regularity, the patient, his mate, and I need to face the question of whether hospitalization is indicated. In the great majority of instances, the knowledge that a treatment program is being developed and that there is a firm contact between the three of us makes it possible for the patient to remain out of the hospital while treatment continues.

In working with severely depressed individuals, drug therapy is an important part of the treatment. The patient's absolute cooperation and trust are essential. During the last twenty-five years the remarkably effective tricyclic antidepressants (Tofranil, imipramine, Elavil, amitriptylene, and so forth) often reverse depressions that have reached a profound level. However, one, two, or sometimes three weeks or longer of continued and faithful drug use may be required before improvement occurs. Sometimes a longer period is required or a change in medication is necessary. The practical problems in this kind of situation are many. The patient, who may well be contemplating suicide, must be told that a long period of time will pass before relief comes. Even a day is a long time for a depressed person.

For the physician, then, in that first appointment there is a great deal to do all at once. A solid contact with the patient and the mate must be established; the doctor must assure the patient that he or she has a sense of what is wrong, must emphasize the necessity of following exactly the medication instructions, and simultaneously explain any possible side effects of the drugs so that the patient does not stop medication prematurely. Many of these drugs have mildly troubling side effects that are discouraging to patients; for example, a dryness of the mouth and sometimes a slight skin rash. Occasionally, some dizziness occurs when one changes from a lying to a standing position. And the first couple of days on any new medicine are likely to be worrisome and disappointing. Patients started on lithium may have similar problems, and in addition they are required to have a number of blood samples drawn in the first month or two of treatment. In my own practice, at least 25 percent of patients will stop medications on their own unless we stay in very close touch at the start of treatment, both by telephone every two or three days and with a visit at least every week. Actually, I may overestimate the level of compliance with my instructions. Some studies show that more than half the patients don't take the medications as prescribed.[9] But I work very hard to see that my patients continue their medication. It's very important. Obviously, prescriptions for large numbers of potentially lethal sleep capsules are inappropriate.

Sometimes, the patient is so very uncomfortable and depressed that hospitalization is necessary. I have found from sad experience that once a decision to hospitalize has been made, the patient should be admitted at once. Changes in the plan, such as a decision to move treatment to a hospital, have led some patients to use the interval before admission to attempt suicide. This becomes more likely if the decision to hospitalize is made and then the patient is left to worry and brood for a day or two. Once in the hospital, higher doses of medications can be given and supervision is better. About one in ten of my patients with endogenous depressive illness receives electrical shock therapy. The others respond to outpatient care, brief hospitalization, emotional support, and medications.

I want to emphasize one other matter at this time. Specifically, by the time a depressive illness is well established, the patient is usually unable on his own to effect major changes in mood. I would never discount an individual's will to health or determination to find his own cure, but in severe depression and in mania, the thermostat controlling mood is out of the reach of the patient. I have worked with some of the world's most stubborn and determined people whose maximal efforts to rid themselves of their depression achieved little or nothing. The urgings to try harder, work more, work less, take a vacation, turn to prayer, retire, or what have you usually help not at all. As the chemistry that underlies brain functioning is more accessible to experiment and the neurochemical disturbances associated with depression and mania are better understood, it has become more evident why "more will power" or "more faith" alone can't routinely accomplish a cure. In this situation, the patient demonstrates great courage by believing in himself, by believing in the honesty and determination of the doctor, and by staying with the treatment. Unfortunately, many already guilty and depressed patients are made guiltier still by those who have a simple exhortative plan. They just don't understand.

OTHER FORMS OF DEPRESSION AND SUICIDAL GESTURE

In assessing the nature of depression, the risk of suicide, and the appropriate management, there are many matters to consider. For example, a considerable number of young people who threaten or make suicide attempts do so impetuously because of some here-and-now matter. They may have had no thought of suicide twenty-four hours earlier, and if, mercifully, little damage is done, thoughts of suicide are forgotten a few hours later. Suicidal gestures in young adolescents and young adults are often a form of emphatic message of frustration or disappointment to a parent, sweetheart, or employer. The message, in translation, may sound something like this: "It isn't fair and I don't like it and won't stand for it! I will kill myself. Then you will be sorry!" Elements of frustration, rage, spite, and a sense of impotence dominate the moment. The suicide attempt is often more gesture than anything else and little or no bodily harm is sustained. At times, the suicidal gesture leads to a change in a girl friend's, boy friend's, or parent's attitude about some disputed matter. A bit of powerfully manipulative behavior may have worked. Of course, it's a terribly dangerous game.

In the case of impulsive, immature individuals who have made an unsuccessful suicide attempt, it is almost always a good idea to insist on a family meeting with *everybody* present. Bringing family members into the same room after a threatened or attempted suicide may open channels of communication that have been closed down for years and bring into the open long-camouflaged fears and areas of misunderstanding. Equally, they also allow family members to make manifest the positive feelings they have for each other. A suicidal gesture represents a moment of crisis for the family. At the same time, it is a unique opportunity. However, a time of crisis represents a time-limited opportunity, that is, the potential for a constructive outcome is one that rapidly disappears. The clinician must carefully avoid sabotage of his or her own therapeutic effectiveness. This most often happens in one of several ways. First, the therapist can undercut the importance of the family conference by allowing a long interval to pass between the suicide attempt and the proposed meeting time. Or, a therapist can *guarantee* the failure of the meeting by agreeing to a conference at which one or more of the important family members are absent. For example, the father may be too busy working to come to the meeting about the suicide attempt of his son. Or the mother may feel that it would be better for the boy and

his father to hold the interview. The spouse may be "working."
When this occurs, the purpose of the family interview will
often have been defeated. *Everybody* has to come! Another
way the therapist can undercut the effort is by assuming (or
being placed in) a commanding, advice-giving, "charismatic"
posture. Often the family arrives and says, "Well, Doctor (or
Nurse), we are here. We want to know what to do. Tell us
what to do." The therapist does well to avoid the honors
offered and seek instead a partnership with the family in the
effort to achieve an honest, open, direct level of communication. At the beginning of the discussion, neither the therapist
nor anyone else knows what should be done. The therapist
advises, "Let's find out what's going on. Everybody is going to
have to help with that. Something good can come out of this
dreadful moment."

Not all suicide attempts by young people are unsuccessful.
Neither are all such efforts perpetrated by impulsive, frustrated adolescents who simply needed to "do something" because of their pent-up frustrations and/or anger. There are
times when the young person who made the suicide attempt
remains depressed, expresses disappointment about recovering,
offers no clear explanation of the circumstances that led up to
the suicide attempt, or talks in an incoherent, obscurely philosophical or morose manner. Or, if the individual utilizes a
particularly bizarre, long-planned suicide method (such as a
sixteen-year-old boy who attempted to kill himself with a bomb
on which he had been working for that purpose over a period
of two or three weeks), he or she is obviously a different kind
of person than the impulsive, immature individual described
previously. The person who after a suicide attempt presents a
somber, depressed, or bizarre clinical picture must be viewed
in a serious light. Some schizophrenic illnesses are heralded
in this way, and there have been a number of first depressive
episodes of what turn out to be endogenous affective disorders
that occur in childhood and adolescence. In that situation,
steps need to be taken to protect the patient from himself or
herself, often through psychiatric hospitalization.

Of course, the widespread use of street drugs by children
from primary school up to young adults and people in their

twenties and thirties adds a very serious element both to the evaluation and the treatment of abnormal mood or disturbed behavior. And as always, social and economic circumstances regularly favor the more affluent. In poorer communities, children and adolescents are more likely to suffer drug abuse, neglect, parental abuse, loss of a parent during the important early years. In general, lower socioeconomic status places both children and adults in double jeopardy. They are members of families that suffer twice the number of serious losses and they have many fewer resources by which to cope. A recent follow-up on the pioneer study of social and economic factors on *Mental Health in the Metropolis,* which was carried out in New York twenty-five years ago, reinforces the original findings. Specifically, two and a half times as many of the young adults from upper socioeconomic levels as children from the lower classes were doing well emotionally. Twice as many from the lower classes were doing very poorly. And as the years pass and the individuals grow older, the gap widens.[10]

But children and young adults from all social levels are vulnerable to the epidemic of suicides, homicides, and accidents that when combined make violent deaths the leading cause of death in Americans up to the age of thirty-nine. Suicide follows only accidents and homicide as the cause of death among young people in the United States.[11] Their rate of suicide is now higher than at any point in American history. The combination of street drugs, social mobility, and the breakup of families serves to strike down many young people. Very possibly, those with genetically determined vulnerability contribute more than their share to the list of fatalities.

There is another kind of person who contemplates, threatens, or attempts suicide as a well-practiced technique for controlling others. He or she may be somewhat older than most who play this game, but he has an essentially adolescent or immature spirit. He feels justified in utilizing the intimidating power that is in the hands of one who threatens suicide. Obviously, people who feel that "all's fair in love, war, or what have you" can be a considerable problem for their families, for friends, and for the therapist.

Case Study 3: *The "Helpless" Woman Who Could Tame Tigers*

Lynn Jefferson, twenty-nine, a language instructor in a large state college, was referred to me by the chairman of her department because of a spotty attendance record, repeated episodes of crying at work, and the suspicion that she might be taking some kind of drugs. She was one of my first patients when I entered practice. In the first interview she presented an uneven picture. At times she seemed a rather sophisticated and intelligent adult woman. This contrasted with an initial set of demands that she tried to impose as her conditions for talking with me. She insisted that I promise never to contact her family, who lived 2,500 miles away (she was an only child and couldn't bear to hurt them), that I promise never to hospitalize her, that I agree to honor requests for medication, and that she be free to contact me at any time she felt the need. She was assured that I wouldn't contact her family without discussing it with her* but that all the rest of her demands were childish. "Miss Jefferson, I'd be quite interested in working with you and I'd do my best. But I learned in 1939 that you can't do business with Hitler and I think your demands are those of a spoiled tyrant." She stormed out of my office but came back a few minutes later, pouted a bit, and finished the first therapeutic hour on a cheerful note. She canceled the next appointment because she had a headache and appeared at my office without an appointment the following day. She was upset and disappointed when I saw her for only a few minutes. Later that evening, she called to complain about an inability to sleep and requested a prescription for sleeping medication. I offered to discuss that request at the next appointment. She slammed down the telephone angrily.

---

* I made the mistake in my early years of seeing some of my patients without seeing their families. I started out that way with Lynn and we both paid a price.

During the next several months, my patient alternately presented herself as a serious grown-up woman trying to understand her problems and as an angry, demanding child with an unending series of explicit and implicit demands. In particular, she seemed to want contacts with me outside our ordinary therapeutic hours and wanted the freedom to call me at home. She engineered several rather obvious attempts to encounter me in a semi-social way, the most colorful effort being positioning herself at the bus stop next to my parking lot on a night when the temperature was ten below zero. She was wearing no coat, and stood shivering and looking helpless. I was irritated at her but more irritated at myself for not driving on. I drove her home. For the next several weeks, she seemed more at peace, less depressed, less demanding, and more friendly.

Soon, however, her friendliness changed into an open wish to become romantically involved with me. She was certain that I must love her, as she insisted she loved me. I offered interpretations and asked her to talk about her feelings rather than attempt to demonstrate them. She denounced my rigidity. During that period a 2 A.M. telephone call from one of her friends brought the news that Lynn had swallowed some twenty aspirin tablets. She was taken to a hospital emergency room and a gastric lavage (stomach pump) was used. She went home the same morning. However, she felt that because of her "suicidal feelings" she should be seen more frequently. When this request was refused, she resumed her nighttime telephone calls and staged a second, carefully preannounced suicidal gesture at 2 A.M. She called me and announced that she had no choice but to kill herself because of the way I had treated her and she murmured, "Good-bye forever," hung up the telephone, and refused to answer it again. I paused en route to pick up an on-duty nurse from the emergency room and made a 2:30 A.M. home visit. Lynn Jefferson was moderately intoxicated, seductively arrayed in a nightgown, and otherwise intact. On three other occasions during the succeeding year, my patient made overt and direct suicide threats, usually as part of some manipulative attempt to dislodge me from what she felt was a cruel, aloof detachment.

She was a very trying person, who, despite relative chronological maturity, used the threat and the gesture of suicide as a powerful manipulative technique not only in her wish to control me but also in her relationships with other important people in her life. I repeatedly asked, "Lynn, is there any amount of reassurance that could convince you of another's esteem for you?" Or, "Does intimacy always present you with a need to test the other person?" Or, in exasperation, "When will you grow up?"

One step that proved very helpful to both Lynn Jefferson and me was her final agreement to allow her mother and father to join us for several sessions during one of their visits to their only daughter. They were older people (Lynn's mother was thirty-nine at the time Lynn was born and her father was forty-five), dignified and distant. Lynn's manner of behavior in their presence was a forced gaiety. And they were the world's most civilized parents. In her earlier years, she had felt that kissing, hugging, and conversations in the family were largely perfunctory. Her seventy- and seventy-six-year-old parents now, as when she was a child, rarely violated her "life space." They treated her in a psychiatrist's office as they were said to have reared her, "aseptically." She grew up hungering for germs, lots of them!

As I indicated, Lynn was a patient rather early in my career and as I later thought over her care, I had a number of regrets. First of all, though she was a great problem for me, she was also a terrible burden to herself. She was very unhappy and had been unhappy most of her life. She fired her own depression by causing people to reject her. But, in part, her behavior was the product of a sustaining depressive restlessness. I should have seen her from the first in the context of her family and her friends. That would have helped in two ways. I might have helped her to be less provocative with everybody (it wasn't just me she was giving a hard time) and I wouldn't have made her so dependent on me. She was twenty-nine, thirty, and thirty-one years old in the years that I worked with her, and she devoted a great deal of her energy, vitality, and (for want of a better word) love to me. That kept her from what might have been a more intense and reciprocated involvement with her friends. But that's over now.

What happened to Lynn Jefferson? The involvement of her parents was a kind of turning point. They were basically very important to her. After their first visit, they returned on two occasions and they were very insistent that Lynn return the visit to them. On that return (to the East Coast) she met a former high school teacher, a man twenty-one years older than she, and it was love at second look. I was unenthusiastic about her sudden decision to displace herself and marry outside her generation. That's what she did.

The first several years of her marriage were apparently somewhat more tempestuous than her former teacher had anticipated. Lynn wrote that she was hospitalized once briefly because of a suicidal threat she made to her husband. She saw a psychiatrist there who treated her on occasion with anti-depression meds, which she felt helped "a little bit." But the marriage sustained. Some ten years later, Lynn and her husband stopped on a transcontinental drive to say hello to me. They were doing well. He was good with her, she the same with him. Her mother lived near to them. Her father had died one year after her marriage. Lynn was teaching part time but enjoyed staying home as much as possible. She and her husband had decided not to have children. She said she felt more than satisfied about our working together. She said she rarely felt suicidal anymore.

In any instance where there is the suggestion of a threat to life, one must take it seriously. Where errors are made, they are better made on the side of overconcern and caution. There has been in recent years a concerted effort to develop predictors of suicidal behavior. Suicide prevention centers and/or suicide "hot line" telephone services have been established in a number of communities. Simultaneously, follow-up of all who threaten suicide over a one-, two-, or three-year period has allowed some refinement in estimating probabilities. Of course, all such data refer to large numbers of people and provide only a general indicator of risk in a specific case. Most vulnerable are people who have lost a mate through death or divorce and who live alone, those who drink heavily or take drugs, those who have recently stopped working, and/or those who suffer manic-depressive illness or other psychiatric and physical illnesses. I also worry more about people in whose family there have been one or more suicides. And I worry a great deal about patients who are depressed and responding slowly at a moment when I am about to leave for a vacation of more than a few days.

SUMMARY

It's important in each and every area of medicine, but nowhere is there greater need for an open and trusting partnership between patient, family, and doctor than in the diagnosis, immediate treatment, and long-term management of depression and mania. And nowhere is there a richer payoff. We don't yet have the final curative techniques and agents, but there have been remarkable gains in the last two decades and there is every reason to hope for considerable progress in the years ahead. In this chapter, I've emphasized the management of the more severe forms of affective disorder in part because of the great recent advances that have been attained in the understanding and treatment of endogenous depression and mania. But there are many other forms of mood disturbance and moody life-styles for which group, couple, and individual psychotherapy, combined on occasion with behavior therapy techniques, are very useful. Many patients with mild to moderate depressions are treated with medications by their family doctors. I've found that some of those patients are undertreated, that is, a minimal dose of medicine is prescribed and, to compound the problem, the patient takes only a part of the prescription. In those instances, the patient may improve "halfway" whereas slight modification of dosage could produce a much better result. Here, the family helps a great deal. They know how good things could be and they often inspire the patient and doctor to settle for no less.

I need to express my own debt and the thanks of countless numbers of my patients and their families to the scientists and scientist-clinicians whose contributions have been so great. Particularly, the unique role of researchers, clinicians, and educator-salesmen and women in the drug manufacturing industry in Europe and the United States deserves full recognition and credit.

11

Alanda's Autobiography: An Introduction to Schizophrenia

The pages that follow contain an autobiography written by Alanda Jenkins, a woman of thirty who had lived a haunted life filled with self-deprecation and torturing agitation for more than a decade. There were times when she was suicidal, confused, and totally unreasonable. Many doctors had diagnosed her difficulty as schizophrenia. She was a sensitive person who was struggling desperately to maintain some semblance of order and dignity in her life. In many respects, she succeeded despite the intense level of her self-preoccupation and the bizarre nature of her symptoms. She was intelligent, sincere, and touchingly grateful. In this woman's autobiography, the reader will sense a continuity between the insecure childhood days and the profoundly disturbed periods of her adult life. However, the relative importance and interrelationship of early life experience and various genetic, metabolic, and neurochemical abnormalities in the development of unhappy, confused, and disorganizing life-styles is only beginning to be understood. One more decade of research may solve many of the remaining questions. On reading Alanda's autobiography, the everyday joylessness, the absence of highs, the subdued sameness of everything in her life are as striking as the descriptions of her periods of "decompensation." One's capacity to "turn on," get excited about, and experience pleasure may be governed from earliest days by the same chemical systems within the brain that become grossly disordered in depression, mania, and schizophrenia. There is currently intensive study being done on these variants of "normal" and "pathological."

Preceding the autobiography are the admission notes of intern and nurses written on the hospital chart on the occasion of her evening arrival at the psychiatric ward of the hospital. The date of admission was February 10, 1974.

Admission Note by Intern (February 10, 1974, 11:00 P.M.)

This thirty-year-old lady is admitted to the hospital with the chief complaint that "my whole life depends upon my hair. It either makes me or makes me not." According to the patient, the most important thing is how her hair feels and how it would feel to her hand. If her hair feels all right then it looks all right too. The patient is afraid to shampoo her hair. Any change or twist of her hair bothers her. If it gets limp or oily, the patient feels very frantic. She would like to fix it and never wash it, only comb it. She wishes it could always be the same. In the morning she always feels that her hair is worse, because there is a change in her hair from sleeping. She spends a great deal of the morning and afternoon grooming and combing her hair. When she is not satisfied with her hair, the patient states, "I can't even sit and visit if my hair is not right. I have to make up some excuse and run to the bathroom and comb it. It's humiliating to leave someone sitting in my living room while I brush my hair like a lunatic." However, if she doesn't feel too bad, she forces herself to go out. There are good weeks and good days, but generally, the patient is upset because of her hair. Problems of less importance are: (1) complexion, (2) gaining weight—"I'm afraid to get fatter and fatter." *In the afternoons, the patient works as a beauty operator doing almost only hair work.* She does not like her work but sometimes a hair case interests her. Sometimes with all these thoughts and feelings she gets confused and worn out. "Sometimes I feel I'm going to die. I would like to pick up the butcher knife and slash my wrists. The only thing that would help me is to be a man and then I would not have to worry about hair."

This patient seems to be very desperate and displays suicidal tendencies. Says she took RAT POISON! Her family doctor pumped her stomach and sent her here. There are no obvious hallucinations, no real delusions. The patient recognizes that her ideas about her hair are abnormal and sick. She appears neat, cooperative, friendly, somewhat depressed, and pessimistic. She is very much handicapped by her ideas.

Medical History & Physical & Laboratory Examinations: Negative or noncontributory except eighteen pound weight loss over two months' period.

Impression: Obsessive compulsive reaction with schizophrenic decompensation.

[End of intern's note.]

Nurse's Notes

February 10, 1974, 10:00 P.M. Patient admitted ambulatory to open unit unaccompanied. Ht. 5' 6½", Wt. 100 pounds, Pupils equal. Although patient cried when she arrived on unit, she soon regained composure and was most cooperative. Alert and oriented. Assigned room 609. Dr. notified. Dr. talking with patient.

February 11, 1974, 6:00 A.M. Patient has had a good night. Slept well. Breakfast: One cup coffee, few bites toast, cereal.

8:00 A.M. Extremely neat—every hair in place. Commented how awful her hair looks in contrast to nurse's. Makes polite small talk only with encouragement. Says little else. Looks sleepy. On bed most of past two hours. Face down. Out of bed with encouragement. Reading. Little facial expression.

12:00 noon. Ate all but potato. States she likes the expensive things to eat.

2:00 P.M. Complains that medication makes her feel so drowsy. Approached nurse to request scissors. Seemed extremely tense. "I just have to cut a bit of my hair. Some is out of place and I can't stand it. Please— you may watch me, I'm not going to poke out my eyes, I just want to trim one spot on my head." Patient's hairdo very neat. Nurse unable to observe one hair out of place.

10:00 P.M. On bed all evening says, "Those pills make me drowsy."

February 12, 1974, 6:00 A.M. Slept fairly well.

8:00 A.M. Readily converses. When nurse entered room to chat, patient began to pat nurse's hair and feel it, wishing hers was like it. Topic changed by nurse and patient continually talked about glasses and food. Supposes she should wear glasses. Interested in obtaining book about health foods and discussing a philosophy of food and life which her next door neighbor is very much a promoter of. Patient is afraid she is not feeding her child right, that he will not, therefore, grow up healthy. Apparently this philosophy attributes life's problems to faulty eating. Patient is not quite sure how she feels about this. Seems very open for suggestion. Enjoys to have someone listen to her.

ALANDA'S AUTOBIOGRAPHY— FEBRUARY 14, 1974

"I have tried to remember as far back into my childhood as I can. This is more difficult than I had thought.

"I was born on a farm, thirty years ago, the second of three daughters. Frieda is two years older than I and Anna two years younger. Therefore, I must have been two years old when my little sister was born, but this event I do not remember. To my knowledge, there were always three of us. But I do recall Anna as a little, blonde, curly-haired girl, not a baby, but probably in her second year. From then on, for three, four, or even five years, life was about the same for me, as far as environment and relationships with other people were concerned.

"It is common to read stories in which the writer recalls the happy days of his childhood. Mine was not that way—not that my general living conditions were utterly miserable, but it was just a dreary, lonesome, unimportant, uninteresting, nil sort of stage that I was caught in. I do not remember really enjoying any activities, or laughing, or having real fun.

"My mother and dad were honest, hard-working farm people—people who believed that children should be seen and not heard. They were kind enough and I respected and loved them—as I felt that was a child's duty.

"We were clothed and fed sufficiently, and the necessities, from their viewpoint, were sufficient. My mother made our big blousy bloomers from bleached feed sacks and I was always embarrassed about wearing them. But they were always clean, not too comfortable, cost little, and that way we were that much less expensive to them and someday, the farm could be paid for.

"Frieda fussed, complained, and grew angry at her home-sewed clothes, long underwear, and long stockings. In turn it made my mother angry and hurt and I felt sorry for my mother. I hated the clothes as much as Frieda, but I hated the wrangling and I didn't want to seem unappreciative, so I never complained—and there I received some praise—I never complained, and I found many times, no matter how unhappy I might be over a situation I did not complain because my mother appreciated me for 'being good and taking whatever I got.'

"Mom always tells of my being a 'good baby.' I would lie quietly, even when awake, and cry very little. When I was older, she says she would put me on a chair and I never moved or spoke until she gave me permission. I will say I was proud of this, and I tried to live up to that reputation and do even better. From then on I guess my ambition was to do what Mama wanted, and to be of as little trouble, expense, and bother as possible. Then she would like me.

"I didn't care for school when I was little. I was afraid I couldn't do well enough. When Frieda was seven, she entered the second grade. I was five then and began first grade. But we were in the same class. At that time, in our country school, grades were combined—first and second, third and fourth, and so on. The same subjects were taught both grades. Therefore, one year would be much easier than the other. I distinctly remember doing, or trying to do, long-division problems when I was in the third grade and I didn't know the multiplication table. I came home with pretty meager grades compared to Frieda's. I was in the eighth grade when for the first time I did not have to compete with Frieda. I enjoyed school a bit more that year.

"I knew I could never be another Frieda. Everything was easy for her, and everything she did, she did so well. I felt and knew people 'took to her naturally.' One aunt was very obvious about it. I especially took notice of the difference in gifts we received from her. I must have enjoyed feeling sorry for myself, because I'd rather have died than mention it, but my heart actually ached when I saw her preference.

"On the other hand was my cute, chubby baby sister, Anna. She was the highlight for her cute, interesting baby ways. And funny as it seems, almost like a hilarious joke, was this awkward character, me, in the middle.

"We were known always as Frieda, Alanda, and Anna, their three girls. I do not know why, but I felt ashamed that there were three of us. It was an odd number. How much more fiitting it would be if there were just Frieda and I (no reflection on Anna). It seemed unbalanced and awkward to be three of us.

"I felt a misfit in our family. My hair was straight and hard to manage; people remarked, 'What happened here? The other girls have naturally curly hair.' Dad cut our hair at home, and he hated cutting mine, because of the way it grew at the back of my neck. I was sorry I was so much trouble. It seemed I made them unhappy and ashamed of me.

"Often I, and that was when I was very young, five, six, seven, eight, or nine even, wished for illness or even death to make them stop and care for me a little, or make them sorry if I would die, and when I was nine, I had an appendectomy —my one greatest childhood experience. I received attention and praise for being so sick and complaining so little.

"My mother was always tired and cross, and I was sort of half afraid of her—in the way that I was tense until she spoke so I could tell what mood she was in. She was cross a lot of the time with my dad. He never scolded her or talked harshly to her but as I saw it, she felt unappreciated. She cried a lot and one of her expressions which haunted me was, 'You kids and your dad take me for a slave, and a dumbbell, and so on' (which was not true) and then she'd say, 'Sometimes I wish I could dig a hole in the ground and crawl in it.' I actually visualized this, but really didn't think she would do it. I knew that her mother (my grandmother, whom I never knew) was supposed to have grown tired and weary of life and lay down on the railroad track in front of a train and died that way. My mother was only nine then and she cared for her two younger sisters until she married my dad at the age of twenty-five and then she still took care of the younger sister. I was afraid she might do something like her mother and I surely didn't want to be the cause of her having any feelings that I did not love or appreciate her.

"Sometime, I suppose when I was five or even four, this thing of masturbation entered the picture. I discovered my body and the peculiar exciting or pleasant feeling I obtained from it. That part of my body, naturally, I had been led to believe was almost unmentionable, secretive, forbidden, unmoral, and nasty. So when I began this bad, embarrassing habit, I felt very guilty and ashamed, and now I was not the good girl I should be. I suppose, even when I was five, it is hard to be sure, I realized where baby animals and human babies came from. I can't remember not knowing. From observing the bulls and cows and other animals on the farm, I assumed their physical contact was the cause of the growth of a baby within the mother. I did not understand or even think of anything passing from the male into the female. I remember holding my two hands over my abdomen and I was sure it was growing larger. I was not a thin child and if anyone mentioned I was heavier than a year ago, or something like that, I was stricken with fear. I remember praying in my simple way, 'God, please forgive me and don't let me have a baby.' When somehow I realized something passed from male to female during sexual intercourse which caused conception, I was amazed. I was almost carefree.

"When I began to menstruate when I was not yet twelve, I was again frightened, ashamed, and horrified. I knew something of it, little ideas here and there, but it was worse and something greater than I had expected. My mother had told me nothing, but I was suspicious of her and of Frieda at certain times of the month. When I told her of myself, she gave me the necessary extra clothing, and so on, and her only words were, 'You will have this every month, but if you don't, something will be wrong, and you tell me.' It had been a secret from me and I felt I must not let Anna know anything of it. I was in misery trying to go to the bathroom to dress and undress, out of sight of Anna. I tried to get her to ask Mom to let her visit an aunt for several days at that time. I nearly wore myself out keeping it secret. Later, that wore away. I suppose when Anna became near that age too.

"Basically, this was my life until I started high school. High school wasn't what I had hoped for. I wished I was a town girl with nice clothes. I was ashamed we were not 'church people' and were definitely not the 'social' type. My clothes weren't right and my hair and my figure were all wrong. There was something about even the homeliest girls that I envied. They all had something, a good figure, clothes, nice hair. I sat in many classes and looked at and studied the girl's hair ahead of me. I felt I didn't have, and therefore, probably actually did not have, one ounce of personality.

"In my junior year I was voted homecoming queen and in the senior year I was voted 'most popular girl.' I did not accept this as 'honest'—to me it was an accident. I felt I knew how it happened both times. Everyone, the girls that is, was jealous of the popular and pretty girls who were candidates and very apt to win so they voted for me, so their pretty friends would not receive the honor.

"I knew my mother was happy when I started my beauty culture career by working as an apprentice and taking a correspondence course. I was earning money and saving it and that was Mom's 'cup of tea.' But I wasn't proud of it or pleased with it.

"Here I was, in this dumpy little town, kids going to college —the kids that really were somebody or wanted to be somebody; but I was afraid to go ahead and take a big step into something I was not sure I could accomplish.

"I began going with Carl four years after I graduated from high school. I was twenty-one and he was twenty-five, really a man. I didn't trust him in the first years of our marriage. When he was late from work, I was sure he was with another girl. I sneaked down dark alleys and watched and waited, but never saw anything.

"Carl always liked my long hair, but soon after we were married, I thought I should have it cut—I don't know why— and with it cut, I also lost the endearing term 'Fluffy' that he had called me. I had my hair cut, and I disliked it and myself. Carl didn't like it, of course, and the one good feature I had finally obtained, I had now ruined of my own accord. I was heartbroken to the point of crying hysterically and had to quit my job.

"Then came the first 'nervous breakdown.' From then on, year in and year out, my hair haunted me. I would get along fair for a couple months and then I couldn't bear it. I recall the misery it caused. If I was not satisfied with my hair, I was 'no good' for anything. I was unsure of myself in every way. I made no definite plans if I could help it, for I never knew what state of mind I might be in. I envied my friends who casually combed through their hair, or nonchalantly stepped into a shop for a haircut. To me, setting or cutting my hair was a major act. I knew something was wrong in this idea—something peculiar. It is my hair, yes—but why can't I do what I can with it and then relax? What funny thing within me lets my hair rule my whole life?

"I had had shock treatments and although everyone marveled how wonderfully they helped me, I did not credit it to the treatment. The treatments frightened me to such an extent I was able to overlook everything, including my hair, to get loose from that horrible 'asylum' I was locked in.

"My life was one horrible mess from one time to another. Carl and I quarreled and actually despised each other at times. I was unhappy, discontented, and unsure of myself in every way possible.

"When I had the second nervous breakdown, as they called it, I thought I would surely lose my mind forever. To me it was six months of sheer torture, more or less before and after, but those months I wanted and prayed for death. More shock treatments, hospitalized, and so on, and so forth, and then a third breakdown, and then a fourth.

"For hours and hours I stood in the bathroom combing my hair and crying until I was actually exhausted. I would tear myself away and try to scrub the kitchen floor, then sit down amongst it all—crying and crying. My friends would drop in, and how embarrassed I was, caught in such a state. They would tell me I just had to 'snap out of it.'

"I begged my mother and dad to help me. It was like being lost. I could see them but they couldn't see me or reach me. I was afraid—I tried to get Dad to talk to me. He told me he could be the same way if he let himself be—in other words, 'You are a weakling who cannot face minor disappointments.' For a long time we saw little of each other. I was not angry, but I realized they could not help me, and I made them feel bad when they saw me in such spirits. So rather than burden them, I felt I was doing them a favor by remaining out of their sight.

"Carl became weary and angry with me very soon, which is understandable, and yet it would have been so comforting if he would have only told me we'd do something, or that he loved me and would help me. But most of the time he was quite harsh and belittled me for not 'wising up and thinking of someone else besides myself.' He would call Frieda and she often came after me and I would spend the day with her. I was off Carl's hands then. Finally, as good as she was to me, I learned that it also made her unhappy to see me that way, and she even told me she'd rather not come at all to see me. Then she could think in her mind that I was probably feeling better and she could go about her happy home without sad thoughts of me.

"On the day I came in here, I had eaten rat poison which did not work. Dr. Berson decided I should see a different doctor and he sent me here."

12

Schizophrenic Living

For twenty-five years I've been helping young psychiatrists prepare for their Board exams by observing and offering comments about their interviewing skills. That was the situation a few months ago when a young woman who had been brought by her friends to the emergency room of our hospital was being interviewed by a student psychiatrist. I'd not seen her before. She was lively, friendly, thirty-ish, seemed pretty behind her dark glasses.

Dark glasses have always represented an impenetrable barrier for me, so, as usual, with apologies, I interrupted to ask her to take her glasses off. She was reluctant. I closed the blinds in my office and asked her again. Her manner changed. She became tense and uneasy. She removed her glasses unwillingly but then, to my astonishment, she held her eyes tightly closed, explaining, "If I look at you, it's like making you a part of my life. Then when you go away, I can't stand the enormous sense of loss and the emptiness I feel." She said she had looked at no one directly for more than six years, even the man she felt she loved.

I remembered a story my wife told me about Marisol, the famous sculptress who came to a party wearing a mask that was painted a ghostly white with purple half moons over the eyes. She wore the mask throughout the evening and finally, at the insistence of everyone present, removed the mask, revealing her face painted in exactly the same manner. Then I thought about the nineteen-year-old airman I had cared for when I was an Air Force psychiatrist in 1954. He had feigned mental illness to obtain his release from military duty in Korea and had been flown to an Air Force hospital in the United States. He told me that, while in Korea, he had written a letter to a friend back home asking for descriptions of symptoms of mental illness that he could claim as his own. His friend replied as he had been asked. The airman practiced and then went to the base hospital and succeeded in being shipped home as mentally ill. He was proud of the successful deception, which he described to me in detail. He had pretended he felt people were talking about him, that he heard voices calling him vulgar names. He told the military doctors he thought there had been some kind of sinister plot and that homosexuality and communism were involved. He laughed at their stupidity.

But my examination revealed a psychotic man with an illness as serious as the one he pretended and one that was not too different in type.

Under sufficient pressure, human beings have thought, said, and done *everything* that is mentally or physically conceivable. And, no matter how unseemly or bizarre, any deed that one person can perform, any other can comprehend. Each person shares a potential for understanding not only the refined and cultivated acts of others but also those that are eccentric, uniquely individual, or even "uncivilized." It is the average man's inescapable intimacy with the very things his society labels as deviant which causes him to shout "bizarre," "sick," "incomprehensible," and "not me!" A sustaining awareness of this tendency to deny parts of one's self well serves students of the history of schizophrenic living. That history is a centuries-old pattern of rejection, gross neglect, or persecution. It is borne to us by more than legend. Sadly, it continues to the present moment.[1]

Only a few decades ago, hundreds of thousands of schizophrenics were warehoused and forgotten in remote dungeons euphemistically called "mental hospitals." Pessimism about these many individuals was so pervasive that the very nature of schizophrenic living itself was confused and falsely equated with living in a dreadful custodial hospital under the most grotesque circumstances. The social and medical consequences that were the direct result of being maintained in a mental hospital were often greater than the impairment from the initial symptoms. Deterioration of the patients was the ordinary, almost the inevitable, course. In such hospitals there were often two or three thousand patients with no more than three or four doctors. Often there were no nurses at all.

I saw my first psychiatric patients in such a setting. I was a medical student at Indiana University and I would go two or three times each week to the state hospital to talk with patients there. I remember those first patients as vividly as any experience in my life. They suffered acute and chronic schizophrenic illnesses. The acutely ill were terrified of the collapse that was occurring in their world. The chronic patients were deep in reverie, refusing to speak, laughing to themselves. They were awesome and dreadful illnesses then—as they are today. In those days we had no major tranquilizing medications. Just as serious, we had little hope. There are people who remember good things about such institutions. I don't. That there are now fewer than 200,000 people in state hospitals in contrast to the 600,000 people permanently hospitalized in 1955 is, for me, a great accomplishment. There is no way to take good care of people in large institutions that are separated from the life of the family and the community.

Sadly, however, the pattern of neglect that was characteristic of the warehousing of the chronically ill in public hospitals in the 1930s, 1940s, and 1950s is now repeated nationwide by neglect of patients released to the streets. The large hospitals are closing and their patients are regularly abandoned to fend for themselves or they are housed in abysmal board- and care-homes in slum areas. It is a national shame. We perpetuate the centuries-old abuse of the severely mentally ill. Until this pattern of neglect is reversed, nationwide, my profession and our society deserve little credit among those who endorse

Schweitzer's belief that reverence for life is the ultimate human value. In part, the neglect is a consequence of the wish to cut public expenditures. In part, the neglect is a reflection of the difficulty of helping those who are gravely ill. Partly, the contemporary philosophy of "it's every man, woman and child for himself" applied to the work practices of mental-health professionals and local and state governments strikes hardest at the chronically mentally ill. They fare badly in our midst.

WHAT IS SCHIZOPHRENIC LIVING?

Despite three millennia of individual, family, and public concern and eight decades of scientific research, a precise explanation of the nature and cause of these astonishing human events is not yet possible. Theories abound and there has been remarkable scientific progress in the areas of diagnosis, treatment, and estimation of prognosis. Still, at this time, no one can say with certainty what schizophrenic living is, why it occurs, and how we can lessen its incidence.

There are many varieties of schizophrenic living. Some who are called schizophrenic are like beaten and dazed fighters; they live their lives aimlessly, staggering without direction in a defenseless state as if awaiting a final blow. Their thinking seems dulled, obtunded. They are extremely withdrawn and unable to function outside a hospital or other protected setting. Such individuals often call forth a feeling of pity and compassion. They are clearly sick. There are others, however, who are much more threatening, whose strange thinking and odd behavior severely challenge the ideas, values, and shared traditions of the "normal" members of the society. Of such individuals, called "paranoid" or "schizophrenic," Talcott Parsons, the sociologist, wrote, "They are the iconoclasts of our time. They refuse to believe what we know to be true. They refuse to do the things human beings are supposed to do." This idea as elaborated by psychiatrist Jules Masserman was earlier noted but bears repetition: almost everyone is made more comfortable by faith in the validity of one or more deeply held beliefs.[2] Many hold to the existence of a transcending

God. A second group has faith in the inherent worth of the work of man and woman and sees purpose in the persistence to develop this planet and ultimately some other planet. For others, a belief in the essential truth of brotherhood, love, and sexuality, a trust in loyalty, fidelity, and the communion between fellow beings, is the treasured basis for life. Many who are called "schizophrenic" refuse to believe and act in accordance with such assumptions. By repudiating the style of life others lead, schizophrenic individuals may be very threatening. Verification of the power of such a threat is evident if you consider the idea of living with someone who believes neither in a transcending purpose nor in the value of any work, or who could never appreciate how good it is to be together.

The question of how best to describe and define the schizophrenic way of living is one that has long been debated but remains unresolved. How much is sickness a "disease of the brain"? How much is a deviant way of life deliberately chosen because of repeated defeat and unhappiness during the years of life shared with others? How much is a period of sickness followed by a determined choice never to return to the former, painful, vulnerable "normal" way of living?

Schizophrenic living is the ultimate "maladaptive life-style," one that is often adopted in the face of overwhelming stress from the psychological, biological, and social circumstances in the life of the individual. The magnitude of this maladaptation is great indeed; the results of schizophrenic living can be death through suicide, starvation, maniacal frenzy, or self-mutilation. It is the "last-ditch stand" of a person who is desperately trying to maintain some semblance of life with self-respect in the face of overwhelming defeat.

Descriptively, schizophrenic living is characterized by a changed manner of thinking and feeling and by a giving up of a shared life with others. That shared life is replaced by a solitary way of living dominated by preoccupation with the sensations, feelings, and ideas experienced in the moment. The schizophrenic life frequently is a moment-by-moment life, a *now* life with little or no concern for maintaining the standards implied by past history and no apparent wish to actualize future possibilities. Instead, the sensations of the moment assume total importance. Passing sounds are listened to with such intense preoccupation that they acquire a significance and complexity beyond that of merely passing sounds. One's face in the mirror on close and prolonged scrutiny is revealed to possess new or previously unnoticed shapes, shades, or areas of creasing. One's eyes are particularly captivating with their blends of red, white, green, blue, black, and with a small round pupil in the middle that changes shape with shifts of light and at times with shifts of mood. Or, a simple word, repeated and repeated, discloses unsuspected sounds and meanings, some harmonic and friendly, some disturbingly cacophonous. Meanwhile, all else in the world is unnoticed. Such highly personalized preoccupation inevitably diminishes the individual's ability to understand or to be understood by others. There is, finally, a deterioration of the capacity to work, to think, and to relate to any other person.

Schizophrenic living when well established dominates every sphere of thinking and behaving. The way in which this occurs was first described by a Swiss psychiatrist, Eugene Bleuler, in the early 1900s, and his descriptions require little modification almost a century later.[3] He pointed out that, above all, schizophrenic living is made of a variety of extreme defensive stances assumed in an effort to avoid further hurt. One such stance is in the form of an actual fleeing or hiding—secluding oneself under a bed, for example. Another retreat is achieved by sitting with one's head buried in one's hands, knees drawn up before the covered face. Or, the retreat and withdrawal may occur through a fracturing of the various mental processes. This form of retreat and withdrawal is accomplished by a blunting or inappropriateness of feeling, a discontinuity or irrelevancy of thought, and ultimately a withdrawal of all concern from the reality formerly shared with others. John Wing, a leader in thirty years of social psychiatric research in Great Britain, has described the vulnerable status of such patients: "Many patients who experience an attack of acute schizophrenia remain vulnerable to social stresses of two rather different kinds. On the one hand, too much social stimulation, experienced by the patient as social intrusiveness may lead to acute relapse. On the other hand, too little stimulation will

exacerbate any tendency already present toward social withdrawal, slowness, underactivity and an apparent lack of
motivation. Thus, the patient has to walk a tightrope between
two different types of danger and it is easy to become de-
compensated either way."[4] While it is possible to describe
separately each of these parts of schizophrenic living, they
come together in a unified way in the form of an extremely
guarded style of living in which control of experience serves
to prevent further loss of self-respect.

The disorder of feeling characteristic of schizophrenic living
may be of several varieties. There may be an overall blunting
of personality, a flatness, an experiencing of other people as if
from afar, a dazed indifference to any and every aspect of life.
Or, the defensive patterning may take the form of a mis-
application and inappropriateness of feeling. The individual's
emotions differ from those ordinarily felt in a like situation.
Instead, an opposite feeling or an apparently incongruous
feeling of amusement, fear, or bewilderment prevails. Tears
accompany a trivial event and laughter marks a tragedy. The
"usefulness" of such a splitting of feeling from life events was
described by a twenty-five-year-old male engineering student,
himself recovered from a period of grandiose, delusional preoccupation with the thought that he was Jesus Christ. He had
been hospitalized for three months.

Case Study 1: *Schizophrenic Living as the Last Effort*

"It isn't easy to describe what I went through. After
you have been badly hurt and humiliated, made to feel
hopeless and it keeps going on, you finally come apart.
That coming apart is the most terrifying thing in the
world. The doctors called it an acute schizophrenic
break. I was sure I was dying. But after a while, something happened and I just stopped feeling the terror.
The horror went away. Something turned off the
switch. Afterward, either I didn't feel very much about
anything or else what I felt had nothing to do with
what others were saying or doing. Whatever came into

my head was the way that I felt. For example, even if everybody else was crying, if I didn't feel sad, then it's not sad! You discover feeling is strictly up to you. It's optional. You don't have to feel any of the things that used to hurt you. That's one of the reasons that I am so shaky these days. Now that I'm better, I'm vulnerable again."

The "usefulness" of this separation of feeling from life situation may be demonstrated in the following imagined dialogue:

ACCUSER: "You are a bad, bad person."

THOUGHTS OF SCHIZOPHRENIC PERSON: "Perhaps he has been hired by the government to protect me and everything he says is to confuse the enemy so that they will not know he is my friend. I will smile at him. It will be a signal."

ACCUSER: "Your job is over. You have been fired. You will have no money to support yourself. Your family will need to go on relief. You are a failure."

THOUGHTS OF SCHIZOPHRENIC PERSON: "I can barely understand the words that he says. Something about money. But I don't have my wallet with me and I can't help him."

ACCUSER: "I want to help you. I am a doctor. I want to restore you to your former functioning self. You are sick."

THOUGHTS OF SCHIZOPHRENIC PERSON: "He is so serious. Is he really a doctor? He looks as if he might cry. But I feel like laughing."

A second characteristic of schizophrenic living is the loss or abandonment of the system of logical thought. No single explanation for the characteristics of schizophrenic thinking is fully satisfactory at this time. The hypothesis that schizophrenic living is produced by abnormality in brain activity and that some form of intoxicated state exists does explain certain aspects of the disordered thought. However, the frequent skilled structuring of schizophrenic thinking to protect a highly defended life-style also needs explanation. Here again, avoidance of further hurt appears to be a predominant matter. There are a number of different ways in which the thinking characteristic of schizophrenic persons differs from normal thought processes. Schizophrenic thought may be utterly concrete and specific so that the symbolic or abstract meanings that are so much a part of ordinary language and conversation may be lost. Or, something of the reverse may be the case. Thinking may be so totally vague, irrelevant, disconnected, or loosely symbolic as to defy understanding. In either case, the disordering of thought serves as a potent defense against the experience of a pyramiding of unpleasant realities. Certain of the characteristics of this way of thinking and communicating may be illustrated in the following examples:

> DOCTOR: "I'm going to ask you the meaning of two proverbs. People sometimes use these statements as a way of describing either an individual or a situation. I want you to tell me what they mean. The first is, 'A rolling stone gathers no moss.' "
>
> PATIENT (a twenty-year-old college student): "Friction will rub off the moss as the stone rolls along the ground."
>
> DOCTOR: "I'm going to give you a different proverb to explain. What does it mean when people say, 'A bird in the hand is worth two in the bush'?"
>
> PATIENT: "A bird that will sit in your hand would cost more. A friendly bird is better than two birds you don't know about. It's like a dog. Well, that's not a good example because of hunting dogs, which go out in the bush to kill birds. But some of those dogs are also expensive. By the way, if you should get lost in the woods when you're hunting, the moss is always on the north side of the trees and rocks. Once when I was a boy, I killed a bird with a stone."

The replacement of ordinary thinking by this kind of disordered intellectual process precludes the building up of ideas that hurt, maim, or degrade. It is, however, an extraordinarily costly defense.

The third major characteristic of schizophrenic living is called autism, "auto-ism." Autism is the ultimate withdrawal into self, the final turning away from a world shared with other people. The individual preoccupies himself with a private realm in which nothing matters except his own bodily sensations or the thoughts being experienced at the moment. The itching of a finger, a word remembered from a childhood rhyme, the configuration of clouds in the sky, any or all of these matters completely absorb all consciousness and over a period of days, weeks, months, or years transcend in importance anything and everything else.

Case Study 2: *The Man Who Looked Only at His Hands*

Arthur Robinson, aged twenty-nine, had lived in a mental hospital for five years. In the hospital, he spent almost all of his time looking fixedly at his hands, turning them over, moving the fingers slowly back and forth, examining the tortuous blue veins, and counting the many creases on the back of each hand. If not required to engage in some other activity, he would spend all day in this manner. He responded to specific requests to go to bed, get up, come to meals, and so forth, but when he was left to himself he turned to the examination of his hands. He never spoke unless first spoken to. In this manner he lived his life, day after day, year after year.

Because I was his ward doctor, one day it fell to me to tell him the sad news that his mother had suddenly passed away. She was the only relative who visited or wrote to him. She came to see him from home seventy miles distant once each week. She wrote letters to him that were never answered. She was a cheerful person, attentive and solicitous to Arthur when she visited. Although I had known her only a few months, I had liked her and felt a personal sadness on hearing the news. Arthur was, as usual, standing by his bed and examining his hands. They were held close to his eyes. He seemed to be counting something. I went over to him and said, "Arthur, I am afraid that I have very bad news for you. I am sad that I must be the one to tell you that your mother was found dead this morning. She apparently had a heart attack. I am very sorry. We will help you go to the funeral if you wish." As I spoke, Arthur slowly dropped one of his hands toward his side, and simultaneously a single tear rolled down his cheek. Then quietly, almost inaudibly, he said, "No, no thank you. I will stay here." And, even as he spoke, the hand that had fallen began very slowly to rise. He was soon, within a moment, examining both hands as before.

Such are the characteristics underlying the myriad symptoms that are associated with schizophrenic living:

* I won't be hurt anymore.
* I feel nothing or, if I feel, my feelings have no relation to what is happening.
* I can't be hurt anymore because my thoughts are disorganized and nothing adds up.
* I can't be hurt anymore because my life has been removed from the world of others.

There are many different kinds of beginnings and endings of periods of schizophrenic living. Most characteristically, at some point between late adolescence and the early years of adult life, following a cycle of mounting stress, disappointment, and failure, there occurs a period of enormous upheaval. The magnitude of this upheaval and the events that follow are astonishing when viewed by an outsider and catastrophic for the individual in whose life they occur. Variously labeled a "psychotic break," "acute schizophrenia," or "severe nervous breakdown," the experience is not easily compared with any other. It is, above all, an overwhelming, terrifying, uncanny series of experiences, an extremity of possible human happenings. With a mounting crescendo, the individual feels he is torn apart from his very world, that he is being betrayed by his own mind. He experiences his imminent annihilation as being at hand. Some respond to these events by a restless pacing leading to a shouting, maniacal state. For others, the mounting terror is signaled by the furtive and suspicious sleepless eyes of a man or woman grown sullen, expectant, and silent. In either instance, whether in shouting agitation or reconciled despair, these moments in time are desperate and frightening, akin to waiting at the bottom of an elevator shaft with the elevator car falling rapidly from above and doom but a moment away. But in acute schizophrenia, the moments of terror continue for hours, days, and even weeks. Individuals who live through this kind of "acute break" may devote much of the remainder of their lives to avoiding its repetition. This is equally true whether the individual recovers and is restored to his ordinary life or if he falls into a chronic pattern of schizophrenic living. One of the main characteristics of the symptoms of chronic schizophrenic living is that they serve to protect against the repetition of another acute break!

One patient I have remembered quite vividly for the last three decades had been hospitalized for several years when I first met him. He spent much of his time secluding himself, often hiding in a bathroom. When as his new doctor I attempted to make contact with him in the bathroom, he began to spend time under the bed. When I joined him there, he struck me. When I returned under the bed the next day, the patient tried desperately to strangle me, saying, "Get away from here! You are not my friend. No friend would want me to go through again what I went through before I came to this hospital. Let me alone or I'll kill you. I'll never leave here."

An ominous event that may follow the first days of an acute break is the development of angry and resentful suspiciousness of other people. The transition is often quite remarkable. After several days of extreme agitation and fearfulness, a strange calm may fall over the individual, a sudden "clarification" having come with the belief that the responsibility for his travail rests not with him but with others. The pioneer

American psychiatrist Harry Stack Sullivan described the process as follows:

> This is an ominous development in that the schizophrenic's state is taking on a paranoid coloring. If the suffering of the patient is markedly diminished thereby, we shall observe the evolution of a paranoid schizophrenic state. These conditions are of relatively much less favorable outcome. They tend to permanent distortions of the interpersonal relations.
> . . . A paranoid systematization is, therefore, markedly beneficial to the peace of mind of the person chiefly concerned, and its achievement in the course of a schizophrenic disorder is so great an improvement in security that it is seldom relinquished. . . . It is for this reason that the paranoid development in a schizophrenic state has to be regarded as a bad omen.[5]

Typically, the events that come before an acute break and the subsequent development of schizophrenic living patterns occur gradually over a period of weeks or months. However, this is not always the case. On occasion, such reactions occur almost precipitously in individuals who are placed in situations of overwhelming stress. Battle-front breakdowns, prison-camp decompensations, the long ordeals of sailors abandoned at sea or travelers lost in the desert are examples of stressful situations so overwhelming that acute schizophrenic decompensation may occur in individuals without a prior history of emotional difficulty. In such circumstances, the relationship between the immediate death threat and the development of a schizophrenic defense against the experience of death may be seen.* Once such a break with reality has occurred, however, it does not always correct itself when the immediate threat is removed. There is a considerable body of evidence that suggests a genetic vulnerability is regularly present in those in-

---

* Paradoxically, just as overwhelming stress may precipitate psychotic illness, there have been occasions when massive stress has provoked recovery in individuals who had long suffered psychotic living patterns.

dividuals who develop a chronic schizophrenic disorganization after an acute decompensation. The matter is still undecided. I don't have information about other family members of the patient who is described below.

Case Study 3: *A Man Whose Illness Began in a Hurricane*

Fred Means, aged twenty-eight, was an officer on a naval vessel that was caught during a severe tropical hurricane in the South China Sea. The storm was so severe that several other boats of comparable size capsized that night. During the height of the storm, he left his duty post and went to bed in his cabin. The next afternoon, he was taken to the ship's doctor, who found him to be confused. He was returned to a hospital in the United States where within a few months he tried twice to hang himself. And on a brief visit from the hospital to his home, he tried to kill himself with a rifle. Despite intensive therapy including medications and electrical shock, he remained preoccupied with bizarre ideas about homosexual practices, the control of human behavior by radar, and the possibility that he was finding human bones in the food that he was being served. He tied these three areas together in his thinking into a vague and disconnected "plot." He remained aloof, distant, and suspicious. He refused to see family members and walked away from them if they came to the hospital. Several times he struck hospital attendants, accusing them of planning his murder. He requested a release from the hospital and when this had been denied demanded an interview with the hospital director.*

DOCTOR: "I can't let you go home, Fred. I think you'd try to kill yourself."

* The hospital director was Dr. G. L. Harrington, a psychiatrist now working in Pacific Palisades, California.

FRED: "I won't pay any attention to my voices. Even if they tell me to kill myself, I won't do it."

DOCTOR: "I have to believe your voices, Fred. You've tried to commit suicide three times now."

FRED: "Suicide is a possibility for any man."

DOCTOR: "For you, Fred."

FRED: "For *any* man."

DOCTOR: "For *you*, Fred."

FRED: "What if you were in the top story of a tall building and the building was burning down and the flames were coming closer and closer to you and you had a pistol with a bullet in it. What would you do in the moment you realized there was no way out?"

DOCTOR: "I'd never live to see that moment, Fred."

FRED: "Then you've never been in a hurricane in the South China Sea!"

As in this example, there are many times when it is tempting to conclude that "this episode of schizophrenic decompensation would never have come to pass except for event X." And in reading the case study that follows, one cannot help but wonder, "Would Joan ever have become so emotionally disabled if her husband had not been called away?" Or, "At what point might his return have interrupted the extending pattern of decompensation?" Frequently, an acute psychotic episode occurring as a response to a severe precipitating stress in a previously well-functioning person will rapidly terminate and there will be a return of normal personality patterns in a matter of days, weeks, or one or two months. No individual ever forgets a psychotic episode, of course, but in such instances, the individual is able to return to his family and work without sustaining permanent loss. There are even times when the patient and family can build upon the disorganizing event and use it to reevaluate goals and relationships in a manner that is life enhancing. Conversely, a gradually developing schizophrenic decompensation in a marginally functioning person is more likely to be followed by a long interval of schizophrenic living. However, even these broad generalizations would probably have been of little use in predicting the pattern of decompensation that occurred in the life of this twenty-nine-year-old wife and mother.

Case Study 4: *Step-by-step Decompensation into Schizophrenia*

Joan was one of identical twins born in a well-established South Dakota family. She was to all outward appearances the more passive of the two girls in personality structure, but she adjusted well within the family unit, school, and community until she left home and went to college. At that time, Joan went west to a California university and her sister went to college in the East.

Within a few days after arriving at the university, Joan became extremely homesick, cried a great deal, and experienced the first gross anxiety of her life. She called her parents a number of times during the first week of school. She also sought medical help at the school infirmary because she feared she was having a heart attack. However, she weathered this crisis and, ten days after arriving on the campus, she met Bob. Within two weeks she had become his steady date. Theirs was an idyllic four-year campus romance. All other friends, teachers, learning experiences, and other factors were subsidiary to this relationship. Joan looked up to Bob and he was grateful for her admiration. They ate most of their meals together, took many classes in common, and were, in a sense, not only sweethearts and lovers but best friends. Joan was very happy during her years at college. Indeed, she thrived.

They were married one week after graduation and moved to a suburban community in Pennsylvania. Two children were born during the first four years of their married life. They remained devoted to each other, yet each was successful in his or her respective areas of community activity and family life. Joan was active in the church, was the prime organizer of a cooperative nursery school, and her health and spirits were good during those years.

However, after eight years of married life, in 1950, unexpectedly, Bob was called to active duty as a pilot during the Korean War. Joan was very shaken and during the weeks before his departure she cried a great deal, experienced much anxiety, but finally pulled herself together and bravely bid her husband farewell. Within a few days after his departure, however, Joan began to experience extreme anxiety and tearfulness. In an effort to retain her self-control, she composed a schedule of proposed work projects for herself. These included a four-month schedule of refinishing furniture in the home to be followed by a four-month project of sewing clothing for the children and new curtains for their room. Ultimately, she outlined a four-month project of sewing new clothing for herself in anticipation of her husband's return. She threw herself tirelessly into the furniture-sanding project, using all her spare time and working late into the evenings.

Two months after Bob's departure, she became concerned about heart palpitations and entered the local hospital for a three-day period of tests and examinations. The results of the hospital examinations were "essentially negative," and she was placed on mild sedatives. Her apprehension continued, however, and she began to supplement the sedatives with alcohol. She was particularly agitated during the late evening hours, and her sleeping patterns were disrupted by early morning awakening, bad dreams, and preoccupation with night noises in the house.

Four months after her husband's departure, she took her children back to the family home in South Dakota and remained there for two months. She settled down somewhat, though not completely. She then returned to her own home in Pennsylvania with the children despite the objections of her parents, who were very concerned about her restlessness. After her return to Pennsylvania there was a steady increase in the level of her agitation. She made a number of contacts with her physician and on two occasions made late evening calls to the police department because she felt the house was being invaded. She drank a good deal, ate sparingly, and sustained a progressive loss of weight. She completely abandoned her work projects. By the seventh month after her husband's departure, Joan's condition had deteriorated alarmingly. She cried a great deal, was extremely anxious, felt certain that she would die of a heart attack before her husband returned, and at times would sit mutely for hours, giving little attention to her home or children. The physician called her mother, who came to help Joan. Seven and a half months after Bob's departure, efforts were undertaken by the family physician through the American Red Cross to return Bob to his family. Joan handled this new development in a peculiar way. There was a sudden demonstration of an outward calm. She insisted on completing dental work before her husband's return, explaining to her mother, "I want to be perfect when he comes back." The family dentist told her that five teeth needed filling and was startled when she insisted that he remove these teeth. He declined her urgent request, and Joan began a search of the community to find a dentist who would remove all of the "decayed and rotten teeth." She was ultimately successful.

Immediately afterward, she became frantically agitated, alternately fearful and elated, grandiose and delusional. She stated that she was the Virgin Mary awaiting the return of God. She was floridly psychotic and actively suicidal when her husband returned.

Within an eight-month period of time in her life, Joan had been a "normal" wife and mother, an anxious and edgy person, obsessively preoccupied, phobic, somatically fixated, dependent on alcohol, suicidally depressed, and finally delusional. She was, to all appearances, normal, neurotic, and psychotic within a relatively short interval.

Joan required two years of almost continuous hospitalization* and she continued to receive out-patient psychotherapeutic help for several additional years after her release from the hospital and full return to her husband and children. Her level of recovery, ultimately, was substantial but not complete. There were certain long-term changes in her attitudes and manner. She was somewhat less dependent on her husband than before her hospitalization, though no less devoted. She was also a considerably less enthusiastic and vivacious person than she had been before. She was more cautious and restrained. Joan described this change in these words: "Maybe it's that I'm more grown-up than I was, not so silly and dependent on Bob. I used to get so excited when we'd start out to do something that he'd say it was cheap to get me drunk. I could get high without drinking a drop. I'm not so much that way anymore. I hold back a lot. I'm quieter, much more careful, maybe a bit moody." Bob felt that "a little something has been taken away from Joan by that dreadful period."

Many of the world's most distinguished scientists have worked much of their lives on the problem of schizophrenia. Over the years, there have been repeated flurries of publications naming first one organ, then another, then one subtle biochemical system in the brain, then another, as responsible for the personality changes seen in schizophrenic living. Early in this century it was discovered that a form of bacteria, the spirochete, was the agent causing syphilis, one of whose late manifestations was the severe mental abnormality called "general paresis." For many years, almost 10 percent of all admissions to psychiatric hospitals were of paretic patients whose symptoms of paresis mimicked schizophrenic living and other forms of serious mental difficulties. The discovery

---

* In all probability, her hospitalization would be considerably shortened today. That hospitalization began in 1952. Major tranquilizers were not yet available at the time of her initial decompensation.

of one specific cause for mental derangement and its frequently successful treatment with antibiotics gave hope that it would be possible to find a comparable explanation and cure in all instances of profound personality change. With the passage of time, however, it has become clear that there is no bacterial explanation for schizophrenic living. It also seems unlikely that there will be a proven viral etiology of schizophrenia, though a few workers continue to explore this line of research. What is quite fascinating to me is the four-decade effort to demonstrate brain pathology as the cause of schizophrenic living patterns. One of my teachers in medical school in 1947 was Doctor Breutsch, a neuropathologist who worked at the Central State Hospital in Indianapolis, Indiana. He conducted detailed microscopic examinations of brain tissue from patients who had died in the mental hospital. He was searching for scarring that might indicate infections, particularly rheumatic fever. Over the decades, the search for anatomical, chemical, and physiological alterations in the brain has continued and at the time of this writing there are some very interesting studies which may, at last, demonstrate that in some patients with schizophrenia there is a measurable abnormality in the density of brain tissue and/or the chemical activity of a part of the brain. Contemporary studies are being carried out with advanced X-ray techniques, radioactive chemicals, and highly refined neuroanatomical and neurochemical studies of brain tissue. The search for subtle physiological and chemical disorders in brain and other body systems continues in hundreds of laboratories around the world. That research is now achieving decisive momentum with one and then another scientific discovery finding its place in an increasingly probable theoretical system. These prevailing theories include a "multiple gene" genetic transmission of predisposition to schizophrenic living patterns, an explanation of the effects of stress in precipitating or prolonging such patterns, and a correlation of change in mood and behavior with predictable alterations in the preponderance of various brain amines. These substances, particularly the indoleamine, serotonin, and the catecholamines, dopamine and norepinephrine, are involved in the transmission of nerve impulse.[6,7,8]

It has always been evident that mental illnesses develop in certain families with much greater regularity than could be explained by chance. This led to conflicting theories emphasizing either genetic predisposition, early rearing patterns, or the effects of social stress. Carefully controlled studies have provided confirmation of a genetic factor in the transmission of schizophrenia through successive generations. Doctors David Rosenthal and Seymour Kety took advantage of extraordinarily detailed childhood adoption and mental hospital record-keeping systems in Denmark that go back several generations, related the two, and demonstrated strong evidence in support of a genetic influence in the occurrence of schizophrenic symptoms in successive generations (even among parents and children who were separated from and unknown to each other).[9] Other studies have followed up and refined techniques applied in the research concerning mentally ill twins undertaken in the 1930s by Dr. Franz Kallman of the New York State Psychiatric Institute.[10] He studied "concordance rates" for schizophrenia in identical and fraternal twins; that is, he was trying to establish how often it happened that if one twin showed the symptoms of schizophrenia the second twin would also show the same symptoms. He reported concordance rates for schizophrenia in 86 percent of identical twins (who share more or less identical genetic inheritance) and 16 percent of fraternal twins (who are, genetically speaking, siblings born at the same time). Contemporary studies generally support Kallman's work, though with considerably lower concordance rates (35 to 50 percent for identical twins, 5 to 15 percent for fraternal twins). Simultaneously, other findings also make it clear that rearing patterns do have at least some effect on individuals with strong genetic endowment for schizophrenia and an appreciable effect on persons without such a background. "Either-or" thinking with regard to psychological, sociological, and biological factors as causative of schizophrenic living patterns usually will lead one astray. But at the same time *there is absolutely no question that many tenderly reared, deeply loved, skillfully nurtured individuals have developed schizophrenic living patterns because of what must be primarily genetically determined factors.*

Equally, despite research in many areas pointing to an association between the incidence of schizophrenic living patterns and the presence of various genetic, metabolic, social class, family relationship patterns, and so on, it is not yet possible to offer a definitive or convincing explanation as to why this person, right here and right now, manifests symptoms characteristic of schizophrenic living or why another person does not! If one could remake the world, it would be as well next time to leave out a genetically determined predisposition for severe mental illness. It just isn't fair. Perhaps that's one of the reasons so many mental-health professionals, including some physician-psychiatrists, prefer to ignore, play down, or refute the relevance of "biological factors." They fear the consequences upon the patient's motivation for self-help if part of what is wrong cannot be overcome by work, talk, understanding, and hope. But in the long run, any approach that denies what is real cannot help the intended beneficiary. Anyway, people already know. You simply tell the truth, both as to the facts as you understand them and as to your intentions in offering to work with the family. For example, "Well, from what you've told me, there does seem to be a tendency for emotional problems and mood disorders to run in the family, very strongly in some, a lot less in others. We'll work to make yours a lot less."

The coming of a schizophrenic episode remains as serious a life event as one can encounter, and of that there should be no doubt.[11] Not only patients and families faced with schizophrenic living patterns but every society in the world has a stake in future scientific discoveries that will refine our prevention and treatment skills. The World Health Organization has identified the improved treatment of schizophrenia as one of the great goals of mankind. It appears that 1 percent of people everywhere suffer its consequences.[12] I have treated schizophrenic patients in the villages of Bangladesh and the plateau country of Ethiopia and talked to patients and their families in three dozen nations. The symptoms, the anguish, and the hope are about the same everywhere. The patients of Asia and Africa, their families, and neighbors, need the same kind of help, advice, and dependable support as patients in

North America. These illnesses and what people require to survive them are part of a basic human condition, tragedy shared across nation, color, and race.

The effective application of what we now know would help many or most of those who suffer schizophrenia, but not nearly to the degree that is needed. As one who has known the suffering of individual patients and their families for as many as twenty-five years, I wait with hope and expectation for future scientific discovery that will improve the therapeutic tools currently in use. I'm relatively certain that many of my patients have already received the benefit of a trial of the psychological, biological, and social therapies presently available. Yet they remain significantly impaired. Tragically, "significantly impaired" is a fair description of the majority of patients who suffer an acute schizophrenic episode, even those patients who are without doubt well treated.

A psychotic episode is an extremely draining event and people who have had the experience are wary of another misstep. This poses a significant dilemma for everyone. Do you advise rest and a slow return, or is the rapid restoration of movement and forward momentum indicated? A young man at college became paranoid. Should he return to school? A working woman who had planned to return to work three months after her baby's birth developed a psychotic episode in association with that birth. Should she remain at home or pick up her career?

Of course, every situation is different. There are many who feel so depleted by what has happened that their motivation to do anything at all is limited. They just don't feel like themselves and going back to work or school is frightening, embarrassing, and seems to require more energy than is currently available. They are understandably self-protective, restrained, and often still troubled by the reverberations of the original illness.

There are limits, but I am very much an advocate of movement and forward momentum in the treatment of schizophrenic illness. I'm a great believer in school, "developing your head," learning a new skill, picking up on a long-time interest. Bleuler felt somewhat the same way. He wrote that it is well to encourage the acute psychotic patient to return from the hospital as soon as possible, preferably in a matter of a few days. This would prevent, he hoped, two serious consequences of schizophrenia: first, the family's getting used to the patient's illness and withdrawal, and second, the patient's discovering another life, one away from daily reality. It's not that simple, of course, but my own experience is that there is often an element of choice that the patient exercises after sustaining so massive an assault. I encourage all my patients to pick up at least some of the pieces of their life as soon as possible. Many of my student patients were back for some of their classes on the second or third day of an acute illness accompanied by a nurse dressed in street clothing. That's not a blanket prescription, but it conveys some sense of the expectation I feel as to what my patient can and should do.

After release from the hospital, it's very important that the patient, family, and clinician have a strong and clear working relationship. What happens next is very much dependent on a contribution to recovery from those three sources. I think the great majority of relapses and rehospitalization episodes could be effectively prevented if the clinician, patient, and family have a good understanding. So, I agree with what Herz and Melville wrote on the subject: "We recommend that the treatment of every schizophrenic patient include a major focus on teaching patient and family to recognize early signs of decompensation and what steps to take to ensure initiation of prompt and effective treatment. Because the prodromal period (before relapse) usually lasts more than a few days, it should be possible to abort an incipient acute psychotic episode."[13] This is especially the case in those many instances in which one of the patient's symptoms may be loss of control and violent outbursts, sometimes against family members. What a terrible disservice it is to people—patients and families alike —to ignore a history of aggressive or self-destructive behavior and send a patient home without preparing the family AS ONE WOULD PREPARE ONE'S OWN FAMILY in such a circumstance. That preparation and the knowledge that treatment will be available precisely when needed makes an enormous difference. It is the moment in psychiatry above all others that lives by the Golden Rule.

Management of medications is both very important and complicated enough so that the patient and family should share responsibility with the clinician. There is absolutely no doubt that the great majority of patients with chronic schizophrenic patterns do better on an appropriate medicine in an appropriate dosage.[14] "Appropriate" means a dose that changes from time to time as the condition itself changes. There are, of course, good reasons why most patients are ambivalent about taking medications. One of my patients said he was never more than 51 percent convinced he should take them even though he admitted they kept him out of the hospital. Some patients do have troubling side effects. Some develop a condition called tardive dyskinesia, with involuntary movements involving primarily the muscles of the lips, tongue, cheeks, and jaw.[15] But, on balance, a well-managed, smoothly functioning anti-psychotic drug program is a gift to the patient and family of considerable importance. Without such a program, an estimated 50 percent and more of patients will have relapses that could have been prevented.

I have written often about the patient and the importance to the patient of support from the family. However, for a given individual, living with close relatives may be more stressful than beneficial and things may go better if the patient lives separately but retains close contact with family members. One of my colleagues, Dr. Werner Mendel, has had extensive experience in outpatient care of very disturbed chronic schizophrenic patients. He believes that all who can should live in their own place. He also feels that many patients should *not* be placed in day-care programs with other psychiatric patients. Instead, arrangements should be made to pay a supervised college student, friend, or neighbor to spend two hours two or three times a week as helper-assistant-companion. Mendel feels that putting patients in an environment of patients teaches chronicity and is basically antitherapeutic.[16]

The patient with a long-term schizophrenic living pattern is inevitably caught up in many conflicting emotions about those who offer help. One of the problems is that the therapist and family support are so desperately needed by the patient that the threat of loss of the relationship(s) is simply unendurable. Worse, it's undignified to need someone that much. And people, no matter how sick, have to protect their sense of dignity.

For some patients, the fear of closeness lest there be loss is compounded by a fear of closeness lest the patient be engulfed by the therapist. Uncertainty about self, the love and fear concerning the therapist, and the clouding of judgment and confused perceptions that may accompany schizophrenia make important relationships tense. It is hard for many such patients to sit back and enjoy the warmth of therapy. The stakes are too high. And often, the patient's past experiences were too disappointing. One of my patients explained, "You're you. I'm me. Don't you get confused. And don't confuse me."

I would like to close this chapter by addressing the sense of helplessness that all patients and all families feel. Particularly vulnerable are those who depend for their care on large public mental-health systems. Many are slow to respond or simply unresponsive. Since most chronic schizophrenic patients and their families have long ago depleted their resources, public care is their only option. If you depend on such care and if it is going badly and you can't obtain the help you need, I have a system to recommend that seems regularly to work. I have named it the "Four Telephone Call Approach." The first two calls should be made to the therapist. The third call should go to the office of the Director of Mental Health Services in the state where you live. The telephone is usually listed in the phone book under "State of, Department, Mental Health." The fourth call should go to the Office of the Governor. The operator will help with the number.

PART FIVE
CONCLUSION

13

Helping

The greatest gift is that which helps another person to become excited about his or her own life—to enjoy it, to be open to it, to be intrigued by its possibilities. The "helping" of a mental-health professional is, at its best, that kind of gift. The ability to share in the excitement and pleasure as another person becomes enthusiastic about his life is the essential personal quality of the effective psychiatrist. Importantly, this wish to share is not to be confused with a need to "tell others how to live," "give people the benefit of my wisdom," or "teach people discipline (or the reverse)." There is an important difference between appreciating and enjoying another person and the wish to govern and control. The nature of that difference is suggested in Theodore Reik's description of his last visit with Sigmund Freud:

> I flew from Amsterdam to Vienna to say good-by to Freud. We both knew we would not see each other again. After we shook hands, I stood at the door and could not say a word. My lips were pressed together so hard that they were unable to part. He must have

sensed what I felt; he put his arm on my shoulder and said, "I've always liked you." (He had never before said anything of this kind.) As I bowed my head wordlessly, he said in a low but firm voice, as if to comfort me: "People need not be glued together when they belong together."[1]

A psychiatrist is privileged to look in, to offer help, and, for what is usually a brief interval, to play a significant role in the life of the patient and the family. Then the therapy is over and each participant continues his search for meaning and satisfaction in other places. Doctor and patient continue on separate paths and no one can foretell what awaits either one of them.

But the truth is that it is hard for a psychiatrist *not* to be helpful. You begin by asking your patient to talk about his mood, hopes, and fears. Because you are really interested, he is careful to make his answers honest and thoughtful. You (must) take a thorough one- or two-hour history that reveals the nature of the patient's earlier experiences, key relationship patterns, genetic endowment, past physical health, and the here-and-now social and economic realities. An hour or two go swiftly, but doctor, patient, and family learn a great deal about each other in that interval. By the second hour's end, I'm usually able to tell people what I think. My recommendations are based in part on the specific information that my patient and members of his family have shared with me. They also reflect my strong convictions concerning the strengths that I believe exist in all people.

Of course, there is no insurance against the exigencies and disappointments of life. Neither psychotherapy, drug therapy, nor any other form of treatment offers entry to a new existence. Into the life of the happiest man ample reasons for despair can come. Even the most successful person may see himself as a colossal failure if he is unlucky enough to meet all of his critics on the same day! Psychotherapy does not ensure that a man's wife will love him or that an unfaithful husband will come home to stay. It will not create a metamorphosis into a new life.

Most of the people who consult a psychiatrist do so because of problems in marital, family, and other loving relationships.[2] Sometimes these problems are the primary difficulty. Often, they are secondary to illnesses affecting mood or to long-standing personality conflicts. The stress of debt, divorce, generational separation, alcohol abuse, and the questioning of belief in religion and family responsibility all contribute to the decision to seek psychiatric assistance. Individuals who traditionally obtain psychological, economic, and spiritual support through affiliation with the family or group suffer and become vulnerable when there is no family and when the group's constituency is constantly changing. Some people can carve out their identity no matter what but most people build their lives on a base of family tradition and family-supported education, within the context of a supportive social and cultural milieu. However, there are many, many people today for whom there simply is no effective loving social-family support system. They face alone a challenge called sink or swim. In this kind of rich, industrialized "every person on his own" society, there are unparalleled rewards for the fleet of foot, for those who do have strong support systems, and for a relatively small percentage of minority citizens who gain their foothold or who are selected as symbolic recipients of the rewards of societal concern. But despite a high financial living standard in North America, there are great gaps in people's lives, particularly in terms of psychological, social, and belief-system supports.

This is the way we live and people are generally adaptive. But it is in great discrepancy with the pattern of our own past history. People before faced terrible problems because of a lack of food and money, in association with disease, war, and oppression. But it was in the context of "belonging," being part of a "we." There is today more food and money, less disease, and so forth, but for many people there is no sense of "belonging" and there is no "we." For many there is more opportunity, for most there is less community. This displacement from the way people have lived in the past is what causes a number of individuals and families to seek psychiatric help. It also constitutes the context in which "helping" must take place. Whatever the nature of the patient's mood or the level of internal stability, whether there is some form of major mental illness present or not, the unstable, rapidly changing social and family systems are regularly significant issues in determining the therapeutic outcome.

The late Carson McCullers wrote compellingly about people and what they mean to each other. My favorite description was spoken by Frankie, aged twelve, in *The Member of the Wedding*.[3] She had decided that she would accompany her soldier brother and his bride on their honeymoon.

> FRANKIE (Suddenly stopping.): No. I just now thought of something. I know where I'm going. (Sounds of children playing in distance.)
>
> JOHN HENRY: Let's go play with the children, Frankie.
>
> FRANKIE: I tell you I know where I'm going. It's like I've known it all my life. Tomorrow I will tell everybody.
>
> JOHN HENRY: Where?
>
> FRANKIE (dreamily): After the wedding I'm going with them to Winter Hill. I'm going off with them after the wedding.
>
> JOHN HENRY: You serious?
>
> FRANKIE: Hush, just now I realized something. The trouble with me is that for a long time I have been just an "I" person. All other people can say "we." When Berenice says "we" she means her lodge and church and colored people. Soldiers can say "we" and mean the army. All people belong to a "we" except me.
>
> JOHN HENRY: What are we going to do?
>
> FRANKIE: Not to belong to a "we" makes you too lonesome. Until this afternoon, I didn't have a "we," but now after seeing Janice and Jarvis I suddenly realize something.
>
> JOHN HENRY: What?
>
> FRANKIE: I know that the bride and my brother are the "we" of me. So I'm going with them and joining with the wedding. This coming Sunday when my brother and the bride leave this town, I'm going

with the two of them to Winter Hill. And after that
to whatever place that they will ever go. (Pause.)
I love the two of them so much and we belong to be
together. I love the two of them so much because
they are the *we* of me.
The Curtain Falls.

There is simultaneously much in the way of scientific information that is required for further advance in helping. The
nature and causes of schizophrenia are not finally known and
a curative therapy is lacking; the management of depression
is very difficult and at times the patient must endure long
weeks of suffering before relief is provided; there are similar
problems in the management of mania. Psychotherapy, family
therapy, group therapy, behavior therapy, separately or in
sequence, sometimes fail to offer the help hoped for by therapist
and patient alike. No psychiatric remedies seem able to undo
the damaging effects of social deprivation, neglect, or persecution, particularly when they continue even as efforts to ad-
minister therapy are underway. Prolonged psychological
treatment is not a good remedy for those who feel isolated
because of divorce, the departure of children, or the obsoles-
cence of their social or work skills. For such problems, the
return to life activities, trying again, and/or coming back in a
new direction are the better approaches.

In the Introduction to this book I shared a carefully guarded
professional secret, one that bears repetition. Specifically, it
is not possible to know with certainty in advance which, if
any, of several potential therapies will be most helpful. The
treatment plan needs to be established with that therapeutic
reality carefully understood. There are some patients who
respond *only* to a sufficient dosage of one of the tranquilizers or anti-depressant medications. All the talk in the world,
no matter how sincere or convincing, will fail to provide relief
of symptoms. For such persons, neither individual, marital-
couple, nor group psychotherapeutic approaches will be useful;
nor will switching from a psychoanalytic to a client-centered
frame of reference make any difference. Medications and
medications alone (and only the appropriate one and in

sufficient dosage continued for a long enough interval) provide relief!

Yet there are other persons who will respond *only* to some form of relationship psychotherapy, that is, to the opportunity to learn about themselves, to reveal long-felt worries and fears, and to review their hopes and plans for the future. For such individuals the administration of drugs provides no help. Worse, there may be a clouding of consciousness, a preoccupation with side effects, and a blunting of motivation for self-help approaches as a result of inappropriate or ineffective drug use.

There are many others among the group called mentally ill who will respond *only* to a therapeutic program that combines the effective use of a specific medication, the effective application of a psychotherapeutic relationship, and specific intervention that modifies one or another of the social and economic problems handicapping their lives. A lesser approach inevitably fails.

And so it goes—patient after patient. Each is different. Each requires an individual approach. Although an experienced therapist can make educated guesses that are often correct, they are only guesses and they may well be incorrect. No matter how wise, how experienced, how careful the clinician may be, it is simply not possible to circumvent or gainsay a therapeutic trial. The importance for the patient to be working with a clinician who can make available the full armamentarium of treatment techniques and perspectives can hardly be overstated. Having begun a specific kind of treatment program, the clinician should be prepared to modify that original plan unless the patient's response is a rapid and fully satisfactory one. At this time in this field, prolonged therapy uninterrupted by experiment with alternative therapeutic programs seems clearly unjustified. For this reason, consultation between professional colleagues should be assigned an important place in the practice of all mental-health professionals. So many therapeutic advances have been achieved during the last decade that no single person can become expert in every area. It should not be an affront if a therapist happens to be expert in techniques that are not effective with a given individual. The incompatibility should be recognized and corrected early in the course of treatment!

THE MANY PSYCHOTHERAPIES

It is now eight decades since the first of Freud's theories were made known to his astonished contemporaries. Hundreds and thousands of books, tens of thousands of articles, and literally millions of hours of discussion have been devoted to the application of the major Freudian ideas that behavior makes sense and that people can change the way they feel. These days, the psychiatrist, psychotherapist, and mental-health consultant are to be found not only in private offices, clinics, and hospitals but also in prisons, primary and secondary schools, colleges, homes for unwed mothers, factories, government agencies, city planning departments, religious seminaries, police departments, advertising agencies, and on the bench with professional football teams. In contemporary North American culture, personal hang-ups are viewed as amenable to change, and the widest variety of counselors, therapists, and group leaders offer their services to those who seek to be different from the way they are.

By now the subject has lost most of its glamour. On radio talk shows, people talk about other things. But every year millions of people build up their courage, make an appointment, and somewhat self-consciously establish themselves as the patient of Dr. X. Even if the drama seems a bit dated on television or in the theater, for the participants in real-life consultation the event is as moving and full of risk as ever.

After all these years, what is the status of talking as therapy? If the goal of life is to learn about, discover, and enjoy it, how much of that can happen while sitting around talking?

Thinking over the three decades of my own experience, certain matters are clear. Those undertakings that featured the patient as student-in-trouble and starred the therapist as impresario of life-living have been duds. Those patients who succeed in trapping a therapist into a "let's pretend" role of teacher of the how-to-feel and how-to-live protected their lives from the risk of change through therapy. Learning to live as the therapist advises is like deciding to do something spontaneously two times daily. No one has figured out how to remember not to remember but to do it anyway. The same problem arose in the process of trying to teach therapists how to make the correct responses. Such instruction went the way of the European academies of art: the more the students copied their teachers, who were copying Rembrandt, the worse the paintings became. I think that this is mostly because psychotherapy (and psychiatry) is not separable from the personality of the participants any more than it is from the life of the times. It does not stand apart. Instead, it is part of the concentric ripples on the waves that make up the tide. The hopes and aspirations of the day, the prejudices that are in ascendance, the economic-political-social realities of the people are not simply matters of relevance. They are the arena in which the person discovers or evades, declares or denies, who he is. The point of focus in the therapy is not the fantasy stirred up in the therapist; it's what happens and doesn't happen in the life of the person called patient. For a therapist, the best strategy is to allow what the patient is saying to live on for a while without dissection, without categorization, and without refutation. Then, after the therapist has listened to and dwelled in the words and life of the patient, suddenly he discovers, "There is much I haven't heard. Is it unnoticed, unspoken, hidden, disguised?"

My own work as a psychotherapist has always been limited (or was it graced?) by my failure to find a highly specialized approach in psychiatry that could regularly encompass the wide variety of problems that unfold in a psychiatrist's office. My own early training included a personal psychoanalysis and the extraordinary scope of Freudian theory has greatly influenced at least one important aspect of my work. Specifically, the indelible imprint of one's early years and their influence on what a person is willing and able to learn about life is a matter reinforced both by my work with patients and by what I have learned about myself. The courses we follow in our lives and the conflicts we spend a lifetime trying to solve come often from the do, the don't, and the do-don't of early years.

In particular, a good many people spend decades and decades worrying about who is the most loved.

Case Study 1: *The Sixty-three-year-old Kid Sister of Shirley Temple the Second*

Mrs. Angie Rogers became my patient during the first year that I went into practice. She was sixty-three years old at the time, a rather forceful person, challenging and sometimes very challenging. I saw her at the request of her family physician, who was puzzled, disappointed, and frustrated because a full year of various therapies had failed to get her up from bed and back to work. She had severe stomach pains and occasional dizzy spells. She was outraged when I first went to see her because I was a psychiatrist and she was practically apoplectic when I asked her to talk about her childhood, her relationship with her mother and father, and her feelings about her only sibling, a younger sister. That sister she called "Shirley Temple the Second." It was still going on! I saw Mrs. Rogers twice in the hospital and listened to her angry complaints about everybody, everything, and me in particular. Then she got up from bed, forgot about her pains, and declared herself my patient . . . "and don't try to get out of it."

There were many reasons for her dissatisfaction. She'd been unhappy as a youngster, felt that she was clearly "number two" behind her sister, and most of her subsequent relationships seemed to reinforce her doubts about herself. Undoubtedly, her techniques for making and holding friends contributed to the unchanging nature of her life. She had evolved a fairly predictable ritual of meeting someone, liking him, assaulting him, and then offering to make friends. Then, after the friendship was established, every once in a while she had to test things. She was often disappointed and she didn't have many friends. Her first husband had divorced her and her second was a quiet drinker who "when we were first married, wanted to make love once a month. Now, he wants to talk once a month."

Mrs. Rogers came to see me once a week for what was to be a fifty-minute hour. Three-quarters of the time she was angry at me about something I said, didn't say, was afraid to say, or had supposedly said the week before. One-quarter of the time she talked about her hopes, her tender feelings toward her husband, her sometime concern about the health of Shirley Temple the Second, and her relief that I hadn't thrown her out of the office.

We'd been working together for five or six months and things seemed to be going fairly well. She went back to work. She also reported some progress with her husband: "It's better. Now he lets me make love with him once a month and talks with me once a month." Her relationship with me seemed to settle down a bit. I began to think about suggesting that her appointments with me could be less frequent. Perhaps she read my mind. Suddenly, I faced the angriest, most unreasonable, most aggrieved and self-righteous person in the world.

I had sensed that something was going on the week before. She was a bit aloof and serious. There was an unfriendly calm about her. At the end of that hour I said, "Well, I'll see you next week," and she replied with some emphasis, "Yes, you will indeed." The next week she was even more remote, mysterious, and unfriendly. One and a half hours after she left my office, while I was talking with a young medical student, a woman, she burst in unannounced, holding a paper with two columns of figures. It was her record of the total minutes I had spent with other patients (average fifty-six) and the scant forty-seven minutes spent with her! She was outraged, deadly serious, and frankly vengeful. All the rest of the world disappeared from her consciousness. She was totally involved in the hurt and betrayal. She even dealt scornfully with the medical student, whom she had misidentified as another of my patients. Her parting words to me were, "I quit this farce!" and to the astonished student who was there she said, "If you want him that much, I'll give him to you."

The next several weeks were made more interesting by a series of angry letters with a carbon to the dean of the medical school where I worked and a number of telephone requests for the name of the young woman student. Mrs. Rogers wanted to "finish the story" that she felt needed to be told. She also decided to see another psychiatrist, but then became angry with him because he wanted to be a "neutral judge." A month later she was back as my patient. She insisted nothing much had happened. There was nothing in particular to learn from that episode. It related to nothing else in her life history. She had a right to be suspicious of me. She might be slightly too preoccupied with such matters but that was perfectly understandable and justified because of her earlier experiences. And, "If that's all you want to talk about, then there's no point in my coming back. That's over. Stop referring to it. I'm no criminal." We worked together another three months. Mrs. Rogers was a little "spent" and I was a bit gun-shy.

I am afraid that I had a clearer sense than Mrs. Rogers did as to how this particular style of drama, occurring with inexorable regularity throughout her life, had restricted substantially what she could learn of the possibilities of life. Freud thought of these kinds of events as a "repetition compulsion," an attempt to detoxify certain painful experiences by repeating them over and over, asserting control over life by making the defeat occur again. This is a kind of perverse victory through defeat. It can come to feel good to feel miserable, particularly if you yourself write the script, orchestrate the music, and manipulate the dialogue. Freud cast the drama in terms of instincts, repressions, unconscious motivation, and compromise solutions between social realities and personal desires.[4]

My own approach to the kind of patient just described takes a different tack. I keep asking, "Why can't I be me and you be you? Why do I have to play out some tired drama with a grubby outcome assured for all?" And more to the center, I try to point out, "In a life that must someday end, you insist on squandering your opportunities to learn and do something new and different." In dialogue form, the confrontation might go something like this:

> THERAPIST: "I am not the mother, father, aunt, uncle, or teacher who preferred Shirley Temple the Second over you."
> MRS. ROGERS: "You look like them."
> THERAPIST: "Look again; it's only me."
> MRS. ROGERS: "I can't tell the difference."
> THERAPIST: "Stop covering your eyes with your hands."
> MRS. ROGERS: "Okay, but can I keep my fingers in my ears?"
> THERAPIST: "No! You need your hands free to reach out."

In this kind of approach in psychotherapy, one assumes that it is not so much the pull from the past that holds people back as it is the fear of the future. But what is it in the future that one fears? Some people are overwhelmingly afraid that they will be made to look foolish. Others fear going into their future because it will mean a final surrender of the (vain) hope of recreating parts of their past. From an existential point of view, that which is most dreadful is our human fate. Some people are willing to do almost anything to avoid living the life of the being who knows his days are numbered.

A major change in my own pattern of practice and in that of many of my colleagues has been the extension of participation beyond doctor and patient to include a wide variety of others. There are now many therapists who treat individuals and their mates. Others work with couples and their children or couples and their parents. Some prefer to work with three-generation family groups. Some therapists include the patient and the group with whom the patient lives or works. In a university setting, this could include ten other members of a rooming house. In skid row, the other participants might be the tenants of a small hotel in which the patient creates a nightly disturbance. Obviously, in this kind of effort, the "sickness" of any single individual rarely remains the exclusive focus of the discussion. Instead, the nature of "our life together" and the reciprocal effects that people are having upon each other becomes the concern of all. Including the wife as a coparticipant in the therapeutic work often reveals that she too is discouraged and depressed and that the marriage they share lacks the hope and warmth for which both privately yearn. After a few shared sessions, it sometimes becomes clear that the unhappiness of this couple seems to make problems for their children and it appears wise to include them in the therapeutic process. When one or another of the grandparents are in the vicinity, it can be very helpful to ask them to add their perspective. When it goes well, what started out as the treatment of one person who bore the label "mentally ill" becomes instead a series of explorations, reevaluations, and reordering of purposes that enriches the life of an entire group. It very often happens that the one who is designated the patient is instead, or as well, the "symptom carrier" for the group, the one who cries "ouch" for a couple, a family, or a society that is aching. Fanon, Halleck, and Myrdal have said it better than I.[5,6,7]

Because people are so accustomed to thinking about psychotherapy as a two-person process, they question how open and candid it is possible to be in the presence of a mate, children, parents, fellow workers, or others. On first consideration, the average individual is likely to be quite wary: "I'm not an exhibitionist!" However, someone who has had the experience of participating in a couple, family, or group therapy program could well reply:

> I felt that way too at first. But actually, it worked the other way. The other patients in the group inspired me and they were as helpful as the therapist. I started out thinking, "Oh God, I can't say anything in here. I don't even know if I can trust these people not to

blackmail me." And then, some other member of the group cautiously speaks up, "I hope I can trust you all because I've decided to tell you honestly why I've come. It isn't easy. . . ."

With the passage of time, you come to feel very close to the others. You get past competitiveness, and you want the other guy to succeed. You help each other. You learned a lot about yourself because someone else took a chance and spoke about things that have been bothering you. And finally, one day, you decide it's time to risk it. You decide: *Today I'm going to get something for myself!* And you do!

I had precisely that kind of experience in 1970 in a group led by Virginia Satir during a one-week "growth" experience at Cambridge House in Milwaukee. I began the week by giving my name as Milton Miller, Chairman of the Department of Psychiatry at the University of Wisconsin. I returned home with a lighter load.[8] Many contemporary therapies focus on the *here* and *now* in search for the answer to why an individual is not able to enjoy and adequately participate in his life. His or her way of dealing with the here and now of the therapy hour (right here! right now!) becomes the issue as illustrated in the following brief vignette.

A marital therapy meeting with husband, wife, and therapist. This is the twelfth appointment. Gene is twenty-nine and Sue is twenty-seven. They have been married for four years and came for treatment after Sue had consulted an attorney to start divorce proceedings. Both Sue and Gene were frequent complainers about the other's indifference.

DOCTOR: "Gene, I'd like you to stop now in what you are saying, and turn your chair so that you are directly facing Sue. Say it to her. You've been talking about her without looking at her. And you don't have a chance to see the emotion she is feeling while you speak."

SUE: "It won't do any good. He never—"

DOCTOR (interrupting Sue): "Wait, Sue, please say it
to Gene, and look at him when you say it. I've
noticed that both of you talk without seeming ever
to talk directly to each other."

SUE (looks at Gene, starts crying): "Oh Gene, please
help me."

GENE (pushing back his own tears and speaking to the
doctor): "This is the first time Sue has ever asked
me to help her."

DOCTOR (standing up, going over and turning Gene's
chair so that he now directly faces Sue): "Gene, tell
it to Sue."

Over a period of many weeks, individuals in a psychotherapeutic relationship are likely to become open and direct
with each other. The give and take, though painful, gives
participants an opportunity to learn that it is possible to become angry, to speak one's mind, to express a foolish idea or a
tender one, and return without shame and fear to the next
meeting. When therapy is successful, there are often changes
in the individual's attitude to other people. They may be less
concerned with pleasing anonymous others and more particular
about what happens with those closest in their lives. That concern sometimes takes the form of a lessened possessiveness and
at the same time a greater reverence and respect. Above all,
there is usually a fuller appreciation of the personal qualities
of self, family, and other people in general. The joys of experiencing and choosing for oneself are desired for one's
fellows. This is the key to a greater capacity for love.

There are important similarities among the various forms
of psychotherapy. As I've said before, I find that the most
successful efforts are clear about the fact that in the future,
therapist and patient will be continuing their searches for
meaning and satisfaction individually. The therapist and the
patient, it is hoped, will each be enriched and made more
curious about life by virtue of their contact with each other.

Psychotherapy cannot be conducted according to a script.
Success, if it comes, may be a consequence more of the spirit
in which the therapy is conducted than of the techniques employed. In the course of my work, I think often of a Hasidic

legend that tells of Zusha, the rabbi, who lay dying. He called his family and students together and told them, "When I meet my creator, he will not say, 'Zusha, why were you not as Moses?' He will say, 'Zusha, why were you not as Zusha?' "[9]

THE USE OF PSYCHIATRIC DRUGS

For the average person, taking drugs of any sort is a rather questionable thing to do. From earliest childhood, people have learned that drugs can be habit forming and the image of the drug addict or of the individual grown dependent upon sleeping capsules is a very negative one. As with the person who becomes dependent on alcohol, people tend to look down on the user of prescription medications. There is a general sense that "one should be able to do it by himself and not have to depend upon a crutch." Prescription of medications has been viewed by some mental-health professionals as a step to be avoided at all costs because it seems to be in opposition to the "self-help" philosophy that is held in high regard. For psychotherapy-minded doctors and patients alike, drug prescribing and drug taking conjure up a cacophony of sounds that include crutch, weakling, addict, dependent, dry-mouth, skin reaction, hooked, suicide, narcotics, drinker, unpsychological, slurred speech, and so on.

However, one fact outweighs all other suppositions, prejudices, "common sense" advice, and other "logical" ideas on the subject: in many situations and to a remarkable degree, *the new drugs work.* For certain kinds of illnesses, they are the only treatment that is regularly helpful.[10,11]

There is no clear dividing line between the many kinds of medications. However, it is possible to consider the most commonly used types in five general categories. The first are the various sedatives, anxiolytics, muscle relaxers, and sleep-producing agents. They include alcohol (ethanol), Librium (chlordiazepoxide), Valium (diazepam), the barbiturates, bromides, paraldehyde, and chloral hydrate. Their various therapeutic uses are as muscle relaxants, mild anti-anxiety agents, and hypnotics. They are generally ineffective in the outpatient treatment of severe agitation* and they are almost totally ineffective in the treatment of severe depression. As with most drugs, these mild agents in sufficient dosage or used over a prolonged period of time regularly have serious detrimental effects. They should not be casually prescribed or self-regulated. There is great concern now about the widespread and long-term use of drugs such as Librium and Valium. That many doctors prescribe them without much worry and that many millions of patients take them with regularity every day has never been a guarantee of their safety. These drugs are now a significant part of stress-filled life-styles and are regularly used with alcohol.

The second category is made up of agents that provide major tranquilization and have specific anti-psychotic properties. They are used primarily in treating the intense agitation, excitement, and disordered thinking associated with schizophrenic living. They are potent agents that produce their own problems, but their use is the main factor in diminishing the morbidity of schizophrenia. It takes an experienced clinician to decide on their use, to persuade hard-to-convince patients to cooperate, to set and regulate the dosage, and to try to prevent and/or manage side effects. All this is very important since there are now data showing that seriously sick schizophrenic patients are more than twice as likely to suffer relapse and require return to the hospital if they remove themselves from major tranquilizers. Unfortunately, many chronically ill patients aren't very reliable when it comes to taking their medications and there are times when it is better if someone else shares that responsibility.

Because Leonard required three periods of hospitalization within six months, I attempted to "hold off" relapses into schizophrenic living patterns by prescribing a daily oral dose of a major phenothiazine tranquilizer Thorazine (chlorpromazine). However, Leonard,

---

* Librium and Valium are used to control the severe agitation in certain alcoholic and drug intoxication episodes. In that situation, they are given in high doses and by injection.

aged twenty-one, responded to stressful moments in his life by giving up responsibility, withdrawing into himself, and stopping all medications. There are several phenothiazine medications that can be given in a single injection and remain effective for two weeks. I finally decided to switch to the injections. Leonard was furious and threatened to withdraw from treatment. His explanation was simple: "I don't ever want to be in a position where I can't go crazy if I need to." Leonard's family helped in the persuasion and he ultimately conceded. On a regular regime of medications he has been free of disabling symptoms for more than seven years at the time of this writing. He was maintained on injections almost continuously for three years. During the last four years there has been some modification of the treatment to allow "drug holidays" when no medications are prescribed, periods when the dosage was kept at a very low level, and there were several (unsuccessful) trials of switching back to the oral route. The goal has been to use the lowest total amount of medication sufficient to prevent relapse in order to minimize the risk of short-term and long-term complications. The attempts to return to oral medications were generally unsuccessful. Though Leonard has been out of the hospital, able to work in a limited way, and has a long-term heterosexual relationship with a girl friend, he forgets with regularity when the full responsibility for taking medication is his. On two occasions after he had stopped all medications, his symptoms recurred. There seemed to be a two- or three-month interval between stopping medication and the threatened relapses.

I need to say that not every patient with a pattern of chronic schizophrenic illness responds well to these medications. There are a few studies that support a different kind of long-term management. They are clearly minority opinions.[12] However, every patient treated with medication deserves careful, individual, constantly reconsidered management.

The third category of medications is made up of the anti-depression drugs. They have been in common use for twenty years though they are still often prescribed in insufficient dosage by doctors unfamiliar with their mode of action. Their target symptom is severe depression and they are often extremely effective. Some of the drugs, the tricyclic anti-depressants, closely resemble in chemical structure one of the major tranquilizer groups, the phenothiazines. The most commonly used of the tricyclic group are Tofranil (imipramine) and Elavil (amitriptyline). A second group, the monoamine oxidase inhibitors, are less frequently prescribed because of the relatively potent side effects, particularly in altering blood pressure. In general, the anti-depressants are remarkable drugs, effective in a majority of instances in which, only a few years ago, prolonged hospitalization and electrical shock therapy were required. Further, they are not only useful in reversing existing depressive states but often can be used to head off a recurring episode. They are also very effective in the management of certain patients who suffer incapacitating phobias.

There are, however, significant problems associated with their use. Most troubling is that an interval as long as two or three weeks may pass before relief is provided. Their delayed effectiveness poses great problems for both patients and therapists. For example, Elavil (amitriptyline) is a very effective anti-depressant. At times, as few as three 25 milligram tablets daily will provide the first relief within three or four days. On the other hand, there are many patients who respond well to the drug but only if it is given in large amounts, ten or twelve tablets daily, and continued for an interval of three or four weeks! Consider the level of trust that must exist between doctor and patient in order for a desperately depressed and discouraged individual to complete this course of treatment. The patient is told initially to take three tablets a day. Then, over succeeding weeks, he is urged to take four, then six, then eight, then ten, and possibly twelve tablets. And relief comes only at the end of three or four long, tormented weeks. Sustaining hope for that interval is very difficult for all participants. The importance of the patient's spouse as therapeutic ally during this period needs no further explanation.

These new drugs, major tranquilizers and anti-depressants, are among the most remarkable scientific achievements of our era. I remember all too vividly what it was like to practice psychiatry without them. For a period of three thousand years people had written of the anguish of the depressive states. For the sufferers, all over the world, there was no greater torture. Now, for the first time in history, and only in these last two or three decades, a group of chemical agents has been synthesized which provide relief. These new drugs accomplish what no amount of talking, no amount of prayer, no amount of other medication, no amount of alcohol, no amount of love, and no amount of self-exhortation could provide. It is unfortunate that there is usually a "lag time" between the development of a major scientific breakthrough and its general availability and effective use. The World Health Organization in its South Asian area now includes a major tranquilizer (a phenothiazine) and an anti-depression medication (tricyclic) among the medications to be introduced in national health planning and treatment programs in nations in the area (Thailand, Bangladesh, India, and so forth). Major psychotic illnesses are present in a generally similar mode in every nation of the world, though there are of course some significant cultural modifications in the symptoms.

In addition to the three major groups—that is, the sedatives and muscle relaxants, the major tranquilizers, and the anti-depressants—as described in the chapter on mania and depression, a compound used earlier and recently rediscovered as effective in controlling mania is lithium carbonate. Where all else had failed, and in one of my patients all else had failed for twenty-five years, this newest therapeutic agent effects rapid termination of the periods of elation, excitability, hyperactivity, and poor judgment which are part of the "manic phase" of a manic-depressive illness. It is also useful in preventing recurrences of mania, and may prevent many of the depressive episodes as well. Further, since studies of families and near-relatives of individuals suffering manic-depressive illnesses reveal a greater than expected number of family members who provide histories of anxiety, alcoholism, and/or aggressive behavior patterns, lithium carbonate is now used experimentally in the treatment of selected patients with these symptoms.[13] A comprehensive family history is very important in the assessment and management of many clinical problems.

Finally, a group of drugs, used to counter certain of the side effects of major psychoactive drugs, are classified as anticholinergic or anti-Parkinson medications. The phenothiazines in particular can produce unwanted and uncomfortable coordination problems, sometimes acute in onset. Most such reactions can be countered or prevented by use of anticholinergic compounds. However, they require careful management by a skilled clinician lest they produce troubles on their own. Cogentin (benztropine mesylate) and Artane (trihexyphenidyl hydrochloride) are commonly used.

Without question, there are many patients who will not benefit from the use of drugs. However, as I have said before, for any individual to be deprived of an adequate trial of at least several of the newer medications in the face of continuing anxiety, depression, mania, or disordered thinking is a serious mistake in clinical judgment. No psychiatrist, psychologist, social worker, psychiatric nurse, or religious counselor deserves the title "professional" unless he or she can, personally or through ready referral, make available medications for any patient who fails to respond to other forms of therapy. Period. Exclamation point!

THE DECONDITIONING THERAPIES

"Behavior therapy," a contemporary extension of principles outlined by Pavlov and others, has come into increasing use during the last decade.[14] As a form of treatment, it usually employs relaxation and psychological desensitization to accomplish the suppression of anxiety and phobic reactions. If the body is relaxed, it is almost impossible to be anxious. Persons who have a localized fear such as a flying phobia, fear of a specific disease, fear of an animal, fear of public speaking, fear of a closed place, and so on may respond best to this form of treatment. For the truck driver who becomes afraid of tunnels and bridges, the businessman who fears airplane travel, or the minister who feels that he will surely faint while delivering a sermon, such symptoms result in severe incapacity. In one of the many deconditioning procedures developed by Dr. Joseph Wolpe, originally a South African, now working in Philadelphia, the therapist begins by teaching the patient a variety of techniques for achieving body (muscle) relaxation.[15] After the patient has some experience in being able to achieve a relaxed state, he or she is then asked to think specifically about the feared situation. When the fear reaction begins, the patient is instructed to reinstitute relaxation efforts immediately. With repeated practice, the feared situation loses its ominous and tension-producing characteristics. Ultimately, the individual is desensitized and deconditioned to his own fear and is able to confront without fear that which he could not even think about before. One young woman described the process as follows:

> Bob had to fly a great deal and since I wanted to go with him, I had to get over my terrible fear. And I did. There were four actual therapy sessions, plus a fair amount of home practice and two not-so-comfortable short airplane rides. But now, about 90 percent of the fear and discomfort is gone and I'm still getting better.
> I learned how to close my eyes and relax every muscle: first the toes, the ankles, calves, knees, and right on up. At the same time, I would imagine that Bob and I were in our boat and that the water on the lake was just a little choppy. And there I'd be, eyes closed, very relaxed and happy, enjoying the mild bumps of the water and quite comfortable as the boat turned starboard. But, after a while, I was really on a 747 jet. I have the comfort of knowing that if I get uneasy on the plane, I can close my eyes, relax, and return to the lake. The last trip I took, the fifth since I had the treatment, I didn't get back on the boat once.

This is a simple example of many varieties of this kind of therapy. One technique, "flooding," provides intense exposure to the frightening object or circumstance. This allows a psychological-physiological "unlearning" of the fear reaction. Other behavioral techniques emphasize the process of symptom substitution. If an individual suffers a particular fear, he can be taught to perform some alternate action or to think repetitively some alternate thought in any moment when the original fear comes to consciousness. Symptom counting is a similar approach, serving as a substituting act. Through counting, a kind of diluting process of the feared subject takes place. That moment of life that was formerly undiluted fear and pain becomes, instead, cluttered with numbers, comparisons, list making, and a process of substitution. Other therapists use a contract in which the patient agrees actually to perform the feared behavior a certain number of times in the interval between therapy sessions. Generally, the process of making the feared matter very specific and then responding to it and overdoing it usually serves to "extinguish" its potency.

These kinds of approaches for dealing concretely with a specific fear or unwanted behavior don't sound particularly elevating in terms of a deepening of psychological or spiritual values. To an outsider they seem mechanical. For participants there is an obvious risk of feeling demeaned in any process of doing "precisely what one is told to do." However, I find that the overwhelming majority of people do a good job in sorting out what is designed to be helpful and what is primarily demeaning. For me, there is nothing contradictory about prescribing drugs or practicing anxiety-relieving exercises in conjunction with a psychotherapeutic program. The new drugs and the various behavioral approaches are often very helpful in freeing people's energy and enthusiasm. So be it!

PRAYER AND RELIGIOUS PRACTICE

The power and meaning of prayerful acts in the lives of the great majority of the people in the world need no documentation or analysis here. In moments when life is least hopeful and equally in moments of ultimate exultation, millions of people find relief and exhilaration in acts of religious devotion. Attempts to analyze or put aside the importance of people's customs or rituals pale in the light of the meaning in people's lives today and throughout human history of their religious practices. Nor can one overlook the unambivalent freedom to make a commitment for service to others that is possible for many of those with strong religious convictions. Of course, the depth and goodness of any belief is limited by the intentions and humanity of the person who interprets the faith. If there are some who focus on the simple ritual and thus evade the profound questions that serve to inspire awe and humility, their perspectives have little to do with the primary religious purpose: to keep the question of human meaning (and an answer as well) in people's consciousness.

In earlier years, there was sometimes a spirit of rivalry or antipathy between clergymen and the various mental-health professionals. Fortunately (for the patients and parishioners), most of that has disappeared. Clinicians are less likely of late to analyze (attack) the spiritual values of their patients. Simultaneously, religious thought has turned increasingly to the nature of the biological, psychological, and social realities that largely determine people's lives. Sometimes in clinical practice I have occasion to feel particularly sorry for an individual who feels guilty because his prayers and faith were not sufficient to control his depression or anxiety. But in the totality of things, that is a smaller matter. For most people, religious beliefs, along with loving relationships, are great strengths in their lives and assets on which to build when things go wrong.

Whether as a part of religious experiencing or as an attempt to gain a deeper awareness of and ability to be "in touch with" self, the process of meditation appears to encompass important anti-anxiety elements. Obviously, meditation, like learned techniques for relaxation, provides the individual with a way of interrupting sequences of anxious moments. Trained meditation probably offers more. Many people have described their meditation experiences as offering significant enhancement of the quality, stability, depth, and sense of appreciation they have for their own lives. Recent research reports would tend to back them up. Formal meditation training apparently has therapeutic effects beyond the obvious inspirational and contemplative dimensions. One of my colleagues at the University of British Columbia, Dr. Juhn A. Wada, a distinguished neurophysiologist, has been studying the possibility that procedures that focus consciousness internally may activate and integrate "silent" parts of the brain.[16] This work, which depends upon highly refined electrical study of brain function, is particularly exciting since it touches on the great hope of all speculation and research: we may discover that the mind (and heart) of mankind is deeper than we knew.

LOOKING AHEAD: QUALITY CONTROL

It is quite likely that the near future will provide an evaluational system that will objectively discover and discreetly inform both the psychiatric clinician and patient as to "how we are doing." This is necessary since, as has been indicated earlier, it is never possible to know with certainty in advance whether a given form of therapy will be effective. Several medical specialties have the beginnings of a system for the retrieval of information built into their practice, particularly when the patient is hospitalized. Most general hospitals have "patient-care committees," which survey the progress of the various doctors' patients, the responses to medicine, the length of time required for recovery, and the incidence of infections. Surgical practice, in particular, has been made much more dependable and precise by the presence in almost all hospitals of surgical pathologists who report back on the examination of all tissue removed during surgical procedures.

In psychiatry, however, and in the other mental-health professions, no effective system beyond his own experience allows the clinician to know early that he is on the wrong track and that some other therapeutic method should be considered. We lack a "tissue committee"* and a "surgical pathologist" for psychiatry and the other mental-health professions.

One possible answer to this problem is the use of an outside

* This was suggested originally by Dr. Martin Loeb, formerly the Dean of the School of Social Work at the University of Wisconsin, Madison.

consultant who shares with both the treating doctor and the patient his or her assessment of the treatment program. Such consultation is considerably less intrusive than it may sound. It is rare for a patient of mine to go longer than a month or six weeks without some other clinician's being asked to consult, either as my cotherapist or in an individual meeting, with the patient. So many patients require weeks and months and sometimes longer to recover that one becomes accustomed to symptoms. The very intimacy of the relationship between therapist and patient can make it difficult to gauge progress objectively.

An additional reason for outside evaluation of treatment progress is that therapists working with slowly improving patients often have difficulty in retaining as the therapeutic goal 100 percent recovery or, better yet, "The patient not only gets well, he gets weller." Seeing a little progress, the clinician and patient may be tempted to stay with the therapeutic program that has some, though limited, effectiveness. A small amount of progress makes it difficult to consider a new approach. The outside consultant can often bring useful perspectives to the participants. Therapeutic relationships that are structured to allow and welcome such "intrusion" will in the long run be most conducive to maximum success.

The use of a computerized evaluation system offers another possible approach to treatment review. This kind of evaluational system would not require the presence within the consulting room of any third party. It might work something like this: The clinician and the patient would each fill out an initial brief description form which would be coded and made part of a computerized record. For the clinician, the filling out of forms might be a three- or four-minute task. For the patient, completing a problem list of forty items might be adequate. Fewer than five minutes would suffice to finish the paperwork. The privacy of the patient would be maintained by a code number. The computer center (serving many hundreds of clinics, hospitals, and individual therapists) would regularly report back to the clinician and patient. At the end of one month of treatment, a second set of reports would be submitted to the computer with the patient stating simply that he is much better, a little better, about the same, or worse. The doctor would record from a treatment checklist the treatment system employed. The computer, after comparing the experience of this doctor and patient with that of hundreds or thousands of others from its data pool, might reply in a friendly but realistic manner:

> At the end of one month on a regime of once-weekly interviews, with two family visits and the use of mild tranquilizers, the patient notes only a limited sense of improvement. The computer's experience indicates that continuing this form of therapy over the succeeding four weeks will lead to improvement in only approximately 15 percent of cases. The computer's further experience indicates that, at this point, the clinician and patient may wish to consider the addition of. . . .

The technology is presently available. What is much less certain is whether its introduction in the name of quality control would introduce a depersonalizing element that would do more harm than good.[17]

I think not. The coming of outside evaluation into mental-health care will produce many changes. But the wish to help, engendered by the words "Please do what you can for me," is a force so powerful that even the awe-inspiring computer can likely be harnessed in its service.

SUMMARY

The relationship between doctor and patient remains as important today as it was ninety years ago when Freud was first undertaking the analysis of his patients' dreams. The addition of a wealth of effective biological treatment tools, behavioral therapy techniques, and family and group therapy approaches makes the stakes of a good therapeutic rapport even higher. The right mix of doctor, patient, family, and a well-chosen treatment program is regularly helpful to a significant number of the people who seek psychiatric help. I'm certain that many more of my own patients do well today than those I treated in years past.

> After having chopped off the arms that reached out to me; after having boarded up all the windows and doors; after having filled all the pits with poisoned water; after having built my house on a rock of No inaccessible to flattery and fears; after having cut out my tongue and after having eaten it; after having hurled handfuls of silence and monosyllables of scorn at my lovers; after having forgotten my name and the name of my birthplace and the name of my race; after having judged myself and having sentenced myself to perpetual hope and perpetual loneliness, I heard against the stones of my gourd of syllogisms the moist attack, tender, insistent, of spring. (From *Eagle or Sun?* by Octavio Paz)[18]

14

If the Patient Is Someone You Love

Have hope, give hope, and, above all, stay involved. I don't subscribe in any way to the school of thought that says it's okay for people to destroy their lives if they want to and that loved ones are supposed to sit by uninvolved. As a matter of fact, in the Great Western Novel I plan to write someday there is going to be a very emotional scene in which one of the characters is about to do himself in when a lasso whips the weapon from the intended victim's hand and a voice cries out, "I can't let you do it, Joe. I'm Tex, your second cousin on your mother's side. You're my family."

I've been watching it for thirty years now and have been forced to choose. I believe the overinvolved families beat the underinvolved families three to one in truly helping their loved ones. There are of course painful moments that come with overinvolvement, but I prefer the shouting and crying to detachment every time. Better still, of course, is the kind of loving support that has an uncanny intuition as to when to move in and when to wait, visible but unobtrusive, nearby.

I have been witness to increasing numbers of tragic outcomes for severely ill patients that are unmistakably the result of the contemporary "freedom," "patients' right advocates," and family disavowal of responsibility for family members. We Americans turn loose and unprotected into our city jungles people that no tribal village would ever dream of asking to fend for themselves.

A young doctor, and a good one, in training with me released a psychotic patient to the streets. The patient promptly walked in front of a car and was seriously injured. When I asked what happened, the young doctor began by explaining to me the law, which does, indeed, emphasize "patients' rights." He said he had advised the patient to remain, but the patient refused, signed a form "releasing" the doctor and hospital of responsibility, and then left. He was hallucinating all the while. The discussion between the doctor and patient lasted ten minutes, during which time the doctor considered contacting the patient's family but decided it would violate the patient's "rights" to do so.

In our heated discussion, I was trying to make the point that the law is basically an effort to spell out the Golden Rule and that in this instance what the law expected was that the doctor talk with this patient for a long time about reasons for staying and that he should call in the nurse to help persuade the patient, and that the patient's family should be asked to use their influence on the patient, and perhaps the family doctor could talk with the patient and the patient's family. And, if all that was to no avail, "Next time, Doctor, call your supervisor," I told him.

We agreed to discuss the matter with our hospital's legal counsel, who said that we were both right.

There are some sad exceptions, of course, but for those with serious emotional problems, the presence of strongly supportive family and friends is a great, great bonus. Over time, a highly troubled, disorganized, or depressed individual whose circle of relationships includes people genuinely and lovingly committed to him may fare better than a seemingly less troubled person who is without close friend or mate. Very often, the best "therapist" is someone who accepts, admires, and loves the person who is also a patient. I find one of the most important goals in any therapy is that of helping those who care for the patient make their caring count.

If the patient is someone you love, your belief in the ultimate success of his or her efforts to improve his life, and thus yours, is very important. *The maintenance of hopes, high expectations, and faith in the recuperative and restorative powers of the patient by those who love him are of almost incalculable value.*

In this respect, I think very often of Martha and of Lenore, women who are strangers to each other but who share an unquestioning, persistent, and ultimately correct faith in the recovery of their supposedly "hopeless" husbands. I respect and admire them greatly.

Martha's husband, Ned, was unable to work at all from his fifty-fifth year until the middle of his fifty-ninth year. He suffered a severe depression, which drained him of hope, strength, and sanity. He was constantly self-deprecating and attempted several times to kill himself. Increasingly, as those years passed, he withdrew into himself. But Martha's loyalty, persistence, and optimism were astonishingly sustaining. She never conceded during those difficult days, weeks, and months that extended into years that Ned would not someday be well. And, in the end, she was right!

The same was true of Lenore, whose husband, Arthur, was not only severely depressed but also was said to be "incurable" because of a neurologist's diagnosis of "early brain atrophy secondary to chronic alcoholism." Arthur, also a man in his fifties, was extremely agitated and unhappy. He reversed day and night, was unable to work or to communicate in any effective manner. And, when left to himself, he would slip off and buy a bottle of wine.

But both men recovered! And they recovered fully! The faith, persistence, and support provided by each spouse helped save both husbands' lives. As a matter of fact, that faith and hope sustained not only their husbands, it sustained me, their doctor. It caused me to keep thinking about them, looking for an answer, trying each new treatment that offered any hope. Their quiet insistence, "Please keep trying!" kept me a full and participating partner with husband and wife in working out what ultimately was a complete recovery for both men. For one, talking plus medicines plus the passage of time seemed to help. For the other, a newly developed combination of anti-depressant medications in high dosage produced a rapid improvement after all other therapeutic approaches had failed. Recommendations in the second instance came from my psychiatric colleague, Dr. Heinz Lehman, of Montreal, who was good enough to see my patient in consultation.

To you who love the patient, I say with sincerity born of many years of working in this field, "Stay hopeful, keep trying, and ask your doctor to do the same!"

There is perhaps only a fine line at times between "stay hopeful" and the refusal to "face reality." But reality changes. Both in the practice of general medicine and the mental-health professions, hope has come often to the hopeless. The possibilities that one clinician could not recognize, a second or a third was able to envision and help bring to actuality. And even more often, what cannot be accomplished at one interval in time becomes possible at a later point. Optimally, the patient and family need not travel from coast to coast in a perpetual search for such assistance. A single clinician who retains hope about his patient, who seeks periodic consultation, and continues to read and study offers as much as the painful, constant migration between health centers.

As with the patient himself, there are times when the best that family and friends can do is "hang on," "don't make things worse," "stay alive," and just *survive*. During such periods, a deeply held hope, a sense of humor, and perhaps a silent prayer may be all the encouragement available to you. Controlling your own guilt feelings is very important in such periods. When the patient is someone you love, his unhappiness is, of course, your unhappiness. But guilt is a much more complicated emotion. Unhappiness and sickness in the life of someone close always raise the question, "What have I done?" To care about someone is simultaneously to be at risk when things go badly for him. But this is an insufficient explanation for the enormous sense of guilt so many feel.

Many family members fall victim to the unfair and inaccurate prejudices put forward to "explain" mental illnesses. Whenever there is no adequate explanation for what is happening and people are experiencing a painful and uncertain time, a search for an evil event or a harmful person is likely to begin. When things go badly, patients, doctors, and family members, like all people, look for someone else to blame. This is a great hazard for patients and families, and a good therapist tries to help people avoid guilt quagmires.

Although there are times in a clinician's office, in the movies, on the radio, in the comics, and elsewhere when it was clear to someone that "X made Y sick," this has *little or no relevance to you.** One needs always to consider Y himself, his personality, his biological constitution, his own life choices, the social circumstances and values of his peer group, and the many other people and events in his life from which you are excluded. Mental-health clinicians are sometimes said to have indicted some person or persons as the X who made Y sick. This is always unfortunate.

Whatever the basis, guilt is such a destructive emotion that you must search for help to become free of it. If the patient is someone you love and if you feel personal guilt about what is happening in his life, by all means tell him how you feel, express your sorrow, and then, as best you can, *put it aside.* Guilt removes the spontaneous, clouds the sincere, and makes easy and open loving too risky to chance.

To describe the good things that can come into the life of a family as a result of one family member's symptoms of mental illness is to risk sounding like a Pollyanna. But symptoms quite frequently represent a "growing edge" in the individual, and it can work that way for the family as well. If the patient is someone you love, openness on your part as to what he or she is working toward may be very valuable. It is tempting to think only of getting him "back on the right track," "as good as new," "back to his old self," and thereby to discount the part of his struggle that can become a thrust *toward* a more meaningful life. However, for many couples and families, the illness of one member has served as a turning point leading to greater

---

* And, in truth, it may have little factual relevance to X or to Y.

honesty, appreciation of the feelings of all family members, and a more open sharing of tenderness and affection.

It is also true that one of the most difficult and painful circumstances that can befall any family is the presence of a family member who is incapable of protecting and caring for himself. It is particularly difficult when someone is too confused, anxious, or angry to recognize his need for outside help and also shuns or fights the efforts of family members and others in his or her behalf. In such dreadful moments, it is almost always a good idea to attempt to assemble *all* immediate family members (preferably with the patient present) to discuss the problems presented by the patient's behavior and needs. Of course, families that are experienced in talking together in an open and mutually respectful fashion are much more likely to be effective in this effort. And conversely, a family that is unaccustomed to talking together to work out ordinary family decisions may find it almost impossible to face confusion, depression, or anger in a family member. Still, it is worth a serious try for two reasons: first, shared family responsibility from the very beginning prevents later misunderstandings; and second, assigning the responsibility to one person is usually unfair to that person and unwise for the family group.

Because these are such painful matters, people often resort to guile or deception. The patient is lied to and tricked in order to place him or her in a hospital. Perhaps, but only rarely, there is no other reasonable choice. In the overwhelming majority of instances, honesty is the better policy, and this is the case irrespective of the patient's age. Honesty and a direct and full disclosure of what the family members are planning help prevent a later guilt compounded by the need to explain "Why we lied." No matter how disturbed the patient may seem to be, no matter how confused, angry, or deluded, there is almost always within him an "island of reason and rationality" that should be addressed. Directing one's efforts toward that unseen area of rational and reasonable thought is frequently effective, though not always immediately. Persistent, honest, sustaining, and gentle efforts to communicate, continued for as long as is necessary, often lead to cooperation that would have been difficult to anticipate. The sequence may be, "NO NO NO NO NO NO—YES."

Fortunately, there are growing numbers of knowledgeable others to whom the family can turn for assistance in protecting and caring for loved ones in such moments. The family physician, the minister, the family lawyer, or another trusted friend may join family members in addressing themselves to the "islands of rationality" within the patient. Suicide prevention centers, Recovery Incorporated, Alcoholics Anonymous, departments of mental hygiene, the local medical society, the judge of family court, and lastly, but often far from least, the local police are also potential resources. Persistence is important. So is patience. Beyond family and friends, every large community and many rural counties have a mental-health center and/or a mental-health association. Very often, such agencies are extremely helpful in offering advice or direct professional assistance. Many will arrange home consultation to help families come together to think about, discuss, and plan for the future well-being of the family member (and the family as well). This outside assistance may be of particular value when the family member in question is an older person no longer able to care for himself at home. Often in such moments the family is divided by guilt. Old disputes and financial concerns arise. The group fails to agree on a unified plan and one person assumes responsibility and the others "wash their hands" of the matter. The family feud begins. The young cousins never get to know each other.

VIOLENCE

There is a great deal of violence that takes place in families and it is time to put an end to it. The battered wife, the abused child, the terrified parents have generally remained silent. Worse, there has been a conspiracy of silence on the subject by doctors, emergency-room staff, other family members, and neighbors. All this is a terrible disservice not only to the people threatened or injured but also to the individual who commits the violence. I am proud that in the mental-health region for which I am responsible in Los Angeles, we've developed a series of women's shelter houses and we have a major child-abuse reporting and treatment system. Abuse in the family feeds on itself. No good comes of it. It's a cancer best treated early.

I have known a number of men and women who have given up their abusive behavior. Most have done so because their victims and other members of the family took action to stop the violence. Otherwise, the person resorting to abuse or assault faces a double problem: "I don't control myself; they don't control me."

If you are one of the very small percentage of patients' relatives faced with the threat of violence toward you or other members of the family, I suggest you take the following steps *today.*

1. Victims sometimes blame themselves. Don't you believe it.
2. Take steps to prevent violence and abuse before they happen. Start out by thinking about what has happened in the past. Was alcohol involved? Street drugs? Was the patient "off medication" contrary to medical advice? How much time, that is, minutes, hours, days, passed between the first suggestion that violence or abuse was coming and the moment of striking out? Who was present in that moment and, more important, who wasn't present when violence or abuse took place?
3. After you decide that you will be a victim no more, talk with someone you trust who knows you and preferably knows the family. It may be a relative, close friend, your doctor, minister, a person in the local police department who specializes in family violence, the local mental-health association, or a psychiatrist whom you consult specifically to consider this problem.
4. I would guess that steps 1, 2, and 3 will lead to correcting the problem more than 50 percent of the time. Knowing what you plan to do is the best preventative of violence. You are not helpless.

5. Part of your plan will include deciding when and under what circumstances you will make known to the individual exactly what you (the family and others who will become involved) plan to do to protect him (or her) and yourself.
6. And do it!

In the great majority of instances of violence by severely disturbed psychiatric patients, there is a failure in the medication program. Usually, the patient has stopped his treatment without the agreement of the therapist. Most of the time, there are many indications prior to the violent moments that trouble is coming. Over and over again, relatives ignore mounting tension and agitation. The result is damage to patient and family. That is one important reason that you should be a part of the treatment program. Certainly, if violence or abuse, including sexual abuse, is part of the illness, the patient's therapist, the patient, and the family *must* talk together. Everyone should have a clear understanding as to what the family should do to protect the patient and himself.

I have never known a situation in which violence was threatened that wasn't improved by facing the problem, thinking about it, deciding to deal with it, developing a plan, and sticking to it.

A good part of the history of progress in mental-health care has been written by individuals who started out as a patient's relative or friend. Those most influential in reclaiming the closed-off and abysmal chronic mental hospitals of the 1940s were more often than not people whose initial commitment had been to a single individual. Similarly, the caring of many who work to enhance the opportunities for the retarded, for the alcoholic, for the troubled adolescent, and the forgotten prisoner began with, but went beyond, a family member. When the patient is someone you love, being witness to his growth and sharing in his recovery is a very moving experience. For most of us, there is nothing quite like it. When it happens, there is a debt accrued which makes the well-being of others one's personal responsibility.

IF THE PATIENT IS YOU

I've seen it happen many times. Out of the most dreadful, unrelenting, and prolonged periods of depression and confusion some of the finest and most effective human beings have emerged stronger and more satisfied than before. So it's important, most important of all, that you not abandon a belief and trust in your abilities and in your capacity to make things right for yourself. There is an inborn righting process in almost every human being that, in time, tends to take over and help put people back on their feet. It's something like air in a pillow pushed under the water. It wants to get back up. I think of this need to survive and grow as somehow inseparable from life itself, a part of the process that put all of us here. This force, that is, the righting process, can certainly be suppressed, pushed down, or drugged. But it can reemerge with awesome determination.

Psychiatric treatment helps many people. But the fundamental basis of your recovery will be you and your ability to use your gifts in your own behalf. If you are going to work with a psychiatrist, find one you like and can trust. This is another way of saying, "Trust your guts." If you are honest with yourself, you'll be right about you more than anyone else will be. In selecting a therapist or rethinking staying on as a "patient" in a particular program, if your feeling about that therapist is "no," look elsewhere. I find it rather predictable that when the patient doesn't like the doctor, the feeling is usually mutual. The most important line in myth, rhyme, or prose is the one that explains,

Why does the lamb love Mary so?
Well, Mary loves the lamb, you know

How soon will things be better? What can you expect in terms of the pace of improvement? This is a legitimate topic for you to take up with your therapist regularly till you are feeling much improved. Almost always there are ups and downs and few individuals with long-standing anxieties or deep mood disorders make overnight turnabouts (though some do). Even in the most successful therapies there are inevitably moments when "holding one's own," "hanging on," "not making things worse" are the best that you or anybody else can do. In retrospect, such days or weeks sometimes seem to have been necessary periods of accommodation and stabilization before improvement could occur. In general, all therapies take some time.

Even the task of learning to be honest about one's feelings can prove to be a more difficult process than one might think. The requirements of living with other people from the earliest days of life include being able to tune into what they want. Some people don't do that too well. On the other hand, a good many people have most of their listening channels tuned into others and don't allow themselves to pay much attention to their own wishes and needs. The role of patient can provide a wonderful opportunity to turn some of that sensitive listening inward. In the process, you can test the present relevance of what you have been assuming are your goals, responsibilities, and commitments. The process of listening to oneself brings into sharper focus the question, "Just how much control can I claim for the life I want to lead?" This in turn calls for a closer look at the attitudes that secretly rule and sometimes ruin people's lives. Pried loose and brought out into the open, they dogmatically assert:

- "You must, of course . . .!"
- "You have no right to feel that way!"
- "I have no choice!"

Once examined, these secretly held, imperative commands lose their exclamation point! They become, instead, questions about self:

- "Who says I must?"
- "How do I really feel?"
- "Who can speak for me other than me?"
- "Dare I experiment?"

This may make it possible for you to undertake the two great risks in life, that is, to be personally responsible for one's decisions by choosing rather than letting it happen and to give up worrying about appearing foolish to others. When these risks are assumed, major change is inevitable. Still, more often than not, long-held relationships with family and friends and one's values and traditions are strengthened by an honest, personal questioning. When the treatment ends, you are still you.

I usually tell my patients that major changes in living patterns are best not made in the first days and weeks of therapy. People who are under stress are inclined to want to change everything in their lives all at once. Later they discover, "There was an awful lot of me in all those things I gave up." Change of job or marital status, moving to a new community, undertaking major financial commitments, and similar matters are best postponed for a *short* time. The relief of anxiety or the lifting of depressive symptoms becomes an important new factor in whatever is to be decided. And clarification of "whose life it really is" usually leads to better choices.

However, undergoing treatment is a poor reason for long postponing important personal decisions and a poor substitute, a dreadful substitute, for getting married, going to school, advancing in work, or traveling around the world. One of my strong professional regrets is that in the early years of my practice I failed to recognize that intense and prolonged commitment to therapy with me made it difficult for several of my patients to live the other parts of their lives. They gave so much of their energy, love, and hope to therapy that there wasn't enough left over for the other people who counted on them. There was too much postponement, too little choosing. One patient's discovery that "he is the one after all" took place only after he had grown tired of waiting and had left. People too often find excuses to explain why *now* is not the moment. Treatment may offer a moratorium of weeks or a few months, indeed rarely a half year, and never a year. More often, therapy ends moratoria by heightening the understanding that by not choosing one chooses.

Although family and friends are no substitute for a needed

therapist, it is also true that, over time, a therapist is no substitute for mate, family, or friends. If your therapy excludes your spouse (which it shouldn't), keep in mind that no person is so totally secure and confident as to be unthreatened by a relationship between his mate and a stranger (therapist). He or she is likely to feel a sense of failure and guilt that the love in the marriage did not solve the problems. People say, "You had trouble long before I met you," but there is almost always the secret self-accusation, "Perhaps it *is* my fault!" The same applies to parents, children, and close friends. Although protecting individual privacy is very important, I find that the exclusion of family members from a role in treatment is a mistake. It's not only the suspicion, jealousy, and sense of guilt that develops which argues against their exclusion, it's the terrible loss of what might have been if those nearest and dearest had been there. It's frightening for most people to think of sharing a therapist's office with mother, father, kids. I'm sure that if my analyst had made the suggestion to me thirty years ago, I'd still remember the moment in vivid detail. But if he had, and if I'd had the courage to agree, it would have been wonderfully useful. In the hundreds of times when I've been privileged to talk with patient and family members, there has never been a single instance when meeting the family didn't elevate my patient in my eyes, deepen my sense of commitment and responsibility to the therapy, and enrich my relationship with my patient. To know a person's people is a very powerful matter. It's inherently elevating for all concerned. So, if you are working with a therapist (psychotherapy, medicines, behavioral therapy, it makes no difference), I hope you, your therapist, and your family will have the good luck to meet together. Sometimes it takes courage to do it, but you'll have no regrets.

A word about medicines. Most of them require days, sometimes weeks to have the right effect—and that's assuming you've been lucky enough to have started on the right choice of medicines the first time. Often a period of trial and error is required to arrive at what will really work. Most people are willing to work with a therapist to find the right dosage of the right drug *if* their relationship is an open one and if the patient knows what to expect with good luck or bad. So you ought to know what to hope for, what to look for, and what to look out for. If not, ask your doctor to give you more detail about what you're taking. I've seen so many people respond in almost miraculous ways to medications that I urge you not to pay attention to those who advise that "you should be able to do it without drugs." If it happens that you're on medication, you are one of a long and distinguished group of individuals. The psychiatric drugs have helped Nobel Prize winners, painters, judges, generals, writers, teachers, doctors, sheriffs, athletic champions, and many, many other people.

Though I've been a psychiatrist for thirty years now, I must confess that ours is still a profession that is in good part trial and error. That would be equally true whether the therapy in progress is medicinal, psychotherapeutic, or whatever. Often, one can predict what will work and how long it will take, but there is no advance certainty. And sometimes the predictions are very far off. It's true in other parts of medicine as well, but that is of little solace. In my own clinical work, there have been times when a second, third, and fourth change in the treatment plan had to be made. You can imagine the great sense of gratitude I feel to my patients—not few in number— who were willing to continue to work with me despite the initial disappointments. Their trust and understanding and sheer loyalty, and that of their families, are among the most moving experiences of my life. The trial and error of so much of psychiatric work seems to me to demand a partnership between patient, therapist, family in which all parties have a responsibility to evaluate the general direction in which things are going.

Not everybody gets well, not nearly everybody. I am sorry indeed if the optimistic tone in these pages doesn't match your own experience. Perhaps whatever interferes with your life has been going on for a long time; you may have been cared for in a "good" hospital, have tried a variety of medicines, spent hundreds of hours and thousands of dollars in the search for improvement that has not come. There are patients of mine whom these words describe. There is a double pain, when so many who are patients have done so well, if the patient who has failed to respond is you.

Some people don't get well because they don't quite fit with the treatment chosen but might respond to the same therapy given more effectively, or to an alternate therapeutic approach. But a substantial number of people fail to make progress because they suffer one of the severe illnesses, punishing and depleting, which are still beyond control. As they have been from the beginning of time, mental illnesses remain among the greatest human problems. If you are the patient who has failed to respond to treatment, you may choose to turn from psychiatry for a time to other ways of working toward your personal goals. If you discontinue treatment and work on your problems in another way, you won't be the first. "Not making it" as a patient is not to be equated with "not making it." There have been many, many people who not only overcame the problems for which they had seen a psychiatrist without success, but went on to achieve success in every area of their personal and professional lives. Actually, all "successful" therapy ends with the discovery that therapy is not the full answer. One continues to look for meaning throughout life.

But before abandoning the hope of psychiatric help, you should make sure you have had an adequate trial of those treatment programs that have promise. In the process of making that decision it may not be easy to decide whether to return to someone with whom you have worked or to consult a new clinician. Should you decide to seek a new consultant, your former therapist may be your best source of referral. It takes courage to say, "I'd like to talk with someone else who uses a different approach. Will you think about who that should be and help me to give him any information he should have?" But if you can do that, it is a tribute to the relationship you and your therapist have established. Otherwise, one of the many hundreds of established mental-health clinics could be a good starting place. Or you may, with the assistance of your family doctor, seek consultation at one of the major university clinics or hospitals in your state or province. Listed in the Appendix of this book are the addresses of the Commissioners of Mental Health in each state and the Ministers of Health in the Provinces of Canada. Listed also are the names and addresses of various public and private organizations to whom you might write for suggestions as to where to turn for help. If you contact someone who is not familiar with you, a brief one-page listing of the therapies you have received should be helpful to whomever you consult. Include in this listing if you can the dates and length of prior hospitalization, the medicines taken, and the dosage and the total period of time medicine was used. The extent of psychotherapy you have experienced and whether this involved other family members should also be described. One practical goal in seeking advice is to find the best source of help close to your own home.

It is terribly discouraging to work in therapy for relief that seems never to be forthcoming. Yet each year, more of those who couldn't be assisted earlier find help in mental-health programs. If all else has failed, I urge that in precisely one year you seek consultation again. In that time, it may have become possible to offer help to you which, till now, has been denied.

Epilogue

My profession has changed a great deal in the last three decades or more—and so have I. I began my career as a psychiatrist by trying to understand and to categorize what was wrong with people. "Advocacy" for my patient, for his or her hopes, needs, endeavors, then seemed beyond the scope of my responsibility. I feared that "advocating" interfered with understanding. I didn't understand at first that where humans and their aspirations are involved, one cannot really understand except from the stance of advocate. A lesson, mercifully early in my career, served to highlight the problem. I had been working closely with a young woman who had become quite depressed after the death of her parents. Shortly afterward, her husband left her and she made a serious suicide attempt. With therapy, she improved rapidly and decided to return to graduate school to resume the education she had interrupted seven years earlier. With permission, she wrote my name on the medical treatment portion of her application and asked that, when solicited, I write a letter indicating my sense of her readiness, her competence, her potential. A few weeks later, a formal request came from the college admissions office along with a letter asserting that an "objective, candid" appraisal was in the interest of the applicant. My letter was impartial, balanced, fair—to patient and school. They turned her down. My patient, wiser and more human than I, abandoned the therapy and explained, "Good-bye! My life is too short to share intimately with people who can be 'objective' about me."

I find that most of the people I have come to know well are happiest if, in their personal lives, they have one or more persons with whom to share their intimate hopes, fears, and love. Money is also of key importance, and I find that asking people about their debts may be as revealing as asking about their sexual relationships. Very, very few people are ungrateful for efforts to help them, yet almost everybody is terrified of being made the fool. I find almost everybody quite as decent as I and as yet have failed to find a concept so complex or a listener so dense as to negate the necessity for 100 percent honesty on my part. Adlai Stevenson, in losing the American presidential elections in 1952 and 1956, advised, "Speak up, not down, to the American people." The results of the balloting notwithstanding, I find his advice altogether correct.

Useful Organizations and Agencies

Alcohol and Drug Problems
Association of North America
1101 15th St., NW, #204
Washington, DC 20005
(202) 452-0990

Alcoholics Anonymous
World Services Inc.
P.O. Box 459
Grand Central Station
New York, NY 10017
(212) 686-1100

American Academy
of Child Psychiatry
1424 16th St., NW, #201A
Washington, DC 20036
(202) 462-3754

American Association for
Geriatric Psychiatry
230 N. Michigan Ave. #2400
Chicago, IL 60601
(312) 263-2225

American Association for
Marriage and Family Therapy
924 W. Ninth St.
Upland, CA 91786
(714) 981-0888

American Association on
Mental Deficiency
5101 Wisconsin Ave., NW
Washington, DC 20016
(202) 686-5400

American Medical Association
535 N. Dearborn St.
Chicago, IL 60610
(312) 751-6000

American Psychiatric
Association
1700 18th St., NW
Washington, DC 20009
(202) 797-4900

American Psychological
Association
1200 17th St., NW
Washington, DC 20036
(202) 833-7600

American Society for
Adolescent Psychiatry
24 Green Valley Rd.
Wallingford, PA 19086
(215) 566-1054

Association of
Mental Health Clergy
5908 Lyons View Dr.
Knoxville, TN 37919
(615) 584-0521

Conference of Social Workers
in Mental Health Programs
Gowanda Psychiatric Center
Helmuth, NY 14079
(716) 532-3311, ext. 300

International Committee Against
Mental Illness
P.O. Box 898, Ansonia Station
New York, NY 10023
(914) 349-8797

Mental Health Association
National Headquarters
1800 N. Kent St.
Arlington, VA 22209
(703) 528-6405

Mental Health Materials Center
30 East 29th St.
New York, NY 10016
(212) 889-5760

National Association for
Retarded Citizens
2709 Ave. E
East Arlington, TX 76011
(817) 261-4961

National Council on
the Aging, Inc.
1828 L St., NW, #504
Washington, DC 20036
(202) 223-6250

National Council on Alcoholism
733 Third Ave., #1405
New York, NY 10017
(212) 986-4433

National Council of Community
Mental Health Centers
2233 Wisconsin Ave., NW, #322
Washington, DC 20007
(202) 337-7530

National Institute of
Mental Health
5600 Fishers La.
Rockville, MD 20852
(301) 443-2403

National Medical
Association, Inc.
1720 Massachusetts Ave., NW
Washington, DC 20036
(202) 659-9623

National Rehabilitation
Association
1522 K St., NW, #1120
Washington, DC 20005
(202) 659-2430

Recovery, Incorporated
(The Association of Nervous
and Former Mental Patients)
116 S. Michigan Ave.
Chicago, IL 60603
(312) 263-2292

CANADIAN ORGANIZATIONS

Alberta
Director of Mental Health
Administration Building
Edmonton, Alberta

British Columbia
Community Health Services
Parliament Bldgs.
Victoria, British Columbia

Manitoba
Mental Health Services
Legislative Bldgs.
Winnipeg, Manitoba B3C OV8

New Brunswick
Director of
Mental Health Services
Fredericton, New Brunswick

Newfoundland
Director of
Mental Health Services
Government Services Bldg.
St. John's, Newfoundland

Nova Scotia
Mental Health Services
Box 488
Halifax, Nova Scotia

Ontario
Canadian Association for
the Mentally Retarded
(Association Canadienne pour
les Déficients Mentaux)
Kinsmen MINR Bldg.
York University Campus
4700 Keele St.
Downsview (Toronto)
Ontario M3J 1P3

Canadian Medical Association
(Association Médicale
Canadienne)
P.O. Box 8650
Ottawa, Ontario K1G 0G8

Canadian Psychiatric Association
(Association des
Psychiatres du Canada)
225 Lisgar St., #103
Ottawa, Ontario K2P 0C6

Ontario Mental Health
Foundation
45 St. Clair St., W
Toronto 7, Ontario

Prince Edward Island
Director of Mental Health
Box 3000
Charlottetown,
Prince Edward Island

Quebec
Department of Social Affairs
Mental Health Programme
1075 Ste. Foy
Quebec, Quebec G1A 1B9

Saskatchewan
Psychiatric Services Branch
Provincial Health Bldg.
Regina, Saskatchewan

State Mental Health Authorities

Alabama
Commissioner
Department of Mental Health
135 S. Union St.
Montgomery, Ala. 36130
(205) 834-4350

Alaska
Division of Mental Heath
Department of Health and Social
Services
Pouch H–04
Juneau, Alas. 99811
(907) 465-3370

Arizona
Division of Behavioral Health
Services
Department of Health Services
2500 E. Van Buren St.
Phoenix, Ariz. 85008
(602) 255-1229

Arkansas
Mental Health Services
Department of Social and
Rehabilitation Services
4313 West Markham St.
Little Rock, Ark. 72201
(501) 664-4500

California
Director
State Department
of Mental Health
P.O. Box 254829
Sacramento, Ca. 95825
(916) 920-6712

Colorado
Director
Division of Mental Health
Department of Institutions
3520 West Oxford Ave.
Denver, Colo. 80236
(303) 761-0220, ext. 201

Connecticut
Commissioner
Department of Mental Health
90 Washington St.
Hartford, Conn. 06115
(203) 566-3869

Delaware
Director
Division of Mental Health
Department of Health and
Social Services
1901 N. Dupont Highway
Newcastle, Dela. 19720
(302) 421-6101

District of Columbia
Acting Administrator
Mental Health Administration
Department of Human Resources
1875 Connecticut Ave., N.W.
Washington, D.C. 20009
(202) 673-6720

Florida
Acting Director
Mental Health Program Office
Department of Health and
Rehabilitative Services
1309 Winewood Blvd.
Tallahassee, Fl. 32301
(904) 488-8304

Georgia
Director
Chairman of Rehabilitative
Services
Division of MHMR, Substance
and Abuse Services
Department of Human Resources
47 Trinity Ave., S.W.
Room 315H
Atlanta, Ga. 30334
(404) 656-4908

Guam
Administrator
Mental Health Division
Substance Abuse Agency
P.O. Box 20999
Main Facility
Guam 96921

Hawaii
Chief
Mental Health Division
Department of Health
P.O. Box 3378
Honolulu, Hawaii 96801
(808) 548-6505

Idaho
Administrator
Division of Community
Rehabilitation
Department of Health and
Welfare
Len B. Gordon Bldg.
327 Statehouse Mail
Boise, Ida. 83720
(208) 384-3920

Illinois
Director
State Department of
Mental Health and
Developmental Disabilities
160 N. LaSalle St., Room 1500
Chicago, Ill. 60601
(312) 793-2730

Indiana
Commissioner
State Department of
Mental Health
5 Indiana Square
Indianapolis, Ind. 46204
(317) 232-7844

Iowa
Director
Division of Mental Health
Resources
Department of Social Services
Lucas State Office Bldg.
Des Moines, Ia. 50319
(515) 281-5126

Kansas
Acting Director
Division of Mental Health and
Retardation Services
State Department of Social and
Rehabilitation Services
State Office Bldg.
Topeka, Kans. 66612
(913) 296-3774

Kentucky
Acting Director
Division of Mental Health
Bureau for Health Services
Department for Human Resources
275 E. Main St.
Frankfort, Ky. 40601
(502) 564-4360

Louisiana
Assistant Secretary
Division of Mental Health
State Health and
Human Resources Administration
P.O. Box 106
655 N. 5th St.
Baton Rouge, La. 70821
(504) 342-2544

Maine
Acting Director
Bureau of Mental Health
State Department of
Mental Health and Corrections
424 State Office Bldg.
Augusta, Me. 04330
(207) 289-3161

Maryland
Director
Mental Hygiene Administration
State Department of
Health and Mental Hygiene
201 West Preston St.—4th fl.
Baltimore, Md. 21201
(301) 383-2695

Massachusetts
Commissioner
State Department of
Mental Health
Exec. Office of Human Services
160 N. Washington St.
Boston, Mass. 02114
(617) 727-5600

Michigan
Director
State Department of
Mental Health
Lewis-Cass Bldg.
320 Walnut St.
Lansing, Mich. 48926
(517) 373-3500

Minnesota
Acting Asst. Commissioner
Mental Health Bureau
Department of Public Welfare
Centennial Office Bldg.
St. Paul, Minn. 55155
(612) 296-2791

Mississippi
Director
State Department of
Mental Health
607 Robert E. Lee Office Bldg.
Jackson, Miss. 39201
(601) 354-6132

Missouri
Director
Department of Mental Health
2002 Missouri Blvd.
Jefferson City, Mo. 65101
(314) 751-3070

Montana
Division Administrator
Mental Health and Residential
Services
State Department of Institutions
1539-11th Ave.
Helena, Mont. 59601
(406) 449-3964

Nebraska
Director
Division of Medical Services
Department of Public Institutions
P.O. Box 94728
Lincoln, Nebr. 68509
(402) 471-2851, ext. 252

Nevada
Administrator
Division of Mental Hygiene and
Mental Retardation
Suite 244
1937 N. Carson St.
State Capitol Complex
Carson City, Nev. 89710
(702) 885-5943

New Hampshire
Director
Division of Mental Health
Department of Health and
Welfare—Okin Bldg.
Hazen Drive
Concord, N.H. 03301
(603) 271-5111

New Jersey
Director
Division of Mental Health and
Hospitals
Department of Human Services
Capitol Place—One
222 S. Warren St.
2nd fl.
Trenton, N.J. 08625
(609) 292-4242

New Mexico
Director
Mental Health Division
Behavioral Health Services
Division
Department of Health and
Environment
P.O. Box 968
Santa Fe, N.M. 87503
(505) 827-5271, ext. 304

New York
Commissioner
Office of Mental Health
44 Holland Ave.
Albany, N.Y. 12229
(518) 474-4403

North Carolina
Director
Division of Mental Health
Services
Department of Human Resources
325 N. Salisbury St.
Raleigh, N.C. 27611
(919) 733-7011

North Dakota
Director
Mental Health and Retardation
Services
Division of Mental Health and
Retardation
State Department of Health
909 Basin Ave.
Bismarck, N.D. 58505
(701) 253-2964

Ohio
Director
State Department of Mental
Health and Mental Retardation
30 E. Broad St.
1182 State Office Tower
Columbus, Oh. 43215
(614) 466-2337, ext. 4217

Oklahoma
Director
State Department of
Mental Health
P.O. Box 53277
Capitol Station
408-A Walnut
Oklahoma City, Okla. 73105
(405) 521-2811

Oregon
Assistant Director
Mental Health Division
Department of Human Resources
2573 Bittern St., N.E.
Salem, Ore. 97310
(503) 378-2671

Pennsylvania
Commissioner
Division of Mental Health
State Department of Public
Welfare
Health and Welfare Bldg.,
Room 308
Harrisburg, Pa. 17120
(717) 787-6443

Puerto Rico
Assistant Secretary of Mental
Health
Department of Health
GPO Box 61
San Juan, Puerto Rico 00936
(809) 781-5660

Rhode Island
Director
Department of Mental Health,
Retardation and Hospitals
The Aime J. Forand Bldg.
600 New London Ave.
Cranston, R.I. 02920
(401) 464-3201

South Carolina
Commissioner
State Department of
Mental Health
2414 Bull St.
Box 45
Columbia, S.C. 29202
(803) 758-7701

South Dakota
Division of Mental Health and
Mental Retardation
State Department of
Social Services
State Office Bldg., 3rd fl.
Illinois St.
Pierre, S.D. 57501
(605) 773-3438

Tennessee
Commissioner
State Department of
Mental Health
and Mental Retardation
501 Union Bldg.
4th flr.
Nashville, Tenn. 37219
(615) 741-3107

Texas
State Department of
Mental Health and
Mental Retardation
Capitol Station
P.O. Box 12668
Austin, Tex. 78711
(512) 459-7315

Utah
Division of Mental Health
Department of Social Services
150 W. Temple
P.O. Box 2500
Suite 336
Salt Lake City, Utah 84110
(801) 533-5783

Vermont
State Department of
Mental Health
Agency of Human Services
Heritage 2
79 River St.
Montpelier, Vt. 05602
(802) 241-2610

Virginia
State Department of
Mental Health and Mental
Retardation
P.O. Box 1797
Richmond, Va. 23214
(804) 786-3921

Washington
Mental Health Division
Department of Social and
Health Services
Mail Stop OB—42—F
Olympia, Wash. 98504
(206) 753-5414

West Virginia
State Department of
Community Health Services
State Capitol Bldg.
1800 Washington St.
Charleston, W. Va. 25305
(304) 348-7898

Wisconsin
Division of Community Services
State Department of
Health and Social Services
State Office Bldg., Room 534
1 W. Wilson St.
Madison, Wis. 53792
(608) 266-2701

Wyoming
Division of Community Programs
Department of Health and
Social Services
The Hathaway Bldg.
2300 Capitol Ave.
Cheyenne, Wyo. 82002
(307) 777-7115

American Samoa
Mental Health
Department of Medical Services
LBJ Tropical Medical Center
Pago Pago, Tutuila
American Samoa 96799

Trust Territory
Mental Health Division
Department of Health Services
Office of the High Commissioner
Trust Territory of the
Pacific Islands
Saipan, Mariana Islands 96950

Virgin Islands
Division of Mental Health
Alcohol and Drug Dependency
Program
Department of Health
P.O. Box 520
Christiansted
St. Croix, V.I. 00820
(809) 773-1992

References

Preface

1. American Psychiatric Association, *Diagnostic and Statistical Manual of Mental Disorders,* 3rd ed., Washington, D.C.: APA, 1980.

Introduction

1. Karl Menninger, "Honoring His 80th Birthday." *Bulletin of Menninger Clinic,* vol. 37, no. 4, July 1973.
2. William C. Menninger and Munro Leaf, *You and Psychiatry.* New York: Charles Scribner's Sons, 1948.
3. Harry F. Harlow and Clara Mears, *The Human Model. Primate Perspectives.* Washington, D.C.: V.H. Winston and Sons, 1979.
4. Carl R. Rogers, Eugene G. Gendlin, Donald J. Kiesler, et al., eds., *The Therapeutic Relationship and Its Impact: A Study of Psychotherapy with Schizophrenics.* Madison: University of Wisconsin Press, 1967, p. 296.
5. Carl A. Whitaker and Thomas Malone, *The Roots of Psychotherapy.* New York: Blakistone Co., 1953.

6. Martin Loeb, Leigh M. Roberts, and Seymour L. Halleck, *Community Psychiatry*. Madison: University of Wisconsin Press, 1966.
7. Norman S. Greenfield and Richard A. Sternbach, *Handbook of Psychophysiology*. New York: Holt, Rinehart and Winston, 1972.
8. W. F. Fey, M. H. Miller, and N. S. Greenfield, "Six Year Specialists: Promise and Problems." *Journal of Medical Education* 46 (1971):615.
9. Seymour L. Halleck, *Psychiatry and the Dilemmas of Crime*. New York: Harper & Row, 1967.
10. Carl A. Whitaker, Graduating Address, University of British Columbia Psychiatrists, June 6, 1975.
11. Karl A. Menninger, quoted in Samuel Silverman, *New Ways to Predict Illness*. New York: Stein and Day, 1973.

Chapter 1

1. Martin Buber, *I and Thou*, 2nd ed. New York: Charles Scribner's Sons, 1958.
2. Richard Stuart, *Trick or Treatment: How and When Psychotherapy Fails*. Champaign, Illinois: Research Press, 1970.
3. Carl A. Whitaker and Edward Olsen, "The Staff Team and the Family Square Off," in *New Hospital Psychiatry*, G. M. Abroms and N. S. Greenfield, eds. New York: Academic Press, 1971.
4. Ernest Becker, *The Denial of Death*. New York: The Free Press, 1973.
5. Jean-Paul Sartre, *Nausea*. New York: New Directions, 1964.
6. Carl R. Rogers, *Client-Centered Therapy*. Boston: Houghton Mifflin, 1951.
7. Ralph G. Martin, *The Woman He Loved*. New York: Simon and Schuster, 1974.

Chapter 2

1. M. H. Miller, "Beginning at the Beginning in Psychotherapy: An Existential Point of View." *Canadian Psychiatric Association Journal* 18 (1973):459–65.
2. Martin Heidegger, *Being and Time*. New York: Harper & Row, 1962, pp. 163–67.
3. Jean-Paul Sartre, *Being and Nothingness*. Hazel E. Barnes, trans. New York: Philosophical Library, 1965, p. 626.
4. Paul Tillich, *Dynamics of Faith*. New York: Harper & Row, 1957.
5. R. D. Laing, *The Divided Self*. London: Tavistock Publications, 1960.
6. Paul Tillich, *Dynamics of Faith*. New York: Harper & Row, 1957.

7. Martin Buber, *I and Thou*, 2nd ed. New York: Charles Scribner's Sons, 1958.
8. Richard Rodgers, *The King and I.* Music by Richard Rodgers, book and lyrics by Oscar Hammerstein II. New York: Williamson Music Inc., 1951.
9. Martin Heidegger, *Being and Time.* New York: Harper & Row, 1962, pp. 163–67.
10. Richard Hovey, "Unmanifest Destiny," in *Masterpieces of Religious Verse*, Morrison James Dalton, ed. New York: Harper & Row, 1948.
11. Lao Tzu, "The Secret," in *Shadow and Substance.* New York: Seabury Press, 1974.
12. Horatio Alger, *Strive and Succeed.* New York: Holt, Rinehart and Winston, 1967.
13. Sloan Wilson, *The Man in the Grey Flannel Suit.* New York: Bentley, 1955.
14. Jack Kerouac, *On the Road.* New York: Viking Press, 1979.
15. Doris Lessing, *Briefing for a Descent Into Hell.* New York: Bantam Books, 1972.
16. Robert M. Pirsig, *Zen and the Art of Motorcycle Maintenance.* New York: Bantam Books, 1974.
17. Hermann Hesse, *Siddhartha.* Hilda Rosner, trans. New York: New Directions, 1974.

Chapter 3

1. M. H. Miller, F. K. Yeh, et al., "The Cross Cultural Student." *Bulletin of the Menninger Clinic* 35 (1971):128–31.
2. M. H. Klein, A. A. Alexander, et al., "Far Eastern Students in a Big University." *Bulletin of Atomic Scientists* 27 (1971):10.
3. Marjorie H. Klein, Milton H. Miller, and Aristotle A. Alexander, "The American Experience of the Asian Student: On Being Normal in an Abnormal World," in *Normal and Abnormal Behavior in Chinese Culture*, A. Kleinmann, T. Y. Lin, eds. Holland: D. Reidel Dordecht, 1980.
4. Isaac Bashevis Singer, *A Crown of Feathers.* New York: Fawcett Publications, 1979.
5. K. Chimin Wong, Lien-Teh Wu, *History of Chinese Medicine.* Shanghai, China: National Quarantine Service, 1936. Reprinted by Southern Materials Center, Inc., P.O. Box 36–22, Taipei, Taiwan, 1977.
6. John J. Kao, *Three Millennia of Chinese Psychiatry.* New York: The Institute for Advanced Research in Asian Science and Medicine, 1980.

Chapter 4

1. J. H. Masserman, "Faith and Delusion in Psychotherapy: The Ur-Defenses of Man." *American Journal of Psychiatry* 110 (1953):324–33.
2. J. D. Salinger, *Catcher in the Rye.* Boston: Little, Brown and Co., 1951.
3. John Dewey, *Art As Experience.* New York: Capricorn Books, 1958.
4. Benjamin Spock, *The Pocketbook of Baby and Child Care.* New York: Pocket Books, Inc., 1946.
5. J. H. Kellogg, *Plain Facts for Old and Young.* Burlington, Iowa: I. R. Segner and Co., 1891.
6. "Singles are Replacing the Traditional Family." *Daily Breeze,* Torrance, California, May 24, 1980.

Chapter 5

1. Frank E. Moss, J. Val, and J. D. Halamandaris, *Too Old, Too Sick, Too Bad: Nursing Homes in America.* Germantown, Md.: Aspen Systems Corp, 1977.
2. Stephen Z. Cohen and Bruce M. Gans, *The Other Generation Gap: The Middle-Aged and Their Aging Parents.* Chicago: Follett Publishing Co., 1978.
3. Bob Dylan, "A Man's Not Busy Living, Busy Dying," in "It's Alright Ma (I'm Only Bleeding)," in *Bob Dylan Song Book.* New York: Witmark, 1965.
4. Seymour B. Sarason, *Work, Aging, and Social Change: Professionals and the One-Life-One-Career Imperative.* New York: Free Press, Macmillan Publishing Co., 1977.
5. *Readings in Psychotherapy with Older People,* Steven Steury and Marie Blank, eds. Rockville, Md.: National Institute of Mental Health, Division of Special Mental Health Programs, Center for Studies of the Mental Health of the Aging, 1977.
6. Paul Conrad, *Los Angeles Times,* December 1, 1978.
7. P. C. Holinger, "Suicide in Adolescence." *American Journal of Psychiatry* (1977) 134 (12):1433–34.

Chapter 6

1. D. O. Lewis, S. S. Shanok, and D. A. Balla, "Parental Criminality and Medical Histories of Delinquent Children." *American Journal of Psychiatry* 136 (1979) (3):288–92.

2. Richard Sarles, "Child Abuse," in *Rage, Hate, Assault and Other Forms of Violence.* D. Madden and R. Lion, eds. New York: Spectrum Publications, 1976, pp. 1–16.
3. L. S. Syme and L. F. Berkman, "Social Class, Susceptibility, and Sickness." *American Journal of Epidemiology* 104 (1976):1–8.
4. Blair Justice and Rita Justice, *The Abusing Family.* New York: Human Sciences Press, 1976.
5. Bertolt Brecht, *Threepenny Opera,* English translation by Desmond Vesey, lyrics by Eric Bentley. New York: Grove, 1964.
6. R. D. Laing, *Knots.* New York: Pantheon, 1970.
7. C. L. Kline and C. L. Kline, "The Dyslexic Child, the Parents and the Schools: A Study in Mutual Futility and Hostility: Analysis of 700 Cases." American Orthopsychiatric Association Annual Meeting, New York, 1973.
8. R. C. Heaton, D. S. Safer, R. P. Allen, N. C. Spinnato, and F. M. Prumo, "A Motivational Environment for Behaviorally Deviant Junior High School Students." *Journal of Abnormal Child Psychology* 4 (1976):263–75.
9. J. H. Satterfield, D. P. Cantwell, and B. T. Satterfield, "Multimodality Treatment: A One Year Follow-Up of 84 Hyperactive Boys." *Archives of General Psychiatry* 36 (1979):965–74.
10. H. Arendt, *Human Condition.* Chicago: University of Chicago Press, 1969.

Chapter 7

1. R. E. Meyer, J. J. Schildkraut, S. M. Mirin, et al., "Opiates, Catecholamines, Behavior and Mood." *Psychopharmacology* 56 (1978):327–33.
2. *Tissue Responses to Addictive Drugs,* Donald H. Ford and Doris H. Clouet, eds. New York: Spectrum Publications (Halsted Press, John Wiley & Sons, distributor), 1976.
3. S. M. Mirin, R. E. Meyer, J. H. Mendelson, and J. Ellingboe, "Opiate Use and Sexual Function." *American Journal of Psychiatry* (1980) 137 (8):909–15.
4. Robert P. Liberman, "Behavior Therapy in Psychiatry: New Learning Principles for Old Problems," in *Controversy in Psychiatry,* J. P. Brady and H. K. H. Brodie, eds. Philadelphia: W. B. Saunders, 1978.
5. *Handbook of Psychotherapy and Behavior Modification,* S. Garfield and A. E. Bergin, eds. New York: Wiley, 1978.
6. WHO Expert Committee on Addiction Producing Drugs, "First Report," World Health Organization Technical Report Series 273, 1964.

7. *Alcoholism Problems in Women and Children*, Milton Greenblatt and Marc Schuckit, eds. New York: Grune & Stratton (Harcourt Brace Jovanovich, distributors), 1976.
8. M. J. Eckardt, R. S. Ryback, and C. P. Pautler, "Neuropsychological Deficits in Alcoholic Men in Their Mid-Thirties." *American Journal of Psychiatry* (1980) 137 (8):932–36.
9. S. J. Wolin, L. A. Bennett, and D. L. Noonan, "Family Rituals and the Recurrence of Alcoholism Over Generations." *American Journal of Psychiatry* (1979) 136 (4B):589–93.
10. Ernest P. Noble, *Alcohol and Health*. Third Special Report to the U.S. Congress. Washington, D.C.: U.S. Government Printing Office, 1978.
11. Carlos Castaneda, *The Teachings of Don Juan*. New York: Simon and Schuster, 1968. *A Separate Reality*. New York: Simon and Schuster, 1971. *Journey to Ixtlan*. New York: Simon and Schuster, 1972.
12. *The Epidemiology of Heroin and Other Narcotics*. NIDA Reseach Monograph 16, Joan Dunne Rittenhouse, ed. Rockville, Md.: National Institute on Drug Abuse, 1977.
13. P. V. Luisada and B. I. Brown, "Clinical Management of the Phencyclidine Psychosis." *Clinical Toxicology* 9 (1976):539–45.
14. C. V. Showalter and W. E. Thornton, "Clinical Pharmacology of Phencyclidine Toxicity." *American Journal of Psychiatry* (1977) 134 (11):1234–38.
15. *The Epidemiology of Heroin and Other Narcotics*. NIDA Research Monograph 16, Joan Dunne Rittenhouse, ed. Rockville, Md.: National Institute on Drug Abuse, 1977.
16. *Research on Smoking Behavior*. NIDA Research Monograph 17, M. E. Jarvik, J. W. Cullen, E. R. Gritz, T. M. Vogt, and L. J. West, eds. Rockville, Md.: National Institute on Drug Abuse, 1977.
17. Albert J. Stunkard and Michael J. Mahoney, "Behavioral Treatment of Eating Disorders," in *Handbook of Behavior Modification and Behavior Therapy*, H. Leitenberg, ed. Englewood Cliffs, N.J.: Prentice-Hall, Inc., 1976.
18. G. A. Bray, M. B. Davidson, and E. J. Drencik, "Obesity: A Serious Symptom." *Annals of Internal Medicine* 77 (1972): 779–95.
19. *Behavioral Self Management: Strategies, Techniques and Outcomes*, Richard B. Stuart, ed. New York: Brunner-Mazel, 1977.
20. R. A. Lantigua, J. M. Amatruda, T. L. Biddle, G. B. Forbes, and D. H. Lockwood, "Cardiac Arrhythmias Associated With a Liquid Protein Diet for Treatment of Obesity." *New England Journal of Medicine* September 25, 1980, pp. 735–38.
21. H. Spiegel, "A Single Treatment Method to Stop Smoking Using Ancillary Self Hypnosis." *International Journal of Clinical and Experimental Hypnosis* 28 (1970):235–50.

22. Peter Suedfeld, *Restricted Environmental Stimulation.* New York: John Wiley & Sons, 1980.
23. G. A. Bray, "Current Status of Intestinal Bypass Surgery in the Treatment of Obesity." *Diabetes: Journal of the American Diabetes Association* 26 (11), November 1977.

Chapter 8

1. Emil Kraepelin, "On Hysterical Insanity," in *Lectures on Clinical Psychiatry*, translated by T. Hohnstone. New York: William Wood & Co., 1904.
2. Jean M. Charcot, *Clinical Lectures on Diseases of the Nervous System*, vol. 3, translated by T. Savill. London: New Sydenham Society, 1889.
3. Joseph E. Breuer and Sigmund Freud, "Studies in Hysteria (1893–1895)," in *Complete Psychological Works*, standard ed., vol. 2, translated and edited by J. Strachey. London: Hogarth Press, 1955.
4. Sigmund Freud, "Fragment of an Analysis of a Case of Hysteria." *1905 Standard Edition.* London: Hogarth Press, 7 (1958):3–122.
5. S. E. Hyler and R. L. Spitzer, "Hysteria Split Asunder." *American Journal of Psychiatry* (1978) 135 (12):1500–04.
6. Isaac Marks, *Fears and Phobias.* New York: Academic Press, 1969.
7. Tennessee Williams, *A Streetcar Named Desire.* New York: New Directions, 1947.
8. William H. Masters and Virginia E. Johnson, *Human Sexual Inadequacy.* Boston: Little, Brown and Company, 1970.
9. Helen Kaplan, *The New Sex Therapy: Active Treatment of Sexual Dysfunction.* New York: Brunner-Mazel, 1974.

Chapter 9

1. Jean-Paul Sartre, *Being and Nothingness.* Hazel E. Barnes, trans., New York: Philosophical Library, 1965, p. 626.

Chapter 10

1. M. T. Tsuang, "Genetic Counseling for Psychiatric Patients and Their Families." *American Journal of Psychiatry* (1978) 135 (12):1465–75.
2. E. S. Gershon, W. E. Bunney, J. F. Leckman, et al., "The In-

heritance of Affective Disorders: A Review of Data and of Hypotheses." *Behavioral Genetics* (1976) 6 (3):227–61.

3. Robert T. Rubin, "Hormones and Human Aggression," in *Handbook on Psychiatry and Endocrinology*, G. Burrows and P. J. V. Beumont, eds. Amsterdam: Elsevier, 1980.

4. M. M. Katz and G. L. Klerman, "Introduction: Overview of the Clinical Studies Program." *American Journal of Psychiatry* (1979) 136 (1):49–51.

5. J. Mendlewicz and J. D. Rainer, "Adoption Study Supporting Genetic Transmission in Manic-Depressive Illness." *Nature* 268 (1977):327–29.

6. J. F. J. Cade, "Lithium Salt in the Treatment of Psychotic Excitement." *Medical Journal of Australia* 36 (1949):349–50.

7. Alan J. Gelenberg and Gerald L. Klerman, "Maintenance Drug Therapy in Long-Term Treatment of Depression," in *Controversy in Psychiatry*, J. P. Brady and H. K. H. Brodie, eds. Philadelphia: W. B. Saunders, 1978.

8. Ibid.

9. J. Amsterdam, D. Brunswick, and J. Mendels, "The Clinical Application of Tricyclic Antidepressant Pharmacokinetics and Plasma Levels." *American Journal of Psychiatry* (1980) 137 (6):653–62.

10. *Mental Health in the Metropolis: The Midtown Manhattan Study*, Book Two, revised by Leo Srole, Thomas S. Langner, Stanley T. Michael, Price Kirkpatrick, Marvin L. Opler, and Thomas A. C. Rennie; Leo Srole and Anita Kassen Fischer, eds. New York: Harper Torchbooks (Harper & Row), 1977.

11. N. S. Weiss, "Recent Trends in Violent Deaths Among Young Adults in the United States." *American Journal of Epidemiology* 103 (1976):416–22.

Chapter 12

1. J. A. Talbott, "An Editorial: Care of the Chronically Mentally Ill—Still a National Disgrace." *American Journal of Psychiatry* (1979) 136 (5):688.

2. J. H. Masserman, "Faith and Delusion in Psychotherapy: The Ur-Defenses of Man." *American Journal of Psychiatry* 110 (1953):324–33.

3. M. Bleuler, "Schizophrenia: Review of the Work of Professor Eugene Bleuler." *Archives of Neurological Psychiatry* 26 (1931): 611–27.

4. J. K. Wing, "The Social Context of Schizophrenia." *American Journal of Psychiatry* (1978) 135 (11):1333–39.

5. Harry Stack Sullivan, *Clinical Studies in Psychiatry*, H. S. Perry, M. L. Gawall, and M. Gibbon, eds. New York: Norton, 1956.

6. Andrew Crider, *Schizophrenia: A Biopsychosocial Perspective.* Hillsdale, N.J.: Lawrence Erlbaum Associates (Halsted Press, John Wiley & Sons, distributor), 1979.
7. *Psychiatric Diagnosis: Exploration of Biological Predictors,* Hagop S. Akiskal and William L. Webb, eds. New York: SP Medical & Scientific Books (Spectrum Publications), 1978.
8. *Annual Review of the Schizophrenic Syndrome 1976–1977,* Robert Cancro, ed. New York: Brunner-Mazel, 1978.
9. Seymour S. Kety, David Rosenthal, Paul H. Wender, et al., "Mental Illness in the Biological and Adoptive Families of Adopted Individuals Who Have Become Schizophrenic," in *Genetic Research in Psychiatry,* R. R. Fieve, H. Brill, and D. Rosenthal, eds. Baltimore: Johns Hopkins University Press, 1975.
10. Franz J. Kallman, *Heredity in Health and Mental Disorder.* New York: Norton, 1953.
11. M. Harrow, R. R. Grinker, M. L. Silverstein, and P. Holzman, "Is Modern-Day Schizophrenic Outcome Still Negative?" *American Journal of Psychiatry* (1978) 135 (10):1156–62.
12. Eliot Slater and Valerie Cowie, *The Genetics of Mental Disorder.* London: Oxford University Press, 1971.
13. M. I. Herz and C. Melville, "Relapse in Schizophrenia." *American Journal of Psychiatry* (1980) 137 (7):801–05.
14. P. May, A. Tuma, C. Yale, P. Potepan, and W. Dickson, "Schizophrenia: A Follow-Up Study of Results of Treatment II Hospital Stay Over Two to Five Years." *Archives of General Psychiatry* 33 (1976):481–86.
15. H. L. Klawans, C. G. Goetz, and S. Perlik, "Tardive Dyskinesia: Review and Update." *American Journal of Psychiatry* (1980) 137 (8):900–08.
16. Werner M. Mendel, *Supportive Care. Theory and Technique.* Los Angeles: Mara Books, Inc., 1975.

Chapter 13

1. Theodore Reik, *Search Within: The Inner Experiences of a Psychoanalyst.* New York: Funk and Wagnalls, 1968.
2. G. J. Warheit, "Life Events, Coping, Stress, and Depressive Symptomatology." *American Journal of Psychiatry* (1979) 136 (4B):502–07.
3. Carson McCullers, *The Member of the Wedding,* in *The Burns Mantle Best Plays of 1949–1950.* John Chapman, ed. New York: Dodd, Mead, 1955.
4. Sigmund Freud, *Collected Papers,* vol. 2. London: Hogarth Press, 1949.

5. Frantz Fanon, *The Wretched of the Earth.* Constance Farrington, trans. New York: Grove, 1963.
6. Seymour L. Halleck, *The Politics of Therapy.* New York: Science House, 1971.
7. Gunnar Myrdal, *The Challenge of World Poverty.* New York: Pantheon Books, 1970.
8. Virginia Satir, *People Making.* Palo Alto, California: Science and Behavior Books, 1972.
9. Martin Buber, *Tales of the Hasidim,* vol. 1. New York: Shocken Books, Inc., 1947.
10. Task Force on Lithium Therapy, "The Current Status of Lithium Therapy." Report of the A.P.A. Task Force. *American Journal of Psychiatry* 132 (1975):997–1001.
11. P. R. A. May, T. VanPutten, and C. Yale, "Predicting Outcome of Antipsychotic Drug Treatment from Early Response." *American Journal of Psychiatry* (1980) 137 (9):1088–89.
12. Maurice Rappaport, "Are Drugs More Than Palliative in the Management of Schizophrenia," in *Controversy in Psychiatry,* J. P. Brady and H. K. H. Brodie, eds. Philadelphia: W. B. Saunders, 1978.
13. Nathan S. Klein and George Simpson, "Lithium in the Treatment of Conditions Other Than Affective Disorders," in *Lithium Research and Therapy,* F. N. Johnson, ed. New York: Academic Press, 1975.
14. Ivan P. Pavlov, *Conditioned Reflexes and Psychiatry.* New York: International Publishers, 1963.
15. Joseph Wolpe, *The Practice of Behavior Therapy.* New York: Pergamon Press, 1969.
16. J. Wada and A. E. Hamm, "Electrographic Glimpse of Meditative State: Chronological Observations of Cerebral Evoked Response." *Electroencephalography and Clinical Neurophysiology* 37 (1974): 201.
17. M. H. Miller, J. E. Miles, and M. H. Klein, "Quality Control in Psychiatric Treatment: 100% Well in Three Weeks or the Doctor Says 'Why'." *Canadian Psychiatric Association Journal* 20 (1975): 267–72.
18. Octavio Paz, *Eagle or Sun?* Eliot Weinberger, trans. New York: New Directions, 1976.

Index